RACING HEARTS AND BURNING CARS

RACING HEARTS AND BURNING CARS

WARD E WILSON
& ROBERT SCHWAB

WEWil Press

For information contact:
ward.wilson@outlook.com

Published byWEWil Press
wewilpress.com

wardewilson.com

Edited by Kristina Kugler
Cover design by Artem Habarov • 99designs
Interior book design by Francine Platt, Eden Graphics, Inc.

This book is based on true events. Names and identifying details have
been changed to protect the privacy of individuals.

Paperback ISBN 978-1-958626-28-3
eBook ISBN 978-1-958626-30-6

Library of Congress Number: Pending

Manufactured in the United States of America

First Edition

TO THE DREAMER IN US ALL
AND
THOSE WITH THE GUTS
TO PURSUE THEM,
NO MATTER HOW IMPOSSIBLE
THEY SEEM

A NOTE FROM
ROBERT SCHWAB

THIS IS NOT A STORY about winning championships, or even winning a race. It's a story of following your dream by discovering who you are, choosing your life's path, and setting goals no matter how impossible they seem. This is my story of utilizing the intangible tools of guts, determination, and turning people's negative comments into motivation. But mostly it's about how I received so much amazing help from so many great people over the years.

I've found the most important thing is setting a clear and defined target. And every time a decision is made, it doesn't matter if it's due to budget constraints, crashing into a wall, or burning up in a fire, make sure the decision keeps you moving towards that target.

I was serious when I told Mathew, "When I get back in that car, it'll be the safest car on the planet." In fact, I was so serious I obsessed over it during the rebuild, and it showed. We were the first funny car team to use a *full aluminum engine belly pan*. We were the first Drag Racing Team to make a *Carbon X fire suit*. And, at the time we tried to get approval for a *crew chief shut down box*, something that is now standard equipment.

Deep down inside I've always felt there's been some sort of divine intervention guiding me. It's been there from the time I left Australia, it's how I survived the crash, and it carried me through the race in Denver. It's also how I've met such great people along the way. Thank you to everyone who's been involved in any way, I hope you all enjoy the book about a simple mechanical thing.

A NOTE FROM
WARD E. WILSON

THE FIRST TIME I heard Robert tell his story, I wanted to laugh and cry, cheer and pause in silence, all at the same time. I couldn't get it out of my mind, it just kept playing over and over. It wasn't long before I realized his story was not in my mind, it was in my heart, and the only way to get it out was to write it. Somehow, I garnered the courage to ask Robert if I could write his story, and that single decision has changed the course of my life.

Though this story happens on race tracks and talks of building cars, crashing cars, burning skin, recovery, and building again. At its core, it's not about any of that, it's about living life, building people, discovering who you are, and following your passion, especially when you're supported by the day job.

His story has inspired me to follow my dream and it has affected every aspect of my life. I show up better at work, in my community, but most importantly as a husband, father, and as of recent, grand-father. I truly hope that Robert's story does for the reader what it has done for me.

"THERE'S A LINE somewhere between complete order and utter chaos. It's a fine line, and it seems my life's quest has been to find it, then ride it. At work, at play, at home, and in the pub, but mostly on the track. The closer you get to that line, the more alive you feel. It's magical when everything comes together in perfect rhythm and time. It's addicting so you get a little closer. The problem is, you don't know when you've found the line because it becomes a blur, and you don't know you've crossed it until it blows up in your face."

SECTION 1

ORDER

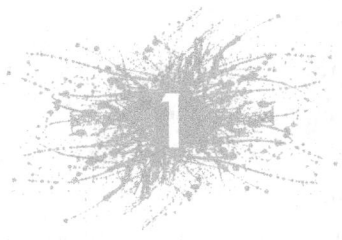

WAKING UP

Rhythmic beeping kept time with the gentle hum of small electric machines, muffling the voices somewhere in the darkness. *What's that irritating noise? And why is it so dark? Are those voices?* Robert thought. "Who's there?" he tried to call out. *Wait, what is in my throat?* Panic threatened and his attempt to run left him twitching in bed.

A voice rose above the pulsing hums. "Look, he's moving!" *I know that voice, that's Bryan! Oh, it's good to hear you, buddy! Lisa, are you there?* Robert squirmed, tilting his head back and forth as if stretching his ears, frantically scanning the voices. "Robert, it's ok. We're here," her gentle voice fell softly on his heart and his entire body relaxed.

"Robert, I'm not sure if you remember the accident, but it was bad. The car is destroyed. You're in the hospital. You've been in an induced coma for five days. There's a tube down your throat and the machine is breathing for you. So just try to relax and know you won't be able to say anything." *That explains a lot,* he thought.

"The accident was really bad, and the fire was even worse. They couldn't get you out for what seemed like forever," her voice quivered and cracked. "There are bandages over your eyes so you're not going to be able to s . . .," her voice cracked again, then broke. She tried to speak, but nothing came out. All she could do was cry, and squeeze his right hand.

Her tight grip kept his fear and panic at bay. *She always knows what to say, even when she can't say anything.*

A strange voice broke in. "Hello Robert, my name is Dr. Steffes. You're a tough one, and lucky too." He drove straight to the facts. "You're in the Burn Unit of the University Hospital. You were in the fire for quite some time. Over 50 percent of your body is covered in second and third-degree burns. As Lisa said, the tube in your throat is connected to a machine that's breathing for you. That's there because your esophagus is severely burned. The damage goes all the way down into your lungs."

With authority, he said what Lisa couldn't, "As for the bandages on your eyes, well, we don't know how deep those burns are, and are unsure of the damage to your eyes. We won't know until the next cleaning. The coma was standard procedure for severe burns like this. It's done to save you from the pain of the burns, the swelling, the changes, everything. You've made it through the worst of the swelling and that's a good sign. But you're not out of the woods by any means." Dr. Steffes hit Robert and his family with the brutal facts as he laid out the plan of recovery.

The doctor's words faded to a sonic blur as Robert drifted off in thought, *Well, ain't this a reversal. I'm the one up on blocks, and they're working on me, wondering if I'm worth the investment. Something I've done with my cars too many times to count.*

Eventually the doctor quit talking and disappeared into the darkness. Robert thought he'd heard the nurse say something about communication. *What was that? Something about a whiteboard and markers?* He began squirming, wriggling, grasping for something—anything. Bryan hollered, "I think he wants to say something. Mark, grab the marker!"

"Here you go," Mark said, gently placing the marker in Robert's right hand while Bryan handed a whiteboard to Lisa. "Robert, we're trying something the nurses suggested. This will be your only form of communication while the breathing tube is in. Just go one letter at a time. I know it's not your writing hand, and I know you can't see, but give it a shot," she said, guiding the marker to the whiteboard.

Marker in hand, he scratched out what appeared to be an O.

"I think it's an O," yelled Mark. "Could be a zero," chimed Bryan. "It might be a 6," Lisa added. No, that's gotta be an O," Mark contested. Robert confirmed with a thumbs up and Mark immediately announced, "it's an O!"

Robert continued and a letter guessing frenzy ensued as Bryan, Mark, Neal, and Lisa each blurted random letters at the first hint of form. Their voices faded into one. "P!" "Q!" "R!" "R, R, R! See that? He said yes, it's an R!"

"I! L! P! D!" "That has to be a D," Lisa blurted. Robert signaled in the affirmative.

"I! L! T! Wait, what is that? I'm not sure. It could be a T, or maybe even a Z." "E. I think it's an E," said Lisa. "E," Mark repeated. Robert gave the thumbs up.

"L! P! R!" "It's another R, isn't it?" Mark exclaimed; Robert confirmed and laid the marker down. "I guess that's it. That's the word. He just spelled out ORDER!" Robert's thumb raised in agreement, then relaxed from exhaustion. "Order what, I wonder?" The boys questioned as they faded off into the distant blackness to debate the issue.

Robert slowly drifted off. He welcomed sleep; it carried comfort in its wake. The quiet moment on either side, the one where the line between wakefulness and sleep becomes a blur, was his quest. For that was where he found true clarity. It's where he dreamed his plans and planned his dreams.

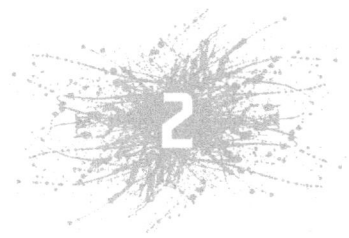

THE KIMBERLY

ELEVEN YEARS EARLIER.
THE KIMBERLY PLATEAU, WESTERN AUSTRALIA.

"Oh, oh, jeez! That's annoying! What the . . . What is that? Oh, my head hurts. Where am I? What happened last night? Oh, oh, yeah. Wait, did that really happen?" I tend to talk to myself as I drift in and out of consciousness; it's something I've always done. That morning, well, afternoon, I found myself lying face down on one of the fancy chairs by the pool at the Kimberly Hotel, trying hard to ignore my pounding head and the urge to heave any remaining alcohol from the last night's bender.

The sun was hot, and I hurt all over, inside and out. I lumbered to my back and gazed into the empty azure sky as the tropical sun continued its slow burn. Drifting between sleep and wakefulness, I found clarity somewhere in the middle and continued the conversation right there, out loud.

"Robert, what are you doing? What are you running from? What's the point? The highlight of life can't be busting loose for a weekend bender, only to be left guessing where you'll find yourself come Sunday morn . . . afternoon. Is this all life's about? Will you be waking up in the same stupor twenty years from now? Will you be sitting at the same stool at the same bar in twenty years? Is this where you're supposed to be?"

I kept asking questions as if someone was going to answer. Then, to my amazement, someone did. Me. At least, I think it was me. I'm not counting out divine intervention, either. I answered out loud, "No, this is not you. I mean, you're good at it—living the bush life, working the mines, and raising hell. But you were meant for something else. You were meant for somewhere else. You were meant for someone else."

Those simple words hit me like none I'd ever heard, and I paused to take them in. Finally, I pleaded, "But what, where, and who?"

"I don't know for sure, but let's start with what. What can I do that'll keep me going, that will give me a purpose?" I began listing the possibilities. "I know I need a good challenge. I could start some sort of business. That would be cool. But then I'm stuck to it for life.

"I could go to college. But I hated school the first time around, so what makes me think I would be any good at it now? No, there's no way I could survive through it.

"I could probably work the mines for a few more years, then go overseas. That sounds fun. Yeah, there's something to that; it's challenging and exciting. But it's too far out.

"I could go backpacking around the world like Jill. She's having an amazing life."

My mind wandered, looking at everything I'd done in my life. There had been quite a bit, and some quite substantial for a twenty-one-year-old. The biggest thrill I'd ever had was standing on the start line with the Southern Thunder, the only Nitro Funny Car in all of South Australia. "Man, I miss that car. I mean, I really miss that car. That's it! That's what I gotta do! I can't deny my racing heart any longer. I gotta pursue racing a Nitro Funny Car. I want to drive one. No, I want to own one!"

A cloud of shame with a touch of reality wafted by, "Who are you to dream such dreams? Nitro Funny Cars are the elite of the elite. Only the best drivers drive them, and only the richest own them.

You're nowhere near their league. You've got neither the knowledge nor the capital."

A ray of sun broke through, "Yeah, but that's the beauty of it all. No one does that, no one just goes out and builds an elite dragster! You can buck the system. You can be the first. Most just find their bar stool and sit there waiting for life to happen. You can go build a life, you can make it happen!"

Another cloud, "You're a scrawny, broke kid from the working side of Adelaide. You're not supposed to dream such dreams. You're supposed to learn your trade, find your stool, and stay there."

Another ray of sun, "That's stupid! I don't need a stool to fill my life. My life is made up of nothing but time, and I'll work it till the end. I can figure out the details when I get to them. For right now I'll focus on what I can do. Challenge accepted!"

"But where is 'there'? I could go back home, but that's never going to happen in Australia. If I'm going to do this, the only way is to do it in America. Yeah, because when I'm successful I want to race the best in the world. Yeahhhh, that's what I'm talking about! Yeah, eff'n-a Mate!"

"I'm going to America and I'm going race my own Nitro Funny Car!" Saying it out loud sent chills right down my spine. I stood from that fancy chair a new man. A man with a purpose, a dream, and a plan. And oh, what a plan it was.

From here on, it's nothing but logistics, I thought, strutting into the crowded Kimberly pub. It felt good to have a plan again, until it didn't. Torpedo asked straight away, "what's up, brother?" With a grin on my face and a cold one in my hand, I said, "I'm going to America, and I'm going to race my own Nitro Funny Car!"

He laughed, "That's funny man! Yeah, that's a good one!"

"What's funny?" I asked, shocked at his reply.

"You, America, Funny Car, that's funny!"

"That's not funny, that's what I'm going to do."

"Look, Fitter, it's a long way from this place to America, and it's even longer from this place to running a race car," he said.

"Yeah, it is." My plan had sounded much better alone out by the pool than in the crowded pub, and for a moment I doubted.

"Well, I think it's brilliant, and I think you should do it!" That was Jill. Sweet Jill, the light of the Kimberly Hotel. Blokes came from miles around to have that beauty serve them up a cold one.

And it wasn't just Jill. The Kimberly was the best pub for 500 miles in every direction. The publican was a smart guy. He knew if he wanted to attract the most miners and station hands, he needed the most attractive staff. So, he'd go on recruiting trips to Perth and offer free bus tickets, room, and board to female backpackers if they'd come to the Kimberly. It worked—folks came from all across the region to be served by the lovely lassies, including myself. But young Jill, the British backpacker—she was a step above.

Looking at her, I stood up tall and proud, raised a beer to the room, and in the loudest voice I could muster announced to all present, "I'm going to America to race my own Nitro Funny Car!" The entire room burst into laughter. No one took me seriously, except Jill. But her approval was all I needed to begin my dream.

"So, when are you heading out?" Jill asked from behind the bar.

"Well, If I'm gonna to do this, I'd better do it soon. I reckon I'll give my notice as soon as I get back to the mine and leave the week after that." I replied.

"Would you like some company? I think it's time for me to get back on the road."

My heart skipped a beat. I couldn't believe my ears. Jill had just invited herself along for the ride!

"Sure, happy for the company." I said calmly, but inside I could barely contain my excitement. "I've been thinking, and the quickest route from here to Adelaide is the Tanami Track," I rambled on. "It's a bit late in the season, but I think it's still the best option." With that, we worked out the details that'd get us home by Christmas.

There are two seasons in the barren inland deserts of Australia; hot and dry, which is most of the time, and hot and wet, which happens occasionally in late summer. When it happens, it floods the washes, roads, and flats, making travel impossible. The Aboriginals just call it "the wet." The locals kept telling us we were crazy for heading out so late in the season and how all it would take was one good wet and we'd be stranded for months. But we were young, and our minds were made up. We had a plan.

Getting to one mine is much like getting to the next. There's lots of wide-open space dotted with scrubby bush, a rise here, a flat there, and an occasional mountain. Somewhere around the 160-mile mark, ya turn left at the burned-out car, then right at the eighth dry wash. The washes all look the same, so ya gotta count careful. You follow that for a spell, then go right at the big gum, then drive another 80 miles or so to the end of the road.

The TripleX was a dry mine, meaning no alcohol. The office, shop, and bunks were nothing more than some old dongas they'd dragged in from some other place and left scattered out along the haul road. A part of me was sad to think it was my final trip in. I'd only been there six months or so, but the place had grown on me. Even the showers were getting to me. They were fed from a tank up top of the hill with about 200 yards of black poly piping. The water was so damned hot most of the time you couldn't touch it. The only safe time for a shower was 6 a.m. after it had the night to cool off, and everyone else had taken their turn.

I smiled at the old fencing wire still strung between the dongas. I couldn't show it to the others, but a part of me was getting sentimental, like I was gonna miss the place.

There were about six of us all living out there in the bush, and not one had thought of bringing a clothes washing machine. Out of reflex, my bush engineering skills had set in. I organized the boys and we went to work. We grabbed the cement mixer from the mine, threw in a bar of soap, a rock or two, and voila, we had a clothes washing machine. Dave rigged the old fencing wire for a clothesline, and the next thing we knew we had clean clothes, until we didn't.

When we got home that first evening, clouds of dust drifted off each shirt, pants, and skivvies with the gentlest of shakes, causing anyone within breathing distance to cough or sneeze. It turned out the trucks on the haul road kicked up red dust with every pass, and they passed every fifteen minutes, all day long. We had to rethink that one.

Did I mention the TripleX was a dry mine? It's probably a good thing as I look back on it. It was extremely remote, and the boys living there came with their own extreme version of crazy. There was Hank, the grader operator. He was always the first up. He headed to work toting his tucker box with a six-pack of Tinny's. I guess you could still call it dry if you don't get caught. Dave was a hauler, Doc was the cook, and Torpedo was the blaster. They were all good. Crazy, but good. I ran a tight mechanic shop and quickly earned every bit of respect I received.

It didn't take long for life to fall into a routine. We worked hard and played harder. About every three weeks or so we'd make a weekend trip into Hall's Creek for a serious bender. Any resemblance of social life in the bush revolved around the pub. I found it interesting how the pubs came in pairs. There was always one set off to the side for the Aborigines and they weren't allowed in the other side. They even bolted the ashtrays to the tables over there so no one would walk off with them. Yeah, it was strange. It was a hard country filled with hard people doing hard drinking. That's how life was out there.

The weekend routine was something like this; we'd start at the Kimberly and stay there until they closed up shop. On the way out, we'd grab a couple of slabs to keep us hydrated until Bluey the baker woke up about four a.m. He was the first one in town to get going and always had a fridge full of coldies he was willing to part with, for the right price. He was our best mate as we drank his beer and watched him make his bread. We'd stay there until the Kimberly opened, and then we'd do it all over, again and again, until it was time to go back to work. Every once in a while, I'd think about Steve and the Southern Thunder, then drink a bit harder to help that memory pass.

Life was pretty much just work punctuated with a trip to town to see the girls and drink some beer every few weeks. That was life. Until one day, it wasn't.

THE TANAMI TRACK

I was in charge of transportation, so I readied the old XW. I loaded two old drums from the mine in the back, one for petrol and one for water, strapped six new spare tires fitted with rims up top, and double checked the old conveyer belt strapped on the undercarriage to keep the rocks from punching holes in the oil pan and fuel tank.

I added a few extra strong spotlights up top, the plan being to drive in the cool of the night and let the spotlights do the job of lighting up the bull dust holes. Those dust holes were big enough to tear the wheels off a Landcruiser, and they'd destroy my XW if given the chance. They blended in with the road during the full light of day but cast an ominous shadow under the spotlights at night.

Jill was in charge of the essentials for the trip. Even though she was a proper Brit, she'd been in the bush long enough to know the dangers looming in the desolate desert of central Australia. She knew if we got stuck, or broke down, we'd need to fend for ourselves for quite some time as no one would be out there that close to the wet season. But she insisted she knew how to survive out there, and well, I had become obsessed about getting to America.

Jill was one of the most popular girls in the area. So, word spread fast when she announced she was leaving. It seemed she had a going away party every night for a week as folks came to say their goodbyes.

I arrived the day before our departure, just in time for the biggest party of all. I'd come to know almost everyone in those parts and they each had their reasons for being there. During those months I'd heard all their stories, and they mine. At least the parts of the stories they wanted me to know, and me them. They were the fun stories folks wanted to share. They'd make you laugh and smile and raise a pint for good effort. But you knew there was a layer of pain or hurt just below the surface.

It was Hank who asked me one last time. "Hey Fitter! Tell me again, how'd a guy like you end up in a place like this?" I raised my pint high and said with a smile, "I turned left at Threeways!" Everyone laughed and carried on. The truth hurt, so I left it buried. The others could see it, but respected my efforts. The collective smiles of the crowd helped, and so did the beer.

There was a moment in the midst of the party when Jill caught my eye from across the room. She had a way of lighting up the room with just her presence. She didn't notice me looking at her standing there in the crowd. She was laughing and toasting to everyone for everything. Part of me was amazed, a bit of me was proud, and all of me was lucky she'd agreed to travel home with me. All me mates, they were just amazed.

The Kimberly was a magical place. The people were rough as guts. Tough, but genuine. I was going to miss them.

With the dark clouds of the first monsoons looming in the rearview mirror, we headed out. We were five miles and five minutes out of Halls Creek when, in a cloud of dust, we turned left off the blacktop and onto the dirt track. "Only 800 miles to Alice," I said. "Here we go," Jill replied. Things got off to a quiet start and we relied on the radio for entertainment.

The road was rough, real rough, and it was giving the car quite a beating. Everything was rattling and shaking about, and it didn't take long before the car literally began falling apart. The interior light was first to go; it dropped right off and landed on the seat between us.

We looked at each other in disbelief as Willie Nelson came on the radio singing "On the Road Again." With smiles, we joined in at the top of our lungs. The song seemed somewhat fitting for the occasion.

Unfortunately, the stereo died shortly after. It didn't fall out of the dash, but into it, disappearing somewhere down in the depths of the car. We heard it bumping around in there from time to time, but it never played music, or anything, ever again.

Silence set in, the stars came out, and Jill drifted off to sleep. I drifted off in thought under the Southern Cross. I figured I could sell the car in Adelaide and use the money to buy a ticket to America. I'd need to get myself to Pomona, California by the first week of February for Winter Nationals. *I'm a good mechanic,* I thought, *I know my way around a Nitro car. I'll get me a job with one of the teams there.* The plan was coming together. I could see it in my mind.

Without warning, the silence was broken by a loud crash. I lost control and we skidded helplessly back and forth from berm to berm. I'd hit a deep pothole, blowing the front tire. Jill woke, screaming for her life, as we skidded to rest in the middle of the road where we sat in blaring silence, afraid to breathe. I wasn't quite sure if she was okay. It would have killed me if she wasn't. She took the edge off by laughing first. I joined in when I knew it was safe, and we spent the next few moments laughing the shock away.

Finally, I jumped out to fix the flat. To my surprise, Jill followed. I pulled the jack, popped off the tire, swapped it for a spare, and put it all back together as she watched. "Next one's mine," she said, jumping back in the car. After that, the traveling was easy, and the conversation flowed freely.

"You know why this road is so bumpy?" She stated it in the form of a question. I wasn't sure if I was supposed to answer or agree, so I just said, "Well it needs a good grading." She went on to tell me all about the track. She'd heard all the stories from everyone coming and going, working in the Kimberly.

She told me about old Ted, the one bloke in charge of maintaining the entire length of track and how he'd finished his grading three months back. "He sets out in the autumn, right after the wet, and he's loaded down with everything he's going to need for the next six months. He loads it all in a trailer and pulls it behind his grader. He spends the entire winter by himself doing nothing but drinking beer and driving his way down the track at five miles an hour. It gets lonely out there, and he can go for weeks without seeing another person. In fact, it's so hot and lonely there's no need for clothes. He grades the entire track in his birthday suit!"

"No! Naked? No clothes?" I replied with a laugh.

"Yeah, for real, completely naked, and there's no one there to care at all!" We laughed so hard I almost lost the road.

We talked about where we came from and where we were going. We talked about life and the way we saw it. We talked about our dreams and how we were going to get there. She told me about her life in the big city of London with her mum, dad, and sister. Jill was good with questions; she had a gentle way of telling me about her, then flipping it around and opening me up.

Then she asked, "How about you, Fitter? Where are you from?"

"Oh me? I'm from Adelaide," I replied.

"Really, that's it? Adelaide? I want more. I want to know about where you're from. Tell me about where little Fitter grew up." She continued probing and prodding until I started talking in a way I hadn't ever talked to anyone before.

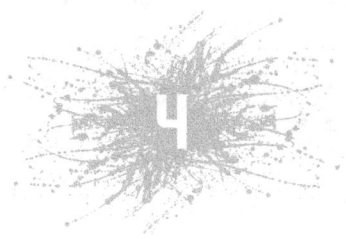

HOME

Me? Yeah, well. Dad, he was from way up in the hills, right at the edge of the bush. That's where he found Mum. The story goes he'd ride his old single-speed bicycle ten miles each way down the rugged dirt tracks for visits. He was a strong and gentle man, full of love for life, and Mum. He was bound and determined to finish school and do what it took to make a life for the both of them. But before he got the chance to do either, World War II broke out and he was signed on to drive the Japs out of New Guinea. He was a navigator on a B24 and flew with the Allies for General McArthur.

He came back just as gentle and full of love for life and Mum as when he left. Together, he and Mum agreed the edge of the bush was no place to raise a family, so they moved to the nearest big city, which happened to be Adelaide. Dad took a job at the local bank, and Mum, well, she got busy making babies. As soon as they could, they bought a house of their own, which happened to be right about baby number three, that's me. I was the first one brought home to the new house.

The Schwab house at 76 Baker Street started out a little two-bedroom bungalow on a big patch of land, but just like the family, it grew over time. A bedroom here, another one there, a family room in the garage. By the time I was a teenager there were eight of us, counting

Mum and Dad, and we lived in a full-fledged five-bedroom house.

It's funny, the things you remember. There was always just the one bathroom, which made for some pretty dramatic mornings. The trick to getting anywhere on time was getting to the bathroom before the girls. I'm still an early riser for that very reason. The toilet started out being outside, but somewhere around the third or fourth bedroom, Dad built in an area so it wasn't outside anymore. But it was still plenty cold. There was never a lock on the bathroom door, and one of the family tricks was to sneak in and dump a jug of cold water over whoever was in the shower.

Much of the large yard was taken up with Mum's garden and fruit trees. There was a shed out back where Dad kept his lawn tools and anything else that needed storing.

Us kids, we were Mum's everything. And well, for Mum, everything wasn't enough, so she adopted the entire neighborhood. She was always feeding our mates, and their mates, and so on. There were always neighborhood kids whose parents were missing for one reason or another. Some were sick, some were off working somewhere else, others were just flat out absent. That's not the important part, the important part was that Mum was out to save the entire world. And she started with Baker Street.

The Schwab home was founded on three simple beliefs, which motivated Mum's and Dad's every move. First, they believed in God, which was kind of a big thing in Australia. You don't find a lot of that. As a Schwab, I went to church every week. That's where I learned to sing and was taught to pray. But just getting the Schwab kids to Sunday school wasn't enough for Mum and Dad, we always brought the neighborhood kids along. You'd be amazed at how many kids can fit into a car on a mission to save souls. It didn't take long before Mum had the pastor sending the church bus out to our neighborhood to pick up all the stray souls Mum was saving.

Second, Mum and Dad believed in hard work, and they led by example. Dad spent his days at the bank investing in people and capital like his job depended on it. He spent his evenings investing in us kids and our home like his life depended on it. The yard was always well kept. He wasn't the one doing the mowing and trimming, but he was always there. Mum's home was also neat and well kept, and she made sure it stayed that way. We didn't spend our school holidays out on the beach like the others. We spent our holidays working odd jobs wherever we could find them. Adelaide was a growing town and there were always paddocks needing to be cleared of rocks, fences needing to be built or mended, or hay needing to be hauled. We kept the money we earned.

Third, they believed in us kids, so much so we ended up believing in us too. There was never any doubt in our minds—we were bound to be useful in this world. We felt it at a young age when love was all we knew. Mum and Dad showed they believed in us by giving us the wisdom of their guidance. Then, they proved it by letting us make our own mistakes, again and again. They always had our backs, Mum and Dad, they never stopped believing in us even when given plenty of reason not to.

Jill interrupted, "Stop right there. This is too much. Please tell me you're kidding!"

"No! I kid you not," I replied, embarrassed I'd showed her the softest parts of me right off the bat. But she had a way of getting to me.

"I don't believe you. That sounds too perfect. Nobody is that perfect."

"Well, that's Mum and Dad. They are truly salt of the earth folks."

"Are you telling me that you, Fighting Fitter from the TripleX, was the model Christian boy from the south at one point in time?" She chuckled. "Tell me, how does one go from being the model Christian boy to Fighting Fitter?"

"Nah, I never said I was the model Christian boy," I replied defensively. "I mean, we all come from somewhere. Me? I just happened to be from a Christian home. Yeah, Mum and Dad, they were the model Christian parents. My brothers and sisters, they were the model children. Me, on the other hand, I tried every bit of patience Mum and Dad had between them.

As for school, my siblings, they took to it really well. But for me, not so much. By the time I'd reached fourth grade, I'd bounced around to several schools, from Adelaide to Glenelg. Most of them were private Christian schools, as they were more to Mum's liking. Some of those schools were nothing more than a willing parent who'd set up shop in the shed, others were full-blown buildings with principals and staff. Either way, it didn't matter much. I had a habit of wandering off when I got bored, which seemed to happen quite a bit.

It started with my first day. They wanted me to wear shoes. I thought I had better places to be than some place that wanted me to wear shoes. So, I left. It about gave Mum a conniption. She had the entire neighborhood on the lookout within minutes of Mrs. Sigg's call.

I was found before I made it home. I'd stopped off at the butcher for a sampling of fritz. Mr. Barns obliged and called Mum while I was filling my face. The whole neighborhood knew everyone, and he knew I didn't belong alone in the middle of town in the middle of the day.

That was just the top of the hill. It was all downhill from there and I kept gaining speed. I'm not sure if it was boredom, curiosity, peer pressure, or what, but I caused Mum and Dad a lot of grief. There's a line between acceptable and unacceptable behavior. And for as long as I can remember, it has been my mission in life to find it, then stay just to the left. The problem is, once you get close enough, it kind of blurs a bit, and you don't know you've crossed it until it's too late. Then everything blows up in your face.

By the time seventh grade came around I exhausted all the private schools, so Mum figured it was time for me to integrate into public schools. That was an eye opener, and where the real learning happened. Unfortunately for Mum, most of what I learned there was on the unacceptable behavior side of things. I had a lot of catching up to do, and I was up to the challenge. It turned out I was pretty good at smoking and cursing. It came quite naturally in fact.

"You're telling me the first thing you learned at public school was how to smoke?" Jill asked.

"Well, yeah. You know, I had a goody-goody Christian boy reputation to shed. Besides, I looked pretty damned cool doing it," I replied as we both burst into laughter at how ridiculous it all sounded when said out loud.

After the laughter subsided, we settled into the gentle rhythmic rumble of the dirt track. I glanced across the seat, the dim glow of the dashboard lights accentuated her soft features and hallowed the wispy curls of auburn hair. She looked like an angel. I finally gathered the courage to ask, "Jill, why are you here?"

She looked over with a bit of surprise, "What? It's time to move on. I'm traveling, you know. It's difficult to travel if you stay in the same place."

"No, that's not what I mean. I mean why did you agree to come with me on such a long and lonely road? I could be a raging psychopath for all you know. Like that other Schwab you'd heard of back at the Kimberly," I said.

She smiled, again like an angel. "No Fitter. You're no psychopath, I can tell. You're a good one."

"But how do you know for sure? There wasn't a weekend at the Kimberly where I wasn't testing the limits of alcohol consumption, or in some kind of brawl or bar fight. I was always busting up some jerk's face, or getting my own face busted up by some other jerk."

"Yeah, that's exactly it. You have a way of sniffing out the jerks." She stopped. "O . . . o, okay, that didn't sound right. In fact, it sounded terrible. But I meant it in a good way, a really good way. What I'm trying to say is, you didn't fight anyone who didn't need a good ass kicking. It didn't take long for me to pick out the blokes you were going to fight. Someone would come into the pub and start pushing someone around or just acting all, I don't know, all jerky. And I'd think, Fitter's going to fix this one. And sure enough, sooner or later, you'd show up for an adventure and you'd have them all busted up and back in their place before the weekend was gone. Most times you even had the decency to take it outside so as not to mess up the place."

"Yeah, well. I hate jerks. Bullies are the scourge of the earth. I can't stand 'em," I said.

"You see, right there. That's what I'm talking about. You wouldn't let anything happen to me. You'd bust up anyone who tried," She replied. I smiled, it felt good to be trusted.

"That was the other thing I excelled at in public school—ass kicking. It's funny how you don't know you're good at something until you do it. I was so scared the first fight I got into. It was with one of the mean kids down by the Bay. That whole family was just mean. He was picking on the littler kids as they entered the gates of the school, shoving 'em, taking their lunch money and such. It pissed me off, so I stood up to him as I walked through the gates.

Real quick, he shoved me back and then went to trashing my bike. He kicked the chain and stomped the wheels, bending them all out of shape. It scared me to death, so I ran to the safety of school. That bike was my only means of transportation. I had to walk it home that day and I cursed him the whole way home and all through the night. He was all I could think about. It just bugged me how he smacked the little kids around, then lit into me for no reason at all.

In the morning I felt something completely new though. It was a strange feeling way down deep in the pit of my stomach. I wanted to run and hide or disappear altogether. I wanted anything but to go back to school. It turns out I was scared. That was new to me. I tried playing sick, but Mum wouldn't have it. She rushed me out the door earlier than usual because I had to walk the whole 3 miles. All I could do was think about my beautiful bike. I loved that bike, it was custom, a real piece of art. I built it myself, and they trashed it. I kept replaying the trashing over and over in my mind and with every step a little bit of fear was replaced by anger. By the time I reached the school, anger was all I had left in me. Yep, I was full to the brim and steaming mad. When I saw those mean kids from down by the Bay doing their thing at the gates. It all turned to rage, and I let them have it. It only took a few punches, and they went running off towards home. Turns out, fighting suited me just fine.

"That was the first time I got sent home from school, but certainly not the last. There developed a true rivalry between me and the kids down by the Bay, and there was always some kid picking on another. I couldn't stand it. I couldn't help myself. It's funny, the only asses I kicked were the ones who deserved it. That didn't really help my goody-goody reputation, but at the same time, it did. You know?"

"Yeah. Yeah, I do," Jill giggled.

Dawn eventually broke and so did my stories. We both marveled at how the dust had piled up deep on the dash and seats, and how it coated every inch of everything inside the car. I guess driving all night through the Tanami Desert with the windows down will do that to a car.

The heat was almost unbearable. We stuck to the plan and sat under an old boab tree on the side of the track. Sleep was light and restless when it came at all. She kept us fed with sliced Spam and a billy of tea. I basked in her voice as she spoke of school and friends. We set out again right about dusk, singing songs, talking, and dreaming.

Eventually she asked, "So tell me, why cars?"

"What do you mean, why cars?" I replied.

"I mean you're going to America to race cars. Why cars?"

"It's simple. I love cars. Besides, I have a bit of a condition."

"A condition?"

"Yeah, a condition. I have what they call a racing heart. I love going fast."

"That's not a condition. It sounds more like a situation or propensity."

"A what?"

"A propensity, you know, something you just tend to do."

"Yeah, no. This goes way beyond a tendency. It's a full on a condition. I love going fast. I mean, I really love it. It's the excitement of it all, I guess. Maybe it comes down to control. When I'm behind the wheel, I'm the one in control. I get to decide how fast or slow I go, where I go, and even if I go at all. And Nitro Funny Cars, well, they are the top of the drag racing world. They are the fastest of the fast, and they're shrouded in mechanical mystery. Everyone talks about these myths of how to tune 'em. They say they have all this voodoo shit about 'em. But I know, deep down in my soul, that they're just simple mechanical things."

"Okay, you've convinced me, you have a racing heart. When did you discover this condition?" she asked.

"Oh, I was just a kid I guess, at camp," I replied.

"Tell me the story. I want to hear about the first time you drove a car."

I smiled.

FINDING PASSION

The belief Mum and Dad had in us kids, that was a real thing. They honestly believed each of us had greatness inside, and they were bound and determined to help us find it. So, all through regular schooling the Schwab kids were exposed to an array of extracurricular activities. It's not easy living in a house full of achievers, because while my siblings' greatness all seemed to be waiting at the surface, my thing was buried quite deep. But that just caused Mum and Dad to work harder to find it. I'm sure I caused 'em to doubt it was even there at all, but both Mum's and Dad's resolve were stronger than my ignorance, and they persisted.

It started with the piano, and man did that suck! "Sit up straight! Keep your fingers up," she'd say. Well, my hands just didn't work that way!

I was so full of energy, it made sense for Dad to point me at every physical thing he could. There was Nippers, the Junior Surf Life Savers. I thought we might have something there, until they made us swim out to sea. Like, way out to sea. Out where the water is dark, and you can't see nothing. I may have been young, but I wasn't dumb. I knew the sea's where the Great Whites lived, and I had no interest in joining them in their natural habitat.

Then came sports. I worked my way through 'em all, one after the other. We started with tennis, but I was clumsy with the racket.

Surely soccer would be better. But it required all of that running, which was something else I sucked at. So, they put me as goalie, which added insult to injury because it required not only hand and eye coordination, but you had to move your feet too. Then you had the added complexity of spatial awareness. I was completely focused on the ball as I went for my first block. I don't remember anything of it, but Adrian said it was spectacular the way my head bounced off the pole and the way the blood ran all down my face and shirt. "It was like a popping ting sound echoing across the field!" he said. All I remember was that was also my last block.

Then came cricket, how bloody boring was that? Nothing happened, and it lasted all day! Aussie rules football was kind of the opposite. There, everything was going on all at the same time. I was out the first game when someone tried jumping on my back going up for a big mark. Yeah, that kind of freaked me out. It just was not for me, and rugby was the same.

It was clear my greatness wasn't going to be found on the sports field, so my parents sent me off to the Sea Scouts. That was quite fun, and I liked it. I didn't have to swim with the sharks, but I knew they were there and from time to time my imagination would run wild as I gazed into the dark blue depths.

Then Dad sent me off to live in the bush for a month-long camp. They taught me bush skills, and I took to it quite well. Yeah, I could easily live out there. The bush always had a special allure. Maybe it was the simpleness of life, or the promise of adventure calling all country folks who'd been forced to find a living in the city. Or maybe it was the extra sense of peace only found in the solitude of the open bush. Any way you looked at it, the folks out in the bush seemed to have an extra dose of freedom the city folk never could find. Mum and Dad were a bit wary when I thanked them for the trip and added, "I think I'm gonna go bush one day!"

Then one holiday Mum and Dad sent me off to church camp. Why I had to spend two weeks of my precious holiday at church camp, instead of working for money out on the farms, I couldn't understand. I was saving to buy a car for when I got old enough, and I was just about there on both accounts. But Mum and Dad knew what they were doing. That camp changed everything for me. There, I found the one thing at which I could excel.

It was a long quiet ride out to the Country Boys Christian Club, or CBCC. A red dust cloud trailed behind Dad's yellow FB Holden as we made our way up from Tepko into the foothills of the Mallee scrub. You could tell where the other campers were and if they were coming or going by tracking the size and direction of their dust clouds. We were early by the looks of it. The country folks living in those parts were homesteaders, and they were as tough as the rocky ground they called home. The only thing tougher, or stronger, was their faith. Which is why they'd built the camps in the first place, I reckon.

Dad parked near the main building. Full of doubt, I dragged myself out of the car and turned a slow 360 to survey the situation. It wasn't much to look at, just a big building in the center with a bunch of tin sheds scattered about.

The bush basher caught my eye first. It was a thing of beauty and looked like something right out of Mad Max, you know, the movie. My interest in camp spiked off the charts when my eye caught ahold of the string of busted-up cars up the hill. They were all lined up on the far side of the tin sheds, which turned out to be our dorms. I wanted to go exploring straight away, but first things first out in the civilized bush. Proper bush etiquette called for a cup of tea and a cucumber sandwich with Mum, Dad, and Mr. Chudles, the camp operator. We followed that up with a tour of the facilities.

I could barely contain myself during the tour. I kept looking up at the cars, wondering and waiting for the moment I could escape and go exploring. But the grownups just kept droning on and on. I heard something about Christian schooling, which pleased Mum. Dad, he had another cucumber sandwich. Eventually Mr. Chudles quit talking, we said our goodbyes, Mum and Dad sped off in a cloud of dust, and I was free.

I dumped my old military ruck sack and home-made swag in my tin room and immediately ventured outside. I came around the last shed to find a red and black XU1 Torana with the bonnet up. It was a thing of beauty. I walked around the side admiring the big wheels and cool scoop. Up toward the front, I startled a teenage lad who quickly snuffed and hid his cigarette. When he saw I was just a kid, he coolly lit it back up and took a big, long drag. His light brown hair straggled in waves down to his shoulders. He wore a red flannel shirt with a black duffle jacket, black skin-tight jeans, and ripple soles. Not the type of kid to be hanging around a churchy camp, I thought, but I quickly learned different.

"G'day mate, how's it going?" I asked.

"I'm Dan," he replied without as much as a hello, or howdy.

"You here for camp?" I asked.

"No, I ain't no camper," he replied. That's when I noticed the CB radio crackling in the background. He continued, "I live down around the way. Me and my family, we go to church down at the main building on Sundays. They let me use the tools up here when my car needs work."

"Cool car. Is it fast? It looks fast," I replied.

"Yeah, fast enough to beat any of the yokoes around here. You drive?"

"Me, no. Not yet, any ways. I am saving for a car though."

"Cool. I guess that's why you're here, eh? To get ready for driving?"

"I'm here because my Mum and Dad just dropped me off. Besides, I'm just fourteen, I don't have a license." I replied.

"That never stopped no one, and besides, that's kind of the purpose of this camp anyway," he said. Then he went on to tell me all about the driving parts of camp and how it all worked with the churchy stuff. I was beside myself to find out the lineup of cars was for the campers and that we'd be learning to drive. He himself graduated from the driving school there.

I quickly decided I liked Dan. I thought, "He may not be the role model Dad expected me to find. But he didn't even offer me a cigarette. So, he couldn't be that bad!"

Dan warned me, "Look, just mind the rest of camp and the cars will take care of themselves."

He was right. I spent the next week doing some of the usual camp stuff you'd expect. The mornings and evenings were heavy on the bush skills. We made damper on the fire, went horse riding, hunted goannas, did some roo shooting, and went rabbit trapping. It was all sprinkled with a dose of churchy learning for added effect.

We'd go on long hikes out into the Mallee after dark. I can't tell you the purpose of those night hikes. Maybe it was to build character, maybe it was to build strength, maybe it was to get us tired before bed, or maybe it was just to get us comfortable walking about in the bush and navigating by stars. Whatever it was, I liked it! It was a great experience for a fourteen-year-old boy with too much energy and an ambition for trouble. Not to mention, it was a great opportunity to be really brave, to walk and talk with girls.

The second week we got to do stuff you wouldn't expect. All those cars, they came to life. Well, kinda. They were in pretty bad shape. They were constantly running out of fuel and always needed fixing. The bush basher from Mad Max, it had a bull bar with old tires wired up and it was used to push start the fleet. The pride of the camp was a red HR Sedan with a 186 engine. She was set aside for the most skilled drivers. If I was going to get to drive it, I had to start from the beginning. Which I did.

Driving school consisted of three stages. Everyone started at level one, which was a simple oval cut out of the Mallee scrub. It was so small, all you could do was drive around in circles in first gear. It may have been a challenge for most, but I was bored within ten minutes.

Stage two was a section of the big track up on top of the hill. There we could change gears, but no passengers were allowed, and we were never to go over thirty mph. The best part of stage two was getting the old Holdens from the sheds up to the track. The road was steep and rocky and more like a goat track than anything, which only added to the challenge, and enjoyment.

I quickly moved up the license requirements and was soon ready for stage three, and my shot at the Red HR. The big track was a full figure eight cut out of the red sandy scrub. The track itself was just a couple of deep ruts with high edges tied in a big knot. Some feared the ruts. Me, I learned to embrace them and use them to my advantage. There was an upside to those ruts. If you lined it up just right, you could fly hands free as they would hold your wheels on the track. The downside—what am I talking about, there was no downside. If you went fast enough, or swerved at the wrong, or right, moment, the wheels would get caught in the berm, sending the car up on two wheels and veering off into the bush. I couldn't get enough! The other kids, they couldn't get enough either. At the beginning, they begged to ride shotgun.

I lived for my chance to drive the HR. When I got it, I was bound and determined to find the limits of what it could do. There was this one corner out on the far side, just out of sight of the camp leaders. If you revved the engine on the approach and cracked the wheels just right, you could spin her sideways all around the corner and then quickly brake back to normal before they could see anything was amiss. That stunt got me kicked off the track a few times.

I was hooked on the adrenaline that came from controlling something completely out of control. I was hooked on the attention from the other lads, and I was hooked on the attention from the girls. They all seemed to be thrilled by my crazy driving, and I seemed to be good at it.

One of the best lessons I learned that summer was how critical it was to have other campers I could count on for help whenever I stalled or rolled a car. It's funny, but by the end of camp no one wanted to drive with me anymore. I never could understand why.

Camp was over as quickly as it had begun. I was so excited on the ride home, I quickly told Mum and Dad everything. I told them about how good a driver I was, and how fast I'd progressed to level three. I told them how I got to drive the Red HR, and how only the best drivers got to drive the Red HR. Then I set in to begging Dad to let me drive. "Come on! Let me show ya! Please! Come on, I'm good. Real good!" I assured in my most enthusiastically whiny voice.

To my astonishment, Dad pulled over and said, "Okay, but only on the dirt track. Let me make this clear so there are no questions: I'm taking over once we hit pavement." With that, Dad slid over, I got in the driver's seat, and Mum got in the back.

The red dust cloud rose high and long in the South Australia evening sun as I slid, revved, and skidded dad's yellow FB Holden around each and every corner from Tepko to Birdwood. Mum was yelling, screaming, and crying around every turn. Dad, he never said a word. He just held on tight with one hand grasping the seat, the other clinging to the dash. By the time he got back in the driver's seat his face and knuckles were as pale as a ghost's. As for Mum, she stayed in the back, mostly to recover, I think. Yeah, I loved that camp and have been chasing the pure adrenaline rush I'd found up in the Mallee Bush ever since.

Boom, screech, skid. Another flat tire in a cloud of dust. "This one is mine," Jill yelled as she popped open the door. I followed. She did a bang-up job with the tire. Of course, I offered my assistance with the heavy lifting of getting the tires to and from the top, but she did the rest. Before I knew it, we were back on the track kicking up a line of dust, shaded by the night.

FIRST CAR, LAST SCHOOL

"So, you learned to drive out in the bush. When did you get your first car?" Jill asked. I glanced over and smiled.

"I was fifteenish, and in high school. It was an old FC Holden, Australia's finest automobile. I paid $100 of my own hard-earned cash for that car. I loved that car."

Mum sent me way across town to Urrbrae Agricultural High School to get away from the boys down by the Bay. It was there I finally found my greatness when I walked into mechanics class. I took to mechanicing real quick. It suited me. I understood the machines. They're simple things really. I started with the demos, but soon enough other kids were bringing their projects in. I asked if I could help, and they welcomed it. It gave me a sense of pride I'd never had before, to help out like that.

When you pay $100 for a car, you can't expect it to run right away. So what I had was a project of my own, and I welcomed the help of the others in class. One day I held off going to school until after Adrian left for work. I needed to borrow his Honda 250 dirt bike without him, or Mum, knowing. I strapped the Holden 6-cylinder 138 head to the seat and headed off. There's a line between brilliant and stupid driving; the fact that I made it to school that day left me feeling on the brilliant side, though that didn't save me from getting in deep trouble.

I was so proud of that car. It was blue when I bought it, but it never made it past primer gray when I was done. I didn't know I didn't like body work until I tried it. I started driving it as soon as it was in working order. I was fifteen and didn't even have a license. But then again, this was Australia and drivers' licenses are more of a suggestion than a law.

It's funny, even after riding forty-five minutes across town I still managed to miss classes from time to time. I was so good at talking with my friends, both in the halls and in class, when I should have been doing some type of schoolwork.

It's ironic. It wasn't the smoking or the fighting that got me kicked out of school. It was an awkward fear of speaking in front of class that eventually got me. Her name was Miss Jury. She was one of the kindest and most caring teachers I'd ever had. She really cared about what she was teaching and how we were learning. She was also drop dead gorgeous and all I wanted to do was impress her. I was doing an okay job at it for quite a while. I even did some homework from time to time, at least for her class.

Then one day she said, "Robert, will you come up and give your report?" "No ma'am, it's not my day," I replied, thinking to myself that there's no way I'm getting up there. "I know, Robert, but you've missed your day three times now. Come on up and just get it over with."

I'm still not sure of a few things from that day. Number one is how I got up in front of the class in the first place. It may have been the way Miss Jury brushed her auburn hair off her big brown eyes the third time she asked. Number two is how long I stood there saying nothing in front of the class. It's not like I wasn't trying. I opened my mouth, but nothing came out. It must have been a long time because it had gotten so awkward even the troublemakers on the back row quit mocking me.

And the last is why I said what I said as I went back to my seat. Finally, Miss Jury relented, "Okay Robert, sit down." Maybe it was out of pure embarrassment. Maybe it was my last-ditch effort to save what little pride I had left. Or maybe it was the disappointment in her voice when she said, "Okay Robert, sit down." That cut me to the bone. I'd let her down and it hurt. I didn't mean it, but I said it under my breath just loud enough to be heard by, well, everyone as I disappeared into my seat. "Bloody silly bitch." Before I had a chance to sink as low as I felt, I was off to the principal's office to think about what I'd done.

I took my usual place on the third chair from the end, waiting my turn to talk with Mr. Mawson, the principal. The wait was a bit longer than usual, but I wasn't worried. I was still too embarrassed to be worried. Besides, I'd been there before and knew the drill. I'd be back in class before long. Then Dad sat next to me. That's when I knew things were bad and the worry set in. "Robert, this is your third strike," said Mr. Mawson, and just like that I was no longer in school.

It was a long, quiet bus ride home that day. All Dad said was, "Well, if you're not in school, you'd better go get a job." And so, I did.

It was right about two a.m. when we passed through the Aborigine reserve. "There's a place somewhere out here called Rabbit's Flat where we can buy some petrol. We won't make it the rest of the way without it," I said to Jill as I turned off the track onto some smaller paths. The XW had a nice growl to her ever since Adrian had put the big engine in her. Now, all the rattling and shaking of the rough Tanami Track had worked a few extra holes into the exhaust system, enhancing the rumble of the engine.

We drove around a bit, weaving through a mesh of paths going every which way. "I think this is it," I said as we moseyed slowly into a small spattering of out buildings.

"It looks deserted," said Jill.

"Yeah, it does. But we're not going to make it much farther without a fill up. And I don't want to waste four hours of driving time sitting around waiting for someone to sell us petrol." I replied.

"We don't even know if this is the right place," she said.

"Look, there's some tanks back there," I said, peering through the starlit night. It was right about then I noticed a long black tube out of the corner of my eye, and it was coming my way. It came right in through the open window and rested on my cheek. In fact, there were two tubes, and they were stuck together in the form of a double-barreled shotgun. A cold hard voice pierced the darkness. "Who the hell are you, and what do you think you're doing? You're on private property, don't you know!?"

I'd never had a gun shoved in my face before, so I was a bit freaked out. And whereas the last sentence was as much a statement as it was a question, I wasn't exactly sure what to do. So I just let out a long, "oooooohhhhhh," with an awkward voice crack somewhere in the middle.

Jill straight up disappeared into the seat. I wondered what she was thinking. Then I thought, *I have to prove myself to her! It is my chance! This is a Titanic opportunity to make an impression.* So, I composed myself quickly and answered, "It's, it's all g-good! We, we, we're not a-a-after any, any t-t-t-trouble, we, we j-just want, want to b-buy some, some p-p-petrol!" To which the voice replied, "I don't give a flying flick what you want. It's the middle of the night, and we're closed! Park around front and wait till the sun comes up! And be quiet! If you wake me up again, I'll be shooting someone!"

"H-How 'bout, w-we j-just wait up, up th-there in f-front," I stuttered. "Yeah, you do that!" the voice replied.

With that, I slowly drove out front with a sinking feeling in my heart. I knew my chance to impress had ended much like the original Titanic. I didn't give her much reason to be impressed.

Sleep didn't happen at all that night; we were both too shaken up with the gun situation, it scared the sleep right out of us. We just sat in our respective seats and stared off into the night.

I'm not sure how much time passed, but she was first to break the silence with, "That was truly some crazy crap!" All I could do was laugh, but she shushed me right away. "Quiet or someone's going to get shot!" And it was quiet, for a second or two. Then we both burst out laughing in muffled giggles. She fought hard to get a few words out between breaths, "I didn't know you stuttered!" Tears of laughter rolled down her cheeks. "Neither did I," I replied just before another burst of muffled laughter. After several minutes the flood of giggles petered down to a trickle.

"I'm not sure how funny this is. It still feels too close to be this funny," I finally said. She agreed, and added, "Yeah, but what are you going to do? When the giggles come, they come, and you just have to go with them."

"Sure enough," I replied.

"Yeah, that was some crazy crap. I don't think I'm going to be sleeping much. Tell me something crazy."

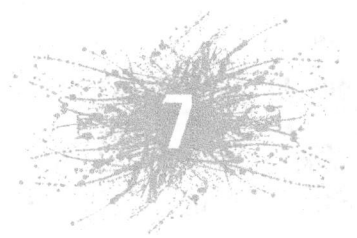

RAISING HELL

I knew at the age of fifteen I was going to be a diesel mechanic, no question about it. The plan was simple. I'd get a job building and fixing mining equipment with old Bill Bleasing whilst getting ready for an apprenticeship with Caterpillar. I'd apprentice with CAT for four years, after which they would hire me on, and I'd live the rest of my life working on only the finest of machines.

My plan worked like a charm, until it didn't. Old Bill brought me on straight away and I spent the next several months building mining machinery out in his shed. But soon enough the building season was over, and Old Bill went back out in the bush searching for black opals. As for CAT, they said they couldn't take anyone who hadn't finished school, and even if I had, I wasn't what they called "CAT material," according to my grades. So, I had to rework the plan.

I bounced around a bit but finally landed a job working the crusher at the quarry. That's where I spent a couple of years making little rocks out of big rocks. I also spent the time looking for a mechanic apprenticeship. That's where I got my plan, and heart, crushed time and time again. But I didn't stop. I kept applying and calling on every lead I could find.

Along the way I found a few more things at which I excelled. First was drinking. There's no better way to make a boy feel like a man than by ending a solid day's work at the pub and laying your own hard-earned money down for a tall pint of well-chilled beer. I loved that feeling.

Another thing that came easy was raising hell. I didn't even have to try. It just kind of followed me around wherever we went. Sometimes the boys were with me, other times they weren't. I respected the responsibility of work, so I had to get all the hell raising in I could on the weekends, and it all seemed to be centered around the old Holden.

Sometimes, when I was alone, and it was raining, and the boredom got to be too much for me, I'd go down to Morphett Park horse track and do donuts out in the grass car park. I'm not sure why the silence had that effect on me. I'm not sure why I couldn't just be. But it seemed the only times I felt at peace were when the adrenaline was flowing as I straddled the line of chaos, spinning loop after loop across the open paddock.

I'd established a craving for speed, so the only natural thing to do was to see how fast that old Holden could go. Sometimes it was at a track, other times not so much. When you're out cruising and racing the streets, you meet others who are out cruising and racing the streets too. That's where I met Knackers. We quickly became mates, he and I. We shared the same quest for speed, raising hell, and pushing the boundaries of crazy. We pushed each other to new heights.

We were so much alike that way, but our quest for crazy stemmed from two very different places. Me, I was hooked on the adrenaline. I loved life. I was running full speed into crazy looking for myself and adventure. Knackers, he was kind of a lost and tormented soul. He seemed to be running from life and used adrenaline to mask something dark and painful deep down inside. Either way, he was a good mate.

Knacker's dad was famous. He was one of the top touring race car drivers in the southern hemisphere. He won races all across Australia and New Zealand. The story goes something like this: He was at the top of his game, but he was having some issues with the car. So, he and the crew worked night and day to set it straight. By the time they got it worked out, they were running way behind schedule. Rather than flying and meeting the crew at the race, he traveled with the crew in the rig to get some sleep.

They were driving through Keith when the mechanic dozed off at the wheel, causing a terrible accident. They hit the earth mover first, then went on to wrap the truck around an old gum tree, trapping everyone inside. His entire crew was killed out on the open road that night. Everyone he had worked with for years was gone, just like that.

He was the only one to survive the accident, though he never fully recovered, and he never raced again. The doctors said it was a combination of brain damage and survivor's guilt. But it didn't matter what you called it; his dad was never the same. He lived for the race team, so when he lost the crew, he eventually ended up losing everything else too. Everything, including his family, which left Knackers with no real parents and no place to live. So, Mum took to feeding him on a regular basis and he took up residency out front of our house, in my car.

Knackers turned to the bottle and didn't look back. He would stumble home from a long night at the Morphett Arms and climb into my wagon parked on the street. I had a job and needed to get to work. So, in the mornings I'd have to wake him up and kick him out of the car. I'm not sure where he went on those cold and rainy winter mornings. I wish I had let him into the house, but Mum was not very happy with his level of drinking and wouldn't have stood for it.

With some hard cruising and harder partying, we'd gathered quite the rowdy crew. There was Smithy, Becks, Fuzz, Tuffta, Lisa, Leanne, and Wayne, all with differing tolerance levels for crazy. Me and Knackers, we were the driving force of course. We had a bond that couldn't be explained; we just fed off each other's need for adventure and adrenaline.

Much of the hell we raised seemed to depend on the weather. When it was wet and rainy, we went mud bashing at the top of Morphett Road. Mud bashing was a simple sport, as all you needed was a car, some rain, and an open field or a dirt road. The amount of mud splashed, and the number of spins achieved was in direct correlation to the amount of speed one could generate on the approach to the bog. That speed also dictated if the spin remained a spin, or if it became a roll. We were known for doing both.

We weren't stupid; we always thought of safety first. We'd cram at least three guys in the front seat to keep us from flying around and losing grip of the steering wheel. When we were mud bashing, we almost always took the toolbox out of the back seat. We didn't need that thing flying around—who knows what it could've broken if given the chance.

I was by far the best bonnet sliding driver in the whole of South Australia. As the name of the sport implies, all you need is a car, a hundred feet of rope, and a bonnet from an old car. I tried 'em all and I prefer the bonnet from an FJ as they have a deep dish and are made of stout Australian steel. Oh, you also need a beach. But not just any beach. To get a proper bonnet slide you gotta to go way out far away from town, where beaches were empty.

Again, we're always thinking safety first and gave the blokes out on the bonnet a helmet and a leather jacket. It only took a time or two before we laid an old mattress atop the bonnet for insulation, to keep the heat from burning the boys out back. And they had it easy. All they had to do was hold on.

The driver, he was the one who had to polish the craft. It wasn't easy making that bonnet swing out wide on demand. You gotta know when to floor the gas, when to slam the brakes, and when to crank the wheel to bring the entire enterprise into or out of a spin at just the right moment. The best was when you could send a bonnet skimming far, fast, and wide across the rolling surf. The goal being to launch the riders off a wave and into the ocean. Of course, Knackers and I always pushed each other for bigger and better, and it wasn't uncommon to get a bit too aggressive and end up fender deep in the surf, but it wasn't anything the boys couldn't push us out of.

It didn't take long before I wore out that first car and started using it for parts to keep the newer Pink FC up and running. We were pretty good at fixing the life back into cars about as fast as we'd beat it out of them. Most of that work happened in Dad's shed out back of our house. It became the hangout for the neighborhood. It seemed there was always something going on down at the shed. If it wasn't me or one of my mates, it was Adrian or one of his.

It was always fun, until it got boring. So just out of principle I'd push the bounds of crazy a bit further with each passing weekend. It's not so easy a task when you have a crazy reputation to uphold. It was bad enough when I was alone, but add the boys into the mix and it only got worse. If you added a few girls, there was no telling what could happen. Somewhere there is a line between crazy and criminal. When you're pushing it, that line becomes a bit fuzzy. As far as I could tell the only determining factor between the two was if you got caught or not.

It was a Sunday night, and in an effort to bid another perfect weekend farewell, I led the charge to find the fuzzy line once and for all. The car was loaded way past full, half of which were girls, which meant there was no hope for sound judgement.

I was out to impress and catch air. We hit the tram tracks going sixty miles an hour. It may have been the thumpity thump of the steel rails launching us airborne, or the bumpety bump of the hard landing that rocked the car. Whatever it was, it brought a moment of clarity with a stroke of genius. I slammed the brakes, cranked the wheel, and yelled, "I know what we're going to do! We're going to ride the tracks!" The whole while, beer is spilling all over everyone, and people are screaming as if something was wrong as we slid to a stop.

All I heard from the back was negativity. Things like, "What do you mean ride the tracks?" "People don't ride the tracks in cars!"

"Wait, you can't ride the tracks! What if a tram comes?" "You can't ride the tracks; no one's ever done that before!"

It was the last whine that cemented my resolve. It just pissed me off that they could be so negative about such a fun adventure. I hollered back with a wild snicker, "Well, we're doing it! Now! We're going to follow them and see where they go."

I straddled those rails like I owned the track. I didn't have a care in the world. The others kept hollering about this or that, but I was in heaven. I can still feel the rhythm of the ties as we danced from one to the next. Mile after mile the crazy kept coming. I can still hear the yells of the guys and screams of the girls! I felt crazy, I felt good, I felt alive!

"Here comes the bridge," someone yelled as if I hadn't already seen it. The desperate cries to stop only stoked my crazy. "What? I'm not stopping!" "But you gotta stop, that's a big bridge, what if we fall off?" The whining continued. I didn't stop the car, but I did slow down a bit. I'm not sure why I slowed. It may have been a momentary lapse of crazy, or it may have been a small dose of reason. For all I know it may have been a bit of divine intervention. But what I do know is, I slowed, a bit.

I was shocked by how quickly everything stopped when we hit the bridge. I mean everything stopped. The car, the laughing, the crying, the screaming, everything. The only sound was the rev of the engine and the buzz of the tire as it brushed against the corner of a lonely tie. I hit the brakes to silence the buzzing and killed the engine to silence the rev. There we sat, suspended about fifteen feet out on the Adelaide side of the Sturt River Bridge in complete silence.

Most were too scared to speak. I was collecting my thoughts and working on a plan. Finally, I broke the silence, "Get out and give me a push!"

"You're crazy! I'm not getting out. We're dangling in midair!" replied Knackers.

"You take the wheel and I'll push!" I insisted.

Turns out, Knackers was right. We were in midair. The front tires were wedged between the ties and the back ones were hanging high between the empty space left by an extra wide gap. That was the only time it was harder to get the girls out of my car than into it. I made trip after trip, showing each the path back to solid ground.

After a few minutes of worry, my sixteen-year-old brain came up with a brilliant idea. I knew just what to do. I popped the bonnet and twisted a wire from the positive battery terminal to the coil to make it look like it'd been hot-wired. Then, with a fist-sized rock, I smashed the driver's window, sending tiny chunks of tempered glass everywhere. "There! The car was stolen, taken for a joy ride, and was abandoned here!" I said.

No one said a word as we walked the quiet moonlit streets back to Glengowrie. Slowly, kids branched off to their own homes. The sun was backlit against the horizon when I finally made it home. Quietly, I snuck in through the back door and into my room. I'd barely had time to slump down inside the sheets when the doorbell rang. Dad answered. I heard voices in the other room and then footsteps coming my way.

"Robert, Robert, do you know where your car is?" Dad asked as he cracked open the door.

I did my best impression of a guy getting woken up from a deep sleep. "Yeah, it's out in the driveway," came my overly tired reply as I wiped the imaginary sleep from my eyes.

"Well, not according to the constables here. According to them, your car is on the tram line straddling the Sturt River Bridge." Said Dad.

"No, it's out on the driveway. That's where I left it," I insisted.

"Well, let's go take a look." So we did. That's when I met the two cops.

"It's not here. It must be your car out there on the bridge," said Dad. I agreed.

"You're going to have to hire a tow truck to get that car off the bridge," said the big cop.

I didn't have money to hire a tow. If I did, I'd have done it already. I replied with, "Well, it's not my fault my car is on your bridge. Someone stole it and left it there. So now it's your problem. You hire a tow and get my car off your bridge."

"Excuse me sir, but I don't think you understand the gravity of the situation. We have two, no, make that three, trams of commuters who are all late to work, because your car is on the tracks," said the lanky constable.

"Just the more reason you should hire a truck and get it off, and get my car back to where it belongs!" I replied.

"Oh, come on, it wasn't stolen. There's glass on the sleepers. The window was broken there! Now go get your car off the tracks before any more trams are late!" he hollered. I'm not sure why, but I felt I was being bullied and it triggered my fight reflexes. I didn't flinch.

Then the big constable walked right up to me. I looked up at him; he glared down at me. I held my ground and there we stood, toe to toe, for what felt like forever, neither backing down. Then, for some reason, we both turned to Dad at the same time. Dad was getting on edge and asked me straight, "Robert, tell me. Did you drive your car out there last night?"

Dad already knew the answer. He knew me, he knew my crazy. He also knew my stubborn streak. I was committed to my story and there was nothing anyone could do to change me from it. "No Dad, it must have been stolen." And that was that.

"You heard him; his car was stolen," Dad said, looking up at the cop.

Eventually they towed the car off the tracks, and eventually the trams got moving again, and eventually all those commuters got to their jobs. It was no thanks to me.

"Your dad seems kind of amazing," Jill said as the story waned.

"Yeah, he is at that. Quiet, but amazing." I replied. "It's kind of funny, the lesson I learned from that little adventure was how much Dad loved me. He wasn't one to tell me, he wasn't one to hug me. But all he did my whole life was show me. Dad always had my back no matter what. He stood behind me because that's what dads do, I guess. They back up their kids as they're exploring those fuzzy lines between crazy and criminal. They're hoping and praying for 'em, but love 'em and stick by 'em no matter what. I guess this is where I confess that I did end up going to court for those shenanigans, and I did end up paying for the tow truck."

"Did you confess?"

"Me? No!" I replied.

"And your dad, did he ever ask about it?"

"Not to this day."

"Yeah, he sounds truly amazing, to have your back like that no matter what," she added.

"Truly," I agreed.

Somewhere shortly after first light things began moving at the Rabbit Flat station. We purchased our petrol first thing. The gent at the station was a bit more pleasant in the early morning light. The last thing he said to us as we settled back in the XW was, "What are you doing anyway, driving around these parts this time of the year? You're going to get yourselves killed. It'll either be by the likes of me protecting my property, or the wet'll flush you down in some wash somewhere, or maybe the dry will bake you and blow you off into the wind. Sure enough, one of them will get you." With that, we set off down the track to find a place to wait until dark. The waiting was always the hardest part.

THE WHITE CAR

"Did I tell ya about my first race car?" I asked as the midday sun made sleep near impossible.

"Race car? You have your own race car?" she questioned.

"Had. But, yeah, sure. Two of 'em in fact. That's why I'm going to America. To race cars," I clarified.

"But you're so young. I thought you were going to America to *start* racing cars. I know you'd worked on cars, but you never said you'd actually owned a race car," she said.

"Yeah, well, I got an early start. And this is serious stuff. Did you know I once drove eight hours to watch a race?"

"What?"

"Yeah, the Bathurst races were on television, and the closest television was over in Broome. I couldn't miss it. I gotta stay up on these things, you know."

"That is some serious stuff. So, what about this race car?"

"It didn't come easy; nothing ever does," I replied, and then just started talking.

Part of the "exploring stage" in life is learning how far you can push things before they break, and we were pushing everything we could find, especially our cars. This resulted in many Monday mornings with a blown diff, gearbox, or engine.

It was after one such weekend I asked Dad over breakfast, "Hey, Dad, can I borrow your car today? I've gotta get to work."

"Not again, Robert! The whole idea of having your own car is to get your own self to work and back!" came his stern reply.

"I know, but I just have to fix up a few things. She'll be ready to roll again tonight, I promise!" I pleaded.

True to Dad's form, he obliged by handing over the keys. Then he did something I'd never seen him do before. He looked me right in the eyes and warned sternly, "This is the last time, Robert! I'm serious!" With that, he turned and slammed the gate behind him as he walked off to catch the bus. Dad was the calmest man you ever met, so seeing him upset like that, it stuck with me all day. It wasn't until that evening that I realized his last statement was not an idle threat. Dad sat me down at the kitchen table when he got home and made it very clear that I needed to find another way to manage my vehicle problems. I'd found Dad's limit.

Later that night, after fixing the car, me and my mates were sitting on the old car bench seat out in the shed. I was studying the paper looking for a junker I could afford when I saw an ad for a 1956 two door Chev. I knew those cars, and I knew there were probably only a dozen or so late-50s model Chevs in all of Australia. *That would make for a pretty spectacular street machine,* I thought to myself, then repeated the thought to the boys. "Oh man, those are beautiful cars," one of them said, which only stoked my interest. The $1500 asking price was way out of my budget, but I wasn't going to let a little thing like money get in my way, so I hatched a plan to get a show quality car. It all depended on Dad.

I set the plan into motion the following evening. "Hey Dad, will you drive me over to Plympton to take a look at a Chev I'd found in the paper?" I asked as kindly as I could. He didn't require too much convincing. After all, it was his idea to get a backup car in the first place.

The plan was to use the one-on-one time of the drive to talk about the car, how rare it was, and how it would make for an extra special show car. Then, once I sold him on what a great project it was, I'd move in for the close by asking him to fund the thing by lending me the money. Surely, he'd be more than happy to help if it meant having a fancy show car in the family.

So, I did. I was the sweetest sixteen-year-old you'd ever seen as we headed off down Baker Street. My mouth was going 100 mph about how you needed a special car if you're going to build a special show car, blah, blah, blah, I went on and on. Dad was his usual quiet self with just the occasional ahhu, yep, and hmmm.

As I listened to myself go on, I realized a few things. First, the thought of spending all that time and money on a really cool street machine, well, it bored me to death. So, I talked a bit slower. Then I realized if I had a nice car, I couldn't go all crazy on it, and where's the fun in that? I talked even slower. Besides, there was no way Dad would've ever lent me the money. He never lent me a cent for anything I wanted. Things I wanted, I had to work for. No, I didn't want any part of that car.

We basked in the silence of each other's company as we rolled up to Canadian Scotty's. There, sitting in the drive was a beautiful two-tone 1956 Chevrolet. It was maroon on the bottom, white up top, chrome wheels, and a perfect stance. Canadian Scotty had obviously cleaned her up for us; the driveway was still wet from the washing. He single-handedly carried the conversation as he went on and on about the car. We kicked the tires and popped the hood. All the while I was struggling because I knew I couldn't afford it, and I just wasn't into it any more. The whole time, there was something in the narrow side yard, way down by the shed, that was catching my eye. I couldn't quite tell what it was through all the weeds, but it looked like some type of roll cage.

Right about the time Dad was to say, "We'll think about it," I found the courage to interrupt.

"Just out of curiosity, what's that over there?" I asked pointing down the yard.

"Oh that? That's just an old digger, some sort of dragster. Junk really," he replied, trying to blow me off.

"Can I take a look?" I asked.

"Sure."

So, the three of us waded back through the weeds, all the while Canadian Scotty was back with his blah, blah, blahing. Somewhere in the string of chatter I thought I heard him say, "You can have it for $100. *Now that I CAN afford!* I thought. At that instant, and out of reflex, my hand went out for a shake to seal the deal as I blurted, "I'll take it, but I need to get a trailer!" And with that, I'd purchased my very own dragster, almost. I still had to pay for it, and I still had to get it home.

I wish I knew what Dad was thinking on that ride home. I could only guess he thought it was absolute craziness. I was running on pure adrenalin. My mouth was going 100 mph and I was telling Dad about how I'm gonna do this, and how I'm gonna to do that, and how I could borrow the $100 from my mates so I didn't have to borrow it from him! Which came as a surprise because I never worked up the nerve to ask for a loan in the first place.

The only thing I recall him saying was, "But you don't know anything about dragsters." "That doesn't matter! We'll learn!" was all I could say. He seemed somewhat happy with my enthusiasm as I made race car noises like a little kid. I imagined I was driving my dragster all the way home.

A few of the lads were hanging out by the shed when Dad pulled into the drive. I was so excited; I was out of the car and halfway to the shed before Dad stopped the car. On my way I blurted out, "I bought a dragster!" They just stood there with blank looks, so I repeated, "I bought a dragster!" and I got the same bland response.

Knackers finally spoke up with, "What do you mean, you bought a dragster?"

"I mean, I bought a dragster! It needs a bit of work, but I bought a dragster! We're going to fix it up and race it!" I yelled with a smile. It took a second for it to set in, but when it finally did, they exploded with excitement and a unified cheer of approval.

In the midst of the celebration I informed them of the details, "Oh, I need to borrow money from each of you."

"Wait, what?" said Smitty.

"Yeah, I need to borrow money from each of you," I repeated.

"I thought you said you bought a dragster," said Tuffta.

"I did, which is why I need to borrow some money. I still need to pay for it," I replied with authority. "And we need to go pick it up as soon as we can, so someone needs to go borrow a trailer!" And they did. All of them! They pitched in what cash they had, and before long Fuzz came rolling up, pulling his dad's trailer.

Word spread fast through the neighborhood. And, before I knew it, we had a convoy going down Bray Street to get the car. Canadian Scotty must have thought us all crazy when three loads of excited teenagers spilled out all over his driveway. We all helped lift the heavy dragster frame onto the borrowed trailer. Then, as quickly as we'd arrived, we were gone.

The excitement was real and the whole group was buzzing on the drive home. As was custom on such a momentous occasion, we drove slowly and took all the detours we could think of. We stopped by the Bay Carpark just to be seen. We cruised slowly down Jetty Road showing off our new pride and joy. She was complete with rusted frame and weeds sticking out from, well, everywhere.

Word continued to travel through the neighborhood. Several more lads had gathered at the shed by the time we made our way home, including Adrian and his mates. I still recall the smirky look on his face. We started laughing and couldn't stop when we finally made eye contact. Unloading was a bit easier with the rest of the lads.

For quite some time we all just stood around with big cheesy grins smattered across our faces, admiring the beauty before us. I think it was the first time Adrian liked something I did. It made me proud as punch to get that level of acceptance from my big brother.

Then all of a sudden, something came over Adrian; it was like he just knew what to do. "We're going to have to strip her down to nothing and build her back up again from scratch," he announced. Then he started barking out orders and telling everyone what to do, and we did it! Within a couple of hours, we had that thing stripped down to the bare frame with all the parts and pieces stacked in piles throughout the shed. "Each one of these parts needs to be cleaned," he said with authority, and we cleaned them. For the next couple of weeks that shed was a hive of activity. That scrap pile of a dragster came to occupy every waking hour outside of work.

We couldn't afford any new parts, so we refurbished what we could, and spent hours scrounging the junk heaps and wrecking yards for the right stuff. If we couldn't find what we needed in the yards, we were not below begging or borrowing from others. It was a true community effort! I donated the souped-up engine out of my gray FC, which kind of had the opposite effect of the intentions which got this whole project going in the first place. Tuffta had a cam and a set of rockers we could use, and the Bruce brothers had a YellaTerra head. Eddie had a set of triple SUs we could borrow, and Martin had a helmet. It was all coming together.

"I can take her to work with me at the rock crushing plant tomorrow and sand blast her clean!" I announced. So, I did. It didn't take long to realize I didn't know what I was doing, so I faked it. The blasting hood was so big, heavy-duty, and old, all I could see were the outlines of whatever was in front of me.

I was bound and determined to do a great job, so I took extra time to get every nook and cranny. When I finally pulled off the hood, I was absolutely flabbergasted to see the panels were all warped and bent out of shape. My first thought was, "It must have been full of

Bondo, and I just blasted it all off." Then old Tom came by to check on my project and said casually, "You gotta be careful when working with aluminum panels. They tend to buckle and stretch if you work 'em too hard."

"That bit of information would have come in handy an hour ago," I said.

"Yeah, I suppose. But now you know," came his reply.

"Well, how do you unbuckle them?" I asked.

He just walked off shaking his head and mumbling under his breath, "dumb kids these days."

The next step was painting. The fact that the primer gray FC was still primer gray was proof me and the lads had failed at body work. We had neither the skills, interest, nor paint, for the job. So, we hit up all the mates in the shed, and everyone declined, except Simon. He actually volunteered first, and second, and then again after each of the other lads declined.

He was quite the character, that Simon, and persistent. He was also ten years old. He showed up right about the same time as the dragster. He'd been begging to help, but we just laughed him off, until it came time for painting. Finally, Adrian relented. "Okay, Simon, you're on, but you gotta find some paint!" With that, Simon disappeared on his pushy. About an hour later he showed back up with a half a can of dried-up paint. It was white, kinda. Apparently, someone in the neighborhood had it sitting on a shelf somewhere for who knows how long. "Well then. Looks like you're ready to paint!" Adrian said. Simon just smiled.

Adrian was always thinking. He turned to me and said, "Robert, go into the house closet. Way in the back is the little tank attachment to Mum's vacuum cleaner. Grab it, and the vacuum cleaner, and bring it here. And be careful not to let Mum see!" I was off, and sure enough, buried way in the back, amongst all the other forgotten treasures, was a glass jar with "Electrolux" spelled in big shiny letters across the front. It had a handle and attachments for the hoses.

"What's this?" I asked as I entered the shed, looking over my shoulder one last time to make sure I'd gone unnoticed by Mum.

"Yeah, most people don't know what this is, but it's a paint attachment," Adrian replied. "See, that end sucks, which means this end blows. Just swap the hoses and bam, you have a paint sprayer."

"Genius," I mumbled. Adrian handed the entire mess to Simon saying, "Here, you figure out the rest."

We moved the car out to the street to save us from fumes. We left Simon out there and went back inside to do our planning and working on engines and stuff. Every now and then we'd look over the gate and sure enough, Simon was just going to town spraying the dragster with Mum's vacuum cleaner. The paint had an orange peel-like surface to it, and really showed how badly I'd damaged the panels. But it didn't matter. We were on a mission. There was a race at the track in a couple of weeks and we were determined to be ready.

We were never alone in the shed. There was always someone there, and there was always something for them to do. It didn't matter how old they were, or if we knew them or not, we put them to work scraping and cleaning parts, holding nuts, bolts, tools, and even lights at just the right angle. None of the neighbors complained when we fired up the engine, no matter how late or early. I think they understood the magic that was happening in the shed. It sure was something to see, so many young folks coming together and working so hard on something.

Mum would come out occasionally and stand in the doorway with her arms crossed in her tartan dress, and just watch. Every now and then she'd sprinkle a few words of wisdom on us. She'd tell us we shouldn't be smoking or drinking so much, and she always invited all us lads to church. Sometimes she'd cook up a dish of her famous goulash and invite us all in for a plate. Dad, well, just gave us space by steering clear and giving up hope of ever using his shed again.

"Wait, your mum invited all you lads to church? Including you?" Jill questioned.

"Yeah, including me. Somewhere through that time I drifted away from the church, not so much from God, but from church. I know it broke her heart, but she never stopped loving me." I stared out the window into the wide-open desert. The conversation died as we drifted off to sleep.

THE FIRST RUN

We were back on the road at dusk. But as it turned out, we weren't the only things drifting out on the Tanami Track. "Look at this!" I exclaimed, not believing it myself.

"Where's the road?" Jill asked.

"Yeah, I'm not quite sure," I replied.

"The dust is so thick," Jill said.

"That's an understatement," I said, clinging to the steering wheel. The wind had blown the dust deep, and drifts piled high. Some places you could tell you were on the road as the dusty drifts exposed the berm. At other places there was no way of telling for sure, so I just kept the car pointed in the general direction and hoped for the best.

"So, did you ever race the car?" she asked as I navigated the dust.

"Oh, yeah. It's funny how things never work out as you plan. But, without a plan, things never work at all," I said, then continued.

Soon enough, we were ready for our first competition. Fuzz borrowed his dad's flatbed trailer, we loaded up the white. . .ish car, and set off to the track. The whole neighborhood came alive, everyone came out to wish us luck, and for that moment, everything was just right. I'll never forget the look on Dad's face when I saw him relishing the moment, or when he caught me looking at him. We both knew it was one of the special moments in life that just happen. You can't force them or plan for them, you just take them as they come, and tuck them neatly away for the days when you need a solid memory of everything good to hold to.

We pulled into the Adelaide International Raceway dragging the borrowed trailer piled high with everything we had. There was our freshly painted car, everything we owned from the shed, everything we'd borrowed from the neighborhood, and our entire cast of mates who'd helped piece the car together. We had everything but a clue. We looked like a circus unloading that car. Not knowing anything, the race officials had to tell us everything, step by step.

It turned out the first thing we needed was a safety inspection. So, we pushed the car to the tech shed. We could feel the eyes of, well, everyone watching our every move. The safety tech got to work, saying, "You gotta fix this, and you gotta fix that." We were all in, saying, "we can do that, yep, that's doable, consider it done."

Then he asked, "Do you have your Chassis Certification?"

"A what?" Adrian and I asked at the same time. We'd never heard of a Chassis Certification. He just looked at us, shook his head, and said, "Look, in order to race you've gotta have your Chassis Certification. Lucky for you, the Division Director is here today. He can come by and inspect it for you."

"Great, meanwhile we'll get busy fixing the other things," Adrian replied.

Eventually this big, tall guy showed up. He recognized the car instantly and set off giving us a detailed history lesson. "That's the old John H Ellers car! It was built by the John H Ellers Holden dealership to show how good the new Holden Red motor was when the 186 Red was released back in 1964! That's quite the historical piece." This guy knew his Australian drag racing history, and he liked talking about it. We all listened intently to the whole story and were feeling pretty proud that we owned it.

Then he started in with the bad news. He told us about a guy who'd bought this car a few years back and tried running it. He told us how they couldn't let him race because the old-style roll cage didn't protect the driver enough. He went on to say how it's just not worth building a whole new roll cage for such an old car. We were gutted at hearing that news, our pride quickly faded into nothing.

As he was giving the history lesson, a few of the senior racers gathered around to check out the new kids and their historic piece. After hearing what was going on, they started heckling the big, tall guy, urging him to at least let us run the car as a trial. After significant discussion, the big, tall guy said, "Look, because you have put so much effort into restoring this car, we will let you run. But just one time tonight, so you can get your license. If tonight goes well, then maybe you can run her again in tomorrow's competition. But after that, you can only run at street meets or at the bush track up in Whyalla." Our entire crew, along with the old timers who'd gathered around, let out a cheer! I knew I'd found my people that day.

As I sat there at the starting line for my very first license run, it was the most amazing experience, the most alive I'd ever felt. It was like all those feelings I'd been chasing my whole life were rolled into one; the adrenaline of that first fight, the excitement of sliding the car out at Tepko, the thrill of driving the tracks, and even the rush of standing toe to toe with the constables. It was all there, and it lasted from the time they strapped me in the car, to when the boys picked me up at the end of the track.

We all seemed to be feeling the same thing. We were so excited! We were just a bunch of kids, but we had a real race car! We had a real driver, with a real license!

We were allowed to race the next day. As we lined up for our first run at competition, that feeling was back. In fact, that feeling has been at every starting line of every race ever since. To our surprise, and everyone else's, we won our first race! We couldn't believe it!

We were parked out on the bowl waiting for the second round

when we found the clutch linkage was bending. Adrian went into action; he pulled the linkage and together we ran at full speed to the Crusaders shed to weld on a bolt for reinforcement. We had so much adrenaline rushing through us we didn't realize how hot the freshly welded parts were, and we didn't notice the burns on our hands and arms until everything was put back together. And we didn't care. We were racing and that's all that mattered.

We lost the next round. But still, just like that we were in love with the sport.

That night, we sat a bit higher with our elbows hanging out the windows as we cruised slowly past every known hangout. We drove up and down Hindley Street a time or two, down Anzac highway to the Bay Carpark, back up Jetty Road, past the Broadway, and on to Holdy's Pub. All eight of us packed into the blue XA Falcon with our dragster in tow on that borrowed flatbed trailer. It was the proudest night of our lives!

Boom, skid, stop. In unison, Jill and I looked at each other and said, "I believe it's your turn." We laughed as we got out of the car. We worked well together. By then, we knew what to expect from the other and we each did our part. Before long, we were back on the road.

WOBITS WAIL
AND A DOSE OF NITRO

"I can't believe you were racing at such a young age," she said.

"It's funny, we never thought of ourselves as young. We were just so caught up in doing the things we wanted to get done, nothing else mattered. I miss that feeling of losing myself in the work, it's like time doesn't exist."

The White Car only lasted that one race, plus a trip or two up to Whyalla, the only bush track we were allowed to run. But we were obsessed and knew if we wanted to compete, we needed a newer, lighter car. So, we went looking and quickly found the makings of a brand-new chassis that someone somewhere had started, but never finished. It was nothing more than a basic frame, a front axle, a diff housing, and the bare frame of a trailer. We had our very own trailer!

The entire neighborhood workforce swung into action as soon as we got the lot home. Once again, the shed was a hub of activity. We had a lot to learn, and we were determined to learn it all. Like how to weld, how to build panels, and how to line up a driveline. Me, Adrian, Knackers, and Simon, we were always there.

The new car came together nicely that winter. It was quite the upgrade. The bare frame was so light, one guy could carry it around by himself. It had a Chrysler automatic transmission, a clutch, a resin filled block, and fuel injection. It was a powerful car. It could carry the front wheels sixty feet down the track!

We even looked the part! We had the car professionally painted by old Scruff. We had matching t-shirts for the dedicated crew. We enclosed the trailer by skinning it with some salvaged Stateliner bus panels.

We were just kids. I'm not sure what made us think we could build a dragster. Maybe it came down to not thinking. We didn't have time to think about what we could or couldn't do, we just did what needed to get done. I fear if we stopped to think about it, we may have thought ourselves right out of some of the best times of my life.

I was on fire the next couple of seasons. We'd raced down at Adelaide International Raceway every chance we could. I won and lost my share. The lads down at the track, the old ones who'd convinced the big, tall guy to let us run that first race, they became mates. I could always count on at least one of them for a bit of advice when needed.

We'd load the car the night before races. On the way to the track, we'd stop by the big gum tree out front of António's Market to load up any additional crew who wanted to watch but didn't have the cash to get into the raceway.

The second year got off to a great start, but it was right about then I finally got a letter from the Engineer and Water Supply Dept (E&WS) offering me a diesel mechanic apprenticeship. The E&WS oversaw the state's reservoirs, pipelines, and sewage works. They had a large fleet of all kinds of earthmoving machines. I was thrilled. I was going to be a real mechanic, like Adrian!

The first year of the apprenticeship was a bit like school, but different. We spent an entire week studying bearings, and I got it! I even built a set of atomizing fuel injectors in the shop. They didn't work of course, but it was the beginning of a trend, a trend where everything I did in my career somehow was used to improve my racecar, and vice versa.

The problem with apprenticeships was they didn't pay hardly anything the first two years. It seemed I was always broke and couldn't even afford beer after work. Some of my mates, like Knackers and the like, were on the dole, and they always had more money than me. Sometimes they would even buy me a beer or two.

Sometimes I wondered why I worked so hard and couldn't buy a beer. Yet, there they sat in the same damned seat, at the same damned pub, all damned day, and they were the ones buying me beer. I reckoned it was just that I liked what I was doing, so I kept on doing it. Yeah, I was always busy learning and building on the Wobit's Wail; it always took all my money.

"Wait, what? What did you say?" Jill interrupted.

"I said it took all my money," I replied.

"No, before that. Wobit's what?" she quizzed.

"Wobit's Wail," I said.

"Why Wobit's Wail? What does that even mean?" Jill asked.

"That's what the kids at the shed called it. It started out as Robert's Rail. But, well, Roger had a bit of a speech thing going on and it came out Wobit's Wail, and it stuck." I said with a smile.

Jill smiled as she giggled.

I was so into that car, until one day everything changed.

I heard 'em first. We were wrapping things up for the night when an unearthly roar rose from the track and rolled like thunder across pit row. Everyone froze with ears cocked and eyes fixed on the track. "What is that?" Knackers and I questioned in unison. "That, is Nitro," replied Adrian.

"Sounds insane," said Knackers.

"Well, that's Nitro," replied Adrian, "Gary Densham is here from America taking on all three Aussie Nitro Funny Cars."

Danny snapped, "The cocky son of a..."

"No. No, he's, he's good. It's just for exhibition, we invited him," Adrian interrupted.

"Who are the Aussies again?" asked Danny. "Graeme Cowin runs the Cowin car, Steve something or other runs the Southern Thunder. And, and . . . who is it that runs the Coke car?" Adrian questioned.

"Yeah. "Nah, I don't know," Knackers replied in a daze as he walked to the car.

"You know, I don't even know who runs the Coke car, someone from Melbourne I think," said Adrian.

I added, "Yeah, I've been reading about Nitro Funny Cars in the magazines, but I've never heard 'em, let alone seen one before."

"Yeah, me either," the rest replied in unison. By then we'd assembled in a line gazing toward the track. We were all kinds of mesmerized by the sound.

"I think we should probably head over there for the next run," Adrian added.

"Yeah," we all agreed from our trance-like state.

"Come on, let's wrap this up and head on over!" ordered Adrian. With that we jumped into action, secured the car, and ran off to the track.

"Finish line! We need to watch this from the finish line," Adrian repeated on the run. We followed him down to the far end of the track and found our perch up top of the dirt mound about twenty feet from the track.

I was intrigued by the fancy paint and flashy designs. But it was what happened next that captured my racing heart, and every other part of me, for that matter. Fire spewed out high on either side, followed a split second later by a thunderous roar, so loud and powerful it shook my insides. A cloud of smoke wafted across the track, and that was just the burnout!

They inched back to the line and waited motionless for the lights. All at once, chaos reigned over the track! The fire! The thunderous roar! Both cars' front wheels popped up off the track. The sheer speed was so far over the top of anything I'd ever seen before! And they were coming straight at me! And I was like, "be still my racing heart!"

My insides shook, my ears ached, and my mind was blown as they flew through the lights!

The Adelaide track has a short shutdown, so the chutes came out right as they passed us. I stood in awe at the raw power of those cars. Each run was an incredible contest between man and machine. The cars bounced around and lifted completely off the track as the driver fought for control.

There was so much power, it was more than I could process at the time. It was all I could think about the rest of the day and into the night. It was all I could think about the next day, and the day after that. To be honest, I'm still processing it to this day. I can't get enough, and I can't get it out of my head.

Jill laughed, "I've never even seen a race car, let alone heard one."

"These are not just regular race cars!" I replied. "Sometimes I try to explain the power of these machines so people can understand, but I can never capture the magnitude. The closest thing I can think of is a fire-breathing dragon. I kid you not! They spit fire and let out a horrifying roar so loud it rumbles your guts. In a cloud of smoke, they rear up on their hind wheels and sprint off faster than any other machine on the planet."

Jill laughed, "it sounds amazing!"

"Amazing doesn't do it justice," I said, then just continued with the story right where we'd left off.

The Nitro Funny Car shook me to the core. I'd found a new passion and had to be part of that world. I didn't know when, I didn't know how, and I didn't know where, I just knew I needed to be a part of it.

There was just one Nitro Funny Car in Adelaide, the Southern Thunder run by Steve Case. So, I did what any other obsessed eighteen-year-old would do; I called him. I was so nervous; I paced the floor practicing what I'd say. "Hello, my name is Robert, you don't know me . . ." no! "Hello Steve, you may or may not remember me, I was at the track the other . . ." No. "Hello Steve, my name is Robert and I'm a mechanic and I think you should let me work on your car." I went on and on. Finally, Knackers threw a can off my head and yelled, "Come on, you're overthinking this. Just call him and talk like a real person."

So, I dialed, and it rang. "Hello, Southern Thunder Racing," came a soft voice on the other end.

"Hello, my name's Robert, is Steve there?" I asked.

"I'm sorry, but he's not in, can I take a message?" came the voice.

"Yeah, sure. Like I said, my name's Robert and I'd like to talk with Steve."

"And what is this regarding?" came the voice.

"Yeah, ah, I'd like to talk with Steve about, well, maybe me being on his crew." I stammered.

"All righty then, I'll relay that message," said the voice, followed by a click.

And that was that. I turned to Knackers and said, "I left a message, he'll call me back."

But he didn't call back, not later that day, not the next day, nor the next week. I couldn't get it out of my head. There was something about the power of that car and the finely tuned crew all working together. I couldn't let it go. So, I called again, and left another message. Then, I called again and left another message, and then another, and another. Denise, the voice on the other end, came to expect my calls. I'd ask when the best time to call would be, she'd tell me, and when I called at the allotted time, she'd answer, "Hello Robert, Steve's not in, but I'll give him the message." She was enjoying herself at my expense. But it didn't stop me from calling again and again. For six months I called.

Then one day a strong and commanding voice answered. "Hello, Steve here!" I was so stunned I stood there in shock. "Hello, hello, is anyone there?" came the voice again. I gathered my wits, "Yes, Steve, my name is Robert and . . ."

"Oh, so you're the one who's been calling me all this time," he interrupted.

"Yeah, that's me. I guess," I replied.

"Tell me something. What's it going to take for you to quit calling me?" he asked.

"Oh, That's easy. Just let me be a part of your crew. I'm a good mechanic and I run my own dragster down at the track. But I'm looking to help on a Nitro car!" I blurted.

"Yeah? Well, if I let you come down for a look around, will you stop calling?"

"Yes sir! You can count on it!" I gushed.

"Okay then, you come down here this one time. If I like what I see, maybe we can make a place for you. But I need to be clear, so you understand, it doesn't pay anything." I was so okay with that!

I was so excited the first time I drove up to the Southern Thunder workshop. I hadn't much reason to be in that part of town and was taken by how huge the houses were. "These must be the richest people in the world," I thought as my rusty HD wagon sputtered to rest next to a shiny late model Statesmen. His house was a beautiful modern red brick two story with a big yard and trimmed shrubs. Behind the side gate I could see a massive truck and trailer alongside a surprisingly normal shed.

Steve's wife walked me through the huge house and out to the shed where Steve was working on a drill press. He came over, shook my hand, and showed me around his shop. By that time, I'd built two race cars and was well into my third-year apprenticeship as a diesel mechanic, so I knew my way around race cars and shops. I went to work organizing and cleaning without being asked. I must have done okay because Steve invited me back, and I came. Then he invited me back again, and again.

Before long I was officially working on the car. I was in heaven! I couldn't believe I was actually working on a Nitro Funny Car. Nitro is the top of the drag racing game, and there I was. I was gaining an education you couldn't buy, no matter what you paid. I was surprised when a couple of crew members left and didn't come back. Then the chief mechanic left, followed by a couple more crew members. Within only a few months I found myself responsible for most of the mechanical assembly of the car, and I loved it.

I became obsessed with Nitro Funny Cars. I was on a mission to learn and understand every aspect. So, armed with tunnel vision and sheer determination, I spent every waking hour outside of my apprenticeship in Steve's shop, and many of the sleeping hours on his couch. It's an amazing thing, to live a dream like that.

It's odd how quickly I lost interest in the Wobits Wail, especially after I'd spent so much time, money, and effort building it. But it just seemed to drop out of interest with a single dose of Nitro. Eventually, things changed so much I had to find another driver. I didn't have to look too far. Rosa, my girlfriend, was the fastest girl around. I mean that literally. She'll happily remind anyone who might forget that Wobits Wail ran faster and won more races with her driving than anyone else.

I was grateful for the education of working on the Southern Thunder, and what an education it was. Because I was on the inside, I learned more than just the mechanics. I learned about the business and the people in the business.

I could see how racing at that level's an expensive habit. Which is why, even with all the fun personalities, big egos, rock stars, and misfits found in the sport, most folks typically fall into three categories: engineers, players, and performers.

Engineers strive to understand the fundamentals of the machines. They are constantly tinkering with things just to prove their understanding is correct. They like winning and all, but they get their satisfaction in a perfectly assembled machine, and a perfectly performed run. They tune these massive machines with data and logic. It's all cause and effect, it all just makes sense, no voodoo shit allowed.

The players are the ultra-competitive ones of the lot. They think about nothing but winning, at any cost. It's all about being the best. It's all about having the best. The best cars, equipment, drivers, tune-ups, and crews. They hold nothing back.

Finally, the performers. They're like the players. For them, it's also about winning. Well, mostly. You need to be competitive just to show up. But showing up is what they do best. It's all about the show, both on the track and off. They have an amazing way of promoting themselves and what they're doing. They seem to be talking all the time. In fact, if there's one thing they enjoy more than being around Nitro, it is talking about being around Nitro. And they talk A LOT! They are both driven by, and tune by, pure emotion. They marvel at all the voodoo shit. But still, it's a business, and as with all things business, it comes down to capital, which brings us to the owners.

Owners can fall into any three of these categories. To be an owner, all you gotta do is buy in. Many buy in with money from somewhere else, either from a successful business they started, or as a successful driver. It is a business, and the business is winning. Most owners are confounded by all the voodoo shit, which is why no one builds their own cars; they have them built. They buy the best of everything. They buy the best cars, equipment, drivers, and crews. Then they hire the best mechanics and engineers to do the rest.

The truth is, it's extremely rare to find an engineer owner. As racing Nitro is an expensive habit, the scarcity of resources typically keeps the engineers on the payroll and out of the driver's seat and owner's box. The engineer is usually the hired gun behind the scenes, making sure everything mechanical is running as it should.

I quickly realized two things. First, I was an engineer. I loved working on the car, I thirsted for understanding and I couldn't get enough. I had to know everything about everything, Voodoo shit and all! You know, when they talk about voodoo shit, all they're saying is there's something going on there, and they don't understand it. Yeah, it was my mission to understand it all.

Second, Steve was a performer. He loved the show and the promotion, and he was incredibly good at it. It was a thing of beauty watching him in his element. He was at home out on the tracks, and on the road. But back at the shop, well, he was a bit of a disappointment. I found it hard that someone who owned one of these cars could know so little about it.

He spent most of his time on the phone talking with others who'd tell him what to do, and then he'd tell me. Eventually, he just introduced me to the people on the other end of the phone. That simple act, of handing me the phone, changed everything. Just like that, I was in. I was talking to the who's who of Australian Nitro Racing.

One week we were prepping for a big race in Adelaide, and of course other drivers started showing up for the competition. Then JB, one of the top Nitro Funny Car owners and drivers in Australia, showed up. He was fresh back from a racing trip to America and he brought some new technology with him. He and Steve worked out a deal and the next thing I knew, the Southern Thunder was set up in the big shop at Steve's place of business. JB showed up with his crew chief, The Ace. We were to modify the Thunder with twin fuel pumps and twin barrel valves, which would double the amount of fuel pumping in from twelve to twenty-four gallons per minute! It took some time to wrap my head around it, but it was such an amazing thing!

The Ace was really good, and he worked with me one on one, teaching me everything he knew about Nitro and Fuel Funny Cars. I was finally learning the stuff that had attracted me to these amazing machines in the first place. We spent the entire week going through the whole car. We rebuilt the bottom end and I learned how to cross-hatch the bearings so they could be reused. Occasionally JB would check up on us. He always listened, and always had a suggestion. JB himself taught me how to dial in a cam. Before long we'd plumbed the new pumps and valves and were ready to go.

I was surrounded by the top Australia Fuel Funny Car Racers, and they were teaching ME! I learned so much I was scared to go to sleep at night, worrying I would lose or forget some of the precious information. It's not often you meet folks who are so open and willing to teach the finer points of a very secretive trade.

We raced all over the country, from Melbourne to Perth. It's the most incredible feeling to stand at the start line when a Nitro car launches. Fire lights the sky and the thunder shakes your insides and rattles your brain. Well, it rattled mine anyway.

There's a line between complete organized chaos, and complete chaos. Complete organized chaos is a thing of wonder, you know it when you see it. It looks like a fire-breathing dragon exploding out of a gate going from 0 to 300 miles an hour in a straight line down a narrow track in three seconds. Amazing, if you stop to think about it. Chaos looks like, well, an explosion. It looks like the dragon tripped over its front toe, landed on its face, and belched up all its reserve fire at once.

The perfect run of a Nitro Funny Car is the closest thing you'll ever get to complete, organized, chaos! And there are no manuals. You're basically pumping massive amounts of this explosive chemical through an internal combustion engine, lighting it up, holding on, and hoping for the best. The cars are incredibly strong, stubborn, and unforgiving. Yet at the same time they are just as delicate, cooperative, and permissive. And you never know which one's going to show up on any given day. Will it be strong and stubborn, or delicate and cooperative? It's almost like the two types of chaos are interwoven. I guess that's why so many of these machines blow up.

We never did fare very well at the races though. Maybe it was because Steve was a performer. Maybe he was just winging it. Maybe I was too young and too green. Maybe I was too cautious and stuck to the organized side of chaos. But one thing's for sure, we never did blow up any cars when I was running the crew. Maybe we'd have done better if he was an engineer and had a better understanding of the tune-up, or if I would have let loose a bit. Maybe it just wasn't meant to be. Whatever it was, it was a great time.

"That sounds truly amazing," Jill said as I stopped to catch a breath.

"Yeah, it was. I hope you understand that what I'm doing, going to America to race, is so unheard of. Nobody does it. It's kind of a crazy dream."

"I still think it's brilliant. But I do have one question. If it's so expensive, how are you going to buy in?"

She knew how to get right to the point. I replied, "Yeah, I've been thinking about that. Quite a bit. I'm a pretty good mechanic and run a tight shop. I'm sure I'll find some work, and then I'll start collecting parts. I'll need a shed, a place to work. Other than that, I'm a bushman at heart. I don't need much, just a bed to lay my head and some simple food now and then. I'm going to have to live on the cheap, and I'm prepared to do it. I'm prepared to do whatever it takes."

"That is brilliant. Don't let anyone tell you that you can't. This is your dream and only you can chase it," she replied, looking off into the darkness.

It meant the world to me, to have someone believe in me like that. But there was no way I was going to tell her that. Instead, I said, "Looky here, black top," as I slowed to make the berm at the transition.

"Wow, that was quite the drive!" Jill said.

"Yeah. That was something. I was a bit nervous on that last stretch there, working our way through all six spares like we did. We couldn't afford one more. And I must say, I'm quite impressed with your tire changing skills. I'll put in a good word to the NASCAR folks in America if you ever want to go pro," I replied.

"Thanks, but I think I'm good. For now, anyway," she smiled. "How's the fuel?"

"Yeah, there's a bit left in there, but not much," I replied.

"Your poor car! Look at this, at least it's still attached," she said as she shook the dash.

"Yeah, she's shook to bits, I don't think she'll ever be the same," I replied. And she wasn't. Red Tanami dust had settled into every nook and cranny. The door panels had all fallen off and were stacked up on top of the drums in back. The door hinges had worn out and rattled with the slightest crack in the pavement, and the wiper motor had broken off and was never seen again.

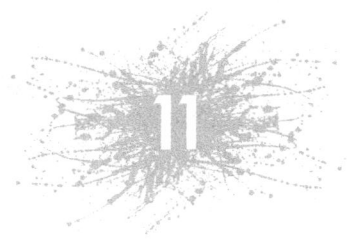

THE OUTBACK, ALICE, HALLS 'N HOME

"**H**ave you been to Alice Springs before?" I asked.

"No, I came across the south, from Adelaide to Perth, before making my way up to the Kimberly," she replied.

"I have," I said uncomfortably. "Did I ever tell you how I got to the Kimberly and the TripleX?" I asked.

"Robert, you told everyone how you got to the Kimberly. You turned left at Threeways," she replied with a smile and a laugh.

"Yeah, okay. You know how I got to the Kimberly. But do you know why?"

"What do you mean? For work, I guess." Jill replied.

"Well, yes and no. The truth is a bit more, well, complicated, and I haven't told anyone. The plan was to turn south for home, but everything changed when I got to Alice."

"What happened in Alice?" she asked.

"How about I start out with how I got to Alice," I replied.

The day after I'd finished my apprenticeship, the union asked me to join. I quit instead. I didn't have a reason for quitting really, other than, I don't know, I just didn't want to be affiliated with the union. So, after four years with the E&WS, I gathered my tools and left.

I was working on a plan for what was next, but that evening some of the boys down at the Broadway pub beat me to it. I'm not sure whose idea it was, mine, Pete's, or John's, but somewhere after the third or fourth round someone blurted out, "we should just go bush!" Someone else agreed and before we knew it, we were all in! We were going bush! In fact, we were going so bush no one would ever find us! By the end of the night, we had it all worked out. We were going to live off the land and build something of nothing, just like the homesteaders before us.

At that moment, we were the best of mates. The camaraderie was so thick, I knew I could count on those guys for anything. So, we made a pact right then and there, "We're going bush, AND we'll stick together, no matter what!" The plan was simple, we'd load up our stuff and drive. We called it THE plan because we didn't need a backup plan.

I just had a couple of things to work out.

First was the Southern Thunder. Steve asked when I'd be back, but I had no way of knowing. When you're heading to the bush for an adventure, there's no telling where you'll find yourself, so there's no telling how long you'll be. I wasn't expecting Steve to be so understanding, but I figured he must have gone bush in his younger days. "Have fun, be careful, and come back, preferably before the season," he said as I walked out of the shop.

Second was the car situation. By that time, my transportation situation had deteriorated down to an XA Ute, which was not going to work for three people. To this day, I'm not sure why Adrian agreed to the swap, but he did. He swapped the XW Wagon he'd modified with a 289 V8 for my XA Ute, certainly not a fair trade. I felt I needed to head out quick before he changed his mind, so we did. We removed the back seat for storage, loaded up my toolbox, our swags, and we were off.

Our first stop was Sydney, the big city. Okay, not quite the bush, but we felt it only proper to start an epic tour of Australia in an epic way. We hit the pubs hard. King's Cross came up a few times as we bounced from pub to pub. After the third time of hearing, "Every young lad visiting Sydney needs to visit King's Cross," we relented and off we went! What an education I received that night. I saw, heard, and experienced things I'd never dreamed. We had our fun, and then some! In fact, we had so much fun we made another pact, "we never talk of this night again, ever!" Yeah, what a night that was!

It took some time for a full recovery the next morning, but before long we were heading north along the east coast of Australia. Back in those days you could get a room above the pubs for real cheap, like five bucks a night cheap. The best meals were at the pub counters, and they were five bucks cheap, too.

We made great time and kinda got into a routine. We'd roll into a town late in the evening, find the pub, grab a bite to eat and a pint to drink, then head to bed. Then we'd do it all again the next day. We never did see much need for doing the touristy stuff, so we didn't. Well, except for the Bundaberg factory, but that wasn't considered touristy stuff, that was important stuff. It was more of a fact-finding mission really. Everything was up to standard, including the samples. Every now and then Pete would mumble something under his breath as we cruised along. I could never make it out, but he never did do that before King's Cross.

We kept the rhythm going and before we knew, we found ourselves up in Townsville, and down on funds. We needed to rethink the plan. New plan, head north up to Wiepa and get jobs in the mines. That version of the plan lasted all of five minutes. The first person we talked with at the pub was quick to inform us we'd have a better chance at work if we headed west. New THE plan, head west, and we did.

Charters Towers was the first real outback town we'd rolled into, it's in the center of Australia's great cattle industry. Life out in the bush is a bit like organized chaos, there's a code, but there are no manuals. The only way to learn the code is to live it. Sometimes you'll stumble across folks who'll give you a pointer now and then, but mostly you learn by things blowing up in your face. You gotta be tough, smart, and adaptable.

Turns out, my mates John and Pete were none of those things. We lost Pete there in Charters Towers. He just kept mumbling under his breath. I thought I may have heard something about King's Cross. I couldn't tell if he was running from the bush, or to the city. He was gone by the morning when John and I set out for Mt. Isa looking for work.

We rolled into Mt. Isa right about quitting time for the local miners. I still feel bad for John, we were learning the code of the bush by sense of feel. If you drifted too far off to one side or the other, you'd feel a miner's fist upside your head to put you back on course. John felt a lot that night!

As for me, I was catching on quick to the subtleties of the code, which left me in one piece and fully aware. Yeah, I saw things in Mt. Isa I never saw in Adelaide. But I did meet a guy who'd talked to a chap whose mate had some work for a mechanic out on the Powder Metals Mine.

I was offered the job straight away, and my funding situation dictated I take it. We were only in Mt. Isa a few days, and I'm still not sure when John disappeared. All I know is, he was gone when I made the long, lonely drive to the Powder Metals Mine. It left me wondering about the pact we'd made, and the camaraderie we felt only a couple of weeks back at the Broadway. Was it real? Was it fake? It sure felt real at the time. I reckoned it was the alcohol talking and resolved to think sober before I made any more major life decisions.

The Powder Metals Mine was where I refined my understanding of the code of the bush. It turns out, it wasn't such a mystery after all. It's a tough breed of people out there, and the key to the code is respect. There's a balance to respect. It needs to be given to be received, and it's not received lightly, it's earned. I took my job seriously, I ran a tight maintenance program, I kept the machines up and running. I earned every bit of respect I got. In fact, my respect was christened in that camp in the way of an official nickname. I became known as Fitter.

It was also there I experienced the chaotic life of a "wet" mine with some crazy mates. There was never a dull moment for sure. But there was something missing. What it was, I wasn't sure. It may have been a longing for home, it may have been me missing racing, but I called it sticking to the original plan to drive and see Australia. I wired up a piece of conveyer belt to the bottom of my low riding XW and headed back to Adelaide by myself.

It's a long way from Mt. Isa to Adelaide, with not much in the way of civilization in between. So, I stopped at the Todd Hotel in Alice Springs to regroup. After lunch, I took a walk to stretch my legs when my eye caught something familiar on a magazine rack in the window of a little shop. It was a National Dragster Magazine with a picture of the Southern Thunder on the cover. Of course, I bought it.

My heart sank, my blood ran cold, and my entire body went numb as I read how the Southern Thunder blew up, then burned to the ground. Everything ran smoothly when I was working her, she had no engine failures at all. Somewhere down deep inside I felt responsible, like the fire was my fault. Like if I'd been there, it wouldn't have happened. Everything changed right then and there. My plan melted. I felt it run right out the bottom of my feet, along with my racing heart, and my longing for home. It hurt. The guilt was so thick I couldn't even call Steve. I knew I could never go back there; it was all my fault.

So, I spent the rest of the evening at the front bar of the Todd Hotel alone, drowning my guilt. Without a plan I was just wallowing in my woes and pounding the pints. Eventually I began contemplating my next move. I picked up an old paper someone had left on the bar and glanced through the jobs section. I saw a posting for a mechanic up in Halls Creek in the Northwest of Australia. I couldn't get much farther away from home, from Steve and the Southern Thunder, and still be in Australia than that. First thing the next morning I called on the job and Fred said it was mine if I wanted it. I told him I'd be there as soon as I could, so without thinking, or planning, I left.

That was the only time in my life I didn't have a plan. And it's not so much that I turned left and went to the Kimberly. It's more like I ran off from something I felt responsible for.

"So that's when you turned left?" Jill asked.

"Yep, that's the spot, and that's why. I just couldn't stand the thought of letting someone like Steve down. It still haunts me to this day." I responded.

Jill replied softly and thoughtfully, "You said it was a fire, and that these things blow up all the time. You know it wasn't your fault. It sounds like he has a racing heart too. From what I gather from what you've been saying, if you've got a racing heart, it's only a matter of time before you have a burning car."

Those words pierced my racing heart, igniting an unchecked sigh. She continued, "he's a big boy and that's his own big boy toy. He's responsible for his own car. Just like you'll be with your own car, once it's built."

Another unchecked sigh escaped. She spoke the truth, and it felt good. It was nice having someone else convincing me of the facts. And after ten months of beating myself up and denying my racing heart, I needed a break. Besides, she was much more persuasive than me. Then just like that, the weight of running was gone, and yeah, it felt good.

"The car, she sure is happy to be back on blacktop. She loves the black top. Looky there, she's purring like a kitten," I said as I patted the dash and wiped my dusty fingers on my dusty pants. Jill smiled as she settled into the hum of the pavement and drifted off to sleep.

Everything we owned, including us, was stained with red Tanami dirt. But I didn't care. She eventually woke and we kept talking, singing, and laughing the rest of the way to Adelaide, just as if we were a couple. Which to my disappointment, we weren't, a fact of which I had to keep reminding myself.

Everyone was surprised when we rolled into Adelaide just before Christmas. It was great to see Mum, Dad, Adrian, and the rest of the family. They were all taken by Jill and liked her right away. I was proud as punch to have such a lovely young lady with me, even though we weren't a thing anywhere but in my mind. She stayed through the holidays.

It wasn't long before I marched into the local travel shop and asked for the cheapest ticket to America. I admired the posters of the far-off places as the friendly agent disappeared behind her monitor and tapped her keyboard. I was fixed on the California poster and I said out loud, "I'm going to be there in two months. The Winternational Races are in February." To which she replied, "the cheapest way to America is an around the world flight for $750." I laid my money down. "Done!"

It felt good to put the plan into action, until it didn't. I must have been beaming, because that evening down at the Broadway one of my mates asked, "What's up? Why are you so happy?" With a cold West End draft in one hand and a freshly printed ticket to America in the other, I held them both above my head and announced with a smile for all to hear, "I'm going to America and I'm going to race my own Nitro Funny Car!"

I'm not sure what I expected, but it wasn't what I got. I'd been around these folks my entire life and I thought they might have a bit more faith in me than the blokes at the Kimberly, but the reaction was identical. "That's funny." "That's a good one!" "You, America, Funny Car, that's hilarious, what a joke!" "You'll be back within two, maybe three months!" "There's no way you can race at that level;

you'll be laughed right out of America." They laughed, all of them, but one.

There was a part of me that knew they were all right, my dream sounded much better in the old XW with Jill than in the crowded pub. Then I heard a familiar voice from behind, "Well, if anyone can do it, you can." It was Knackers.

"Knackers! How's it going mate?" I yelled as I put my arm around his skinny shoulders and pulled him in.

"I'm okay, I guess. It's sure good to see you," he said, but I could see he wasn't okay. I could see he was hurting and holding tight to yesterday's pain as we wandered to a table on the far side. "You're serious about America and race cars?" he asked.

"Sure am, I got my ticket right here. I leave on the eleventh," I answered.

"Well, how about that. If anyone can do it, it's you! And don't let nobody tell you otherwise. Screw all these pricks. They'll still be sitting here when you come back," he added.

"Thanks, I appreciate that, Knackers," I said. As I was about to apologize for kicking him out of my car on those cold and rainy mornings—it'd been weighing on me for some time—he started talking and didn't stop. So, I sat there and listened.

"And what those other guys were saying? Don't let that bother you. That's just people talking to make themselves feel better. I'm not sure why they do that, it seems they thrive on bashing anybody who wants to step out of the box and achieve something for themselves. Screw 'em! They've been bashing me my whole life. First, they bashed my dad for being at the top of his game and then me for being what I was to him. Then they celebrated him for being at the bottom of his game, and me for joining him there. I guess them seeing me, somehow it makes them feel a bit better about themselves. Don't let them do that to you, Robert. You were the one who believed in me, don't listen to them. Don't let them question your dreams or celebrate your defeat."

I bought him a few cold ones that night and we kept talking and drinking until the wee hours. I dropped him off down by the bay and stayed there idling for a bit thinking about what had just happened as he wandered off into the darkness.

What Knackers said that night has stuck with me and helped me formulate my outlook on what "they" say. When "they" are bashing me, it means I'm on the right track. It means I have dreams, goals, and plans, and I'm working on them. In my mind, I've been able to take the negative talk of others and make it my own personal motivation. Whenever anyone dared to question my dreams, I've taken it as a compliment. I've vowed never to let anyone celebrate my defeat.

That was the last time I saw Knackers.

Jill soon left. She was chasing her dream of seeing the world and was on her way to Sydney, then on to Thailand. I still smile when I think about a bush Fitter and a British backpacker traveling down the Tanami Track in an XW.

It's interesting how people can drift into your life, even if for just the briefest of moments, and have such a strong and lasting impact. That trip down the Tanami Track with Jill changed me. I'd opened my soul to her by shared my deepest dreams and highest aspirations. Dreams so big they defied logic. Dreams so big most folks lacked the courage required to dream them out loud. But she got them out of me, she had me dreaming out loud and then convinced me to chase 'em. A chase that would take me across oceans and continents.

SECTION 2

A

BACK IN THE HOSPITAL

"What do you think he means by ORDER?" asked Bryan.

"I don't know," replied Mark.

"Maybe he wants a Big Mac," said Neal.

"Yeah, and get some fries with that," said Bryan. They all laughed.

"Lisa, can I talk with you?" Dr. Steffes leaned in from the hall.

"Sure," she answered as she handed the white board to Bryan.

"Lisa, what we just saw in there was a good thing, promising, but we can't get our hopes up too high just yet."

"Is there something else wrong?"

"No, nothing else. This is enough for sure. There's no way of telling how bad his lungs have been burned. Another reason for the coma, the reason I didn't want to say in front of him. Well, we do it in cases like this when we're unsure if the patient will live through the initial trauma, and here he is. He's still fighting, and that's what we hope for. "

Those words simultaneously silenced her, and pushed her back a step. A moment later, and on the offensive, she stepped forward in reply, "Well, he knows how to fight, that's for sure."

"I have no doubt about that. I only wanted to check expectations and see how you're doing."

"Me? I'm fine," she said clearing her throat. "He's never quit anything before, and I don't see him quitting this fight now. And I'll be with him every step of the way."

"Hmm," He muttered looking to the floor. "Well, we'll keep him heavily sedated for the pain, so he'll be drifting in and out of consciousness over the next several hours. He'll tire quickly, so let him sleep when he needs to sleep. Just be here for him as much as you can, let him know you're here. For now, that's about all we can do." And with that, he walked off down the hall.

That little interaction with Dr. Steffes was the most anyone had said over the past five days. Everyone was so unsure of everything that no one dared say anything. All they could do was give the facts. Fifty percent of his body was burned. The wounds needed to be cleaned, the burns needed to be scrubbed, and the bandages needed to be changed. Everything was so overwhelming she found a secluded corner in the hall where no one would see, curled up against the wall, and cried. She felt so alone and so exposed as she sobbed aloud, "Don't do this, don't leave me. I need you. I need your strength. I need your energy. I need your love. I need you to live. You saved me when I needed someone. I'll do what it takes to save you, just don't leave."

She thought back to the first time they'd met. She was working the front desk of the dental office when he walked in. She didn't think much of him at first glance, he was much like the thousand patients before. Until he wasn't, which was when he opened his mouth.

"I need to get this tooth pulled; it's bloody killing me!" he said in a thick Australian accent as he marched up to the counter.

"What do you mean, pulled? Let's slow down a little. What you mean is, you have a tooth ache, and can we have a look?" she'd responded.

"No. That's not what I said at all. I just need it out," he demanded.

"We can't determine that just yet, not until we take a look. But you might need a root canal," she answered.

"No, are you kidding? I just need this thing out of my head. It hurts!" came his reply.

"It's hurting and swollen because it's infected. The tooth is probably still good. We should be able to save it with a root canal. Then you'll keep all your teeth all nice and pretty as they are."

"Well, you're the first one to ever tell me my teeth are pretty, but that's beside the point," he replied.

"What is the point?" she fired back.

"Do you know how many race car parts I could buy for the price of a root canal?" he asked. "All I need to finish my car is an injector hat. That's $1500.00. Your root canal will cost that much!"

"What on earth are you talking about?" she asked, intrigued.

"I'm talking about how I'm building a race car and I don't have the time or money to be bothered with a rotten tooth. I just need this thing out of my head as quickly and cheaply as possible, so I can be on my way," he said, half smiling at the fight in the little lady across the counter and half wincing with pain.

"I think you just might be crazy," she said with the same half smile.

"He's back! Mom, grab the marker!" Mark yelled down the hall as Bryan grabbed the white board. Lisa paused for a moment, pulled herself together, putting her game face on for the boys, and confidently walked through the door. Something she'd done so well for so long. She needed Robert; he was her anchor. He was the one who'd pulled her through the hard times and helped her find the strength she thought was lost. He helped her find her a way to live for the boys. But then, as she sat down beside her love, she felt so alone, again.

Everyone resumed their proper positions. Lisa held the white board while the boys huddled around, and they all watched in anticipation as the marker scratched out the next bit.

"What's with the A?" said Bryan.

"I think it's an H," said Neal.

"Me too," said Mark.

"That's gotta be an E," said Lisa.

"It is an A," Bryan barked with confidence. Robert followed with a thumbs up and a point to Bryan as his hand relaxed and he drifted off.

"So, we have ORDER A," said Mark.

"I wonder where he's going with this?" asked Neal.

"Maybe he really is ordering a Big Mac," Mark joked.

"Let him rest," said Lisa.

"OK," replied Bryan as he gathered the marker and white board.

TO AMERICA, TO PHOENIX

I studied the rough texture of the popcorn ceiling and marveled at the randomness of it all. It made no sense. The white fluff and silver sparkles spread overhead for no one to see. A part of me felt like I was waking up back at the Kimberly Hotel, but without the hangover. "Robert, what are you doing?" I asked myself out loud. I was surprised by Susan's response, "What? What's going on, is it time already?" "Nothing, no, go back to sleep," I replied, knowing I had to take my soul-searching conversation internal.

Robert, you've been here over a year now and you're no closer to running a car than you were when you stepped off the plane. You know your stuff. You're paying your dues, you're putting in the work, but for what? Is it getting you where you need to be? You're working hard with grand intentions, but that doesn't mean anyone's going to give you anything. If you're going to get it, you've got to go and get it.

But where, I said to myself, starting a long string of questions and answers.

I don't know. Wherever it takes you. Wherever you need to go to build a car, and that ain't here.

But what about Susan?

Susan's great! If she loves you, she'll help make the dream come true. And the kids?

The kids are young, they'll adapt. They'll love life no matter where they are, as long as they have their mom and you.

What about work?

Work! Work feels just like the Water Works in Adelaide and the dead-end pubs in the bush. They don't care about you. You'd only been there four months when they promoted you to shop supervisor. All that did was give you another couple of bucks an hour and pissed off all the guys who'd been there for years. You remember what they did and what they said when you told them your plans. The latest National Dragster Magazine had just arrived, and you were trying to impress them with your history with the Southern Thunder. As if they'd know what that was. Then you just had to keep on going and tell them the dream. They laughed, didn't they? They laughed when you told them about building and driving a Nitro Funny Car. I don't know why you told them in the first place. Their reaction was the same as all the others along the way. They don't want to see you, or anyone else, do or achieve more than them. Out of self-preservation, self-pity, or just straight up meanness, they cut down anyone who dares try anything worth doing.

I continued to myself, *You'd better get busy working on the dream or you're going to wake up one day under the same sparkly ceiling, going to the same lame shop with the same miserable people who couldn't care less about you. You'd better start chasing that dream or it's going to end up chasing you in your nightmares. That's what regret looks like.*

But how and where?

You're a diesel mechanic, you love adventure, you know the mines, and love the bush. What's the biggest adventure you could have, and where is the most money you could make? Alaska!

It hit me so hard it knocked me out of third person dialog and back into first.

I'd heard there was work in Alaska, lots of work with all the oil and mineral exploration going on. Alaska was calling and I was going to answer. So, I hatched up a plan right then and there, in bed, under the gentle twinkle of the popcorn ceiling as dawn broke through the lace curtains. I'd drive up there and get on with one of the big outfits. I'll earn triple the money, which would leave plenty for a car.

"Susan, you awake? Come on, Susan, you up?" I asked with a gentle nudge.

"I am now," she replied.

"I'm done," I said.

"What?" she exclaimed, jumping right out of a dead sleep to a sitting position. "Why? Wait! What? With us?" she questioned as tears welled just under the surface.

"No, no, not with us, I love you." I replied and continued, "I mean I'm done with this life here and what I've been doing and working for. I came here to pursue a dream and I've gotta catch it before it slips away. I'm a certified diesel mechanic with real bush mining experience, I can make two or three times what I'm making now if we go up to Alaska."

"Alaska, what do you mean Alaska? That's crazy," she said.

"Maybe a bit, but that's never stopped me before. I know I can get work with one of the exploration companies up there. They are always looking for solid, reliable folks."

"Really? Alaska?" she questioned.

"Yeah, that would mean we'd have enough to build a Funny Car and we can catch that dream," I said.

"What about the kids? They're in school. Granny's only five minutes away, and they love Granny!" she replied.

To which I responded, "They have schools in Alaska. As for Granny, we'll be making enough we can get you and the kids down for visits. Heck, she can even come on up and visit us! Besides, all the kids really need is you."

The hottest part of the brutal Phoenix summer had faded. I spent the fall and winter planning the route to Alaska. I figured we'd head straight up the Alcan highway and try our luck in Fairbanks, then

Valdese as a backup, and then on to Anchorage if needed as a last resort. Spring is a great time for new beginnings, so we loaded up the wagon on the first of April and headed north. Everything our little family of four would need was either stuffed in the back or strapped to the top of that old station wagon.

We'd hardly made it out of town when it started. "Are we there yet?" Jeremy yelled from the backseat.

"No, not yet, Sweety. Here, color in your book," answered Susan.

"How much longer," whined Krissy.

I boomed in with a question, "Have I ever told you about my first day in America?"

The kids both smiled, giggled, and yelled, "Yes! Tell us, tell us again!"

"Attention, passengers, we are on our final approach to Los Angeles. Please secure your seatbelts and prepare for landing. Local time is two a.m.," came the voice over the intercom.

"This is it," I said to Angie, the Canadian backpacker I'd been sitting next to for the past several hours.

I'd shared my plan with her over the course of the flight. It was simple, really; I would land in LAX and walk to Venice Beach where I'd sleep on the beach until I could buy a car. Then I'd get some temporary work. I just needed enough money to carry me through the three weeks to the Winternationals in Pomona. Then I'd get a job with one of the Nitro teams and I'd be set.

She insisted my plan needed some more work. She was adamant about two points. First was that two a.m. was not the time to be walking from LAX to Venice Beach. Second was Venice Beach was not the place to sleep. She suggested the local youth hostel.

"What's a youth hostel?" Jeremy questioned.

"It's like a hotel, but cheap," replied Susan.

"Yeah, real cheap," I added, and continued.

I set off on foot at first light. Out of habit, I stopped at the first shop I saw to buy a Hot Rod magazine. As I thumbed through the ads in the back, I saw the Boulevard Speed shop was located on Sepulveda Blvd in Los Angeles, California.

I thought to myself, *Well hey, I'm on Sepulveda Blvd right now. I think I'll swing on by there on my way to Venice Beach.* I headed off down the sidewalk to find the speed shop. The only problem was, I didn't know how far it was to 110206 N. Sepulveda Blvd. After an hour or so of walking I noticed the street numbers weren't going up very quickly.

Back in Adelaide, the cops had always been a friendly lot and ready to help. So, when I saw an officer, I didn't think anything of it. He was standing on the passenger's side of a dark blue Cutlass Supreme chatting with the folks inside.

I walked right up and gave him a gentle tap on the shoulder. What I'd planned to say was, "Pardon me mate, do you know how far 110206 Sepulveda Blvd is?" I got as far as, "Pardon," at which point he about jumped clean out of his shoes. While in midair he'd drawn his gun, had it pointed at my face, and was yelling at me to freeze, turn around, raise my hands, and grab on to the fence, all before he hit the ground. Such a feat as freezing, turning, moving up to a fence, and grabbing ahold all at the same time was a task I'd have told you was impossible. But I figured it out, quick!

The poor cop, I didn't realize he was in the middle of pulling over what, on second look, appeared to be a gang banger car loaded down with a gang banger types. I thought I was being friendly, but it turned out I was being stupid.

The cop was spread wide open with his gun pointing at me. His empty hand up in gun position, fully locked and loaded, bare fingers pointing at the carload of bangers. He was yelling frantically at us, "Be calm! Be calm! Don't move!" His head anxiously bounced back and forth from them being calm in the car to me being calm at the fence, then back again.

Each time he looked my way I'd yell, "It's all right mate! No worries! I was just looking for directions!"

"Directions? What do you mean directions, directions to what and where?" he yelled back.

"Directions to the Boulevard Speed Shop, it's somewhere on this road."

"Speed shop, what are you talking about?"

"I'm talking about I've just got off a plane from Australia. I've come to America to build a race car and I am looking for the Boulevard Speed shop, just to check it out."

"You stay put right there; I'll be right back! If I see you so much as move a muscle, I'm shooting!"

"Yeah, you got it, whatever you say, officer!" I said calmly as I hugged the fence with my fingers braided in the links.

"Were you scared?" Jeremy hollered from the back.

"Yeah, I was scared, Jeremy. Sometimes scared is the thing to be," I replied.

Both kids were awed into silence that big old Dad could be scared.

The cop, he finally holstered his gun and finished up with the bangers. It may have been the frantic way I clung to the fence, or the Aussie in my voice, but he was much more pleasant when he walked back my way. He smiled when I explained it was my first day in America. I went on to tell him all about my plans and he told me why he became a cop. After a few stories, he responded to some chatter on the radio and said he had to go. He wished me luck and left me with a bit of advice upon parting, "You ain't in Australia anymore. You may want to think twice before you just walk up to a cop who's in the middle of a police activity." I followed his advice, but I never did find that Speed Shop.

The kids laughed, and Susan smiled.

"Tell us more, tell us more!" the kids begged. I was talking to Susan as much as the kids. We hadn't been together all that long, and I wasn't sure if she'd heard all the ins and outs of my first few weeks in America, so I continued.

"After experiencing the special place that is Venice Beach, I took Angie's advice and found the youth hostel. That's where I fell in with a batch of backpackers about my age. They were nice enough and reminded me of the packers who'd pass through the Kimberly back home. They were a colorful lot from around the world, and I fit right in.

"I bought the very car we're driving at a police auction just down the street from the hostel. It was the cheapest car on the lot, a bit of a fixer upper, but nothing I couldn't handle, and it was full of clothes that just happened to fit. In fact, this shirt right here came from this very car," I said with a smile as they giggled.

I told them how it was the Swedish girls who'd painted the Australian flag on the bonnet, and the Swedish flag on the tailgate.

The miles ticked away as I told them about how I'd dumped most of my money on the car, which left me with not much for anything else. So, the station wagon became my primary residence. I parked out front of the hostel so I could spend the daylight hours with my fellow international team of adventurers, while the nights were spent in the car out on the street.

"As for food, well, what little money I had was devoted to beer, so my main source of nourishment was the hostel food closet. The closet was a conglomeration of leftovers, the stuff packers couldn't carry with them when they left for whatever was next for them. I ate a lot of crackers and jam in those days.

"Finding work was a problem, and I needed money. It wasn't long before someone said they'd heard from somewhere that there was plenty of work in Phoenix, and someone else agreed. They asked if I was in, but I declined. I wanted nothing to do with it. I had Pomona to think about. That was until I found out Phoenix was only 400 miles away.

"The backpackers seemed a bit surprised when I told them how I'd driven farther than that to watch the races on television back in the bush. They thought me crazy even after I explained that the closest television was eight hours away in Broome. The lot of them pooled their money and nominated me as their ticket to Arizona, and the next thing I knew, I was in Phoenix."

"Is that when you met Mommy?" asked Jeremy.

"Well, not quite. I still had a bit of wandering to do, but eventually I found her," I replied.

The kids giggled some more. Susan smiled and shook her head yet again. A silence fell over the car as they all drifted off to sleep.

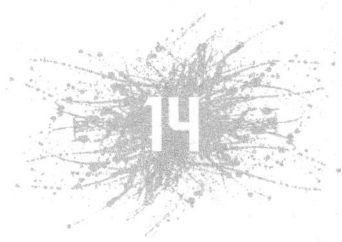

TO POMONA, TO ELKO

lost myself in thought as the Joshua trees passed and my passengers slept. There were parts of the story that still hurt too much to talk about, so I didn't. I just played them over and over in my mind from time to time, as a form of self-torture, I guess.

The hostel in Phoenix was much like the one in Venice Beach. The same kind of people, just different faces. We laughed at the same lame jokes and drank the same lame beer. My priorities were petrol for the car and beer for my belly. So, just like in California, I slept in my car and ate leftover food from the community cupboard. I would sneak in for a shower every now and then, and occasionally, I even paid a couple of dollars for one.

Finding work in Phoenix was easy, but getting it was a completely different story. I was a trained Journeyman Diesel Mechanic; I was in high demand. Every door I knocked on swung wide open at the prospect of hiring skilled labor. But those same doors slammed shut just as quickly when I couldn't produce the proper documents.

The door at Johnny's Truck Shop was rigged with a little bell that sent two dainty chimes through the empty office, one when the door opened, the other when it closed. The office was empty, so I poked my head through the shop door and let out a loud, "Hello, anybody home?"

"Hey, hold on, give me just a minute," came a muffled voice from under the truck in the second bay. I liked this place right away; I could tell whoever ran it was a real professional. The shop was well kept, the tools were in their places, even the boots sticking out from under the far end were polished and kept. Things only got better when he made his way up front.

I introduced myself, telling him I was a trained and professional Diesel Mechanic looking for work. He smiled big like he'd just hit the jackpot and told me his name was Johnny. I went on to tell him how much I liked his shop and how I could tell he was a professional by how he kept things neat and in their place. Johnny smiled even bigger and offered me a job right then and there. "You can start immediately," he said, so I did. I spent the rest of the morning acquainting myself with the shop by straightening up the already straight tools and sweeping the floor. I even fiddled a bit with the truck in the second bay.

Things were great, until they weren't. "Okay Robert, let's make this official. I'll need your driver's license and Social Security Number for the paperwork."

"Yeah, about that," I replied. "I have a driver's license, but it's from South Australia."

"You're killing me, Robert. I hate to say this, but I'm not going to be able to keep you if you don't have proper documentation. There was a time maybe I could have. But not now, not with all the immigration hassles going on."

"Oh man, I'm sorry, Johnny. All I've got is my Aussie license."

"Come with me," Johnny said as he marched off to the little Mexican restaurant across the street. "Order what you'd like—lunch is on me," he said as he introduced me to his Italian cronies. They were all very well dressed, with nice hair. They obviously enjoyed their daily lunches.

I kept them entertained with my Aussie accent and wild stories of home. I told them about Old Ron at the water works, and how

I was his apprentice for about nine months. I told them how Old Ron knew every pub in Adelaide, and how he knew which had the best counter meals, the best draft beer, and the best girls to keep him entertained. "Entertain him they did, but they straight up terrified me. I couldn't afford them anyway, not on an apprentice wage!" I said with a smile.

Johnny laughed so hard he choked on his beer. "And all of this was on the job?" he asked in disbelief.

"Sure thing, and many days Old Ron never did quite find his way back to the shop. That was the road I was on, and I just didn't see me having a life like that. So, when it came time to join up, I just couldn't do it. I had to go and chase my dream. And now here I am."

"Well I wish there was something I could do. I really could use the help and I think you'd fit in just fine, but I just can't. Not without proper documentation," Johnny said apologetically.

"No worries mate, I understand," I replied.

"Here, here's your pay for the work this morning," Johnny said as he stuffed a wad of cash in my palm followed by a vigorous handshake. "I really do wish I could hire you. Good luck finding work and good luck with your race car!"

Just like that I was on my own again, with a wad of cash and no other prospects for work. Johnny was quite generous; that wad of cash was worth much more than three hours of work. If it wasn't for him, I wouldn't have made it to Pomona.

"This is it!" I said out loud as I drove under the big California Fairplex sign. "This is where it all begins and ends. This is my chance to make it happen. I have the passion, I have the skill, and I have the experience. I've worked on Nitro engines before. Who else can say that? I've got this!" I kept the solo conversation going as I found the perfect parking spot on the far end of the empty lot.

It was a surreal moment, and there's no way of telling how many times I'd lived it in my mind. I'd dreamed of being in Pomona since I first raced the white car. It's not often a body gets to live a dream. I marched across the empty lot and right up to pit row with an air of confidence that let them know I was coming. Then I just stood there for a minute taking it all in, enjoying the sight of the crews bustling around readying their stations and tuning their cars. The sound of the track staff prepping the grounds echoed through the pits. The smell of oil, exhaust, and hot dogs filled the air. I was standing on a little slice of heaven.

There, near the back of the stands, not far from the Food Plex, was Al Segrini, a four-time winner of the WinterNationals. I couldn't believe my eyes. I could tell the crew chief straight away; he was directing the rest as they scurried about. Continuing with the same air of confidence, I marched right up to the chief and said, "Hey mate, how's it going? My name is Robert. I've come all the way from South Australia where I was lead assembler on the Southern Thunder Nitro Car. I've come to offer my services as a member of your crew."

"Oh? Hey, my name's Jake. And, well, you couldn't have come at a better time. We've been waiting for a good mechanic. Can you start right now?" he asked.

"Yeah, I suppose if you need. I was hoping to get a little lunch first, and I have a few tools out in my car. You okay if I get them?" I replied.

"Oh, I'm not sure we can wait. We've got this cam that's giving us all sorts of trouble," Jake said.

I replied, "Oh, well, yeah. cams, they can be tricky. I can help with that. I've been trained by the best in Australia!"

"That's what I wanted, no, needed to hear. Hurry up, come on!" Jake urged, and I did. I dialed it into a state of perfection. Then on race day I stood at the starting line as our finely tuned machine launched off into the record books.

Sometimes I like dreams more than reality; the endings are so much better, and so much less work. There were a few similarities though; I did drive under the "Fairplex" sign, I did park the car, I did walk confidently, and I did stand in the middle of pit row to take in the sights, sounds, and smells. And that's about as far as the similarities between the dream and reality went.

It was much quieter than I expected. The Food Plex was closed and wouldn't open for another couple of days, so there was no smell of hot dogs. It just smelled like an abandoned parking lot, like a million little dried oil leaks baked in the sun. As for Al Segrini's team, Well, I did find his pit, but it was a lonely place. I lingered fifteen minutes before seeing any sign of life. I marched right up with my well-rehearsed introduction and an air of confidence. "Hey mate, how's it going? My name is Robert. I've come all the way from South Australia, where I was lead assembler on the Southern Thunder Nitro Car. I've come to offer my services as a member of your crew."

He responded with, "Oh, I don't actually work here. I'm just stopping by to see a friend. Someone should be here soon."

It was another fifteen minutes before the "friend" walked by. I gave him the same introduction and he said, "Oh, I'm not the crew chief. You may want to come back this afternoon. Everyone should be here then." I promised to return.

The pit two stalls down had a few folks muddling around, so I walked up and delivered the same rehearsed intro. One gent looked down, another smiled, and yet another just laughed right out loud. "Hold on there, Aussie, let's slow things down a bit. Do you care to know my name?" asked one.

"Oh, yeah, sorry about that. I'm just a bit excited. I've been dreaming of this for so long. I can't believe I'm actually here. Pomona! I mean, this is the place, this is the real deal!"

"You really are excited!" he replied.

"Yeah, just a bit. I mean, I'm really here!" I said.

"My name's Dan," he continued. "This is Eddie and Vance. Since you were so direct with your approach, I'll be very direct with my reply. No. I don't have any "open" positions. In fact, we have a waiting list of people who want to be on this team. With all the prepping, testing, and tuning for the new season and all, I've been fully staffed for months."

Those words hit me square in the face and about knocked me over. *Oh no! What was I thinking? I should have come to America months ago and hit up the teams in the off season. This is it. This is the big league. No one is showing up without a fully assembled crew.*

"Yeah, right, no worries," I responded out of habit as I regrouped my thoughts.

"Sorry I can't help you with work, but hey, tell me more about this Southern Thunder. That sounds like something," he added.

"Yeah, it was." I went on to tell him all about how I called for months on end to get the job, and how we drove all over Australia from Sydney to Perth. He handed me a beer somewhere about halfway through, and that felt right. He told me about how he got on his crew there in California and how he'd been traveling the US for the past several seasons. It was quite a nice conversation when all was said.

"Well, I better head out. With any luck, I'll find someone who needs some help. It was good to meet you. Thanks for the beer and the stories," I said.

"Right back at you. Good luck finding work. It may be a bit tough at this point, but best of luck just the same. And Robert, I'd recommend starting your conversations a bit less direct. Maybe start with some of your Aussie stories," he added.

He didn't tell me anything I didn't already know, it's just that it'd been so long since I was on the fan side of things. It's funny, when I was driving and crewing, I used to make fun of the folks doing the very thing I just did. I'd been an insider since the age of sixteen, I was used to folks coming up to me and acting all giddy. But there I was, acting like a totally goofy fan. But I couldn't help it. It's funny how different things are when you're in the moment on the other side of the rope.

That's about how the rest of the day went. I met a lot of great people, had a lot of good conversations, and drank a lot of mediocre beer. But I never did find any work. I ate the crackers I'd taken from the hostel cupboard for dinner and spent the night in my car. The next day I woke up and wandered back down to pit row to give it another try.

There were more people bustling around with the qualifying runs starting the next day and I knew it was my day. It just felt different. But it wasn't.

It's no wonder. I'd come straight out of the bush, and I never thought to shave or cut my hair. I'd been sleeping in my car and hadn't had a shower in days. With super sponsors like Budweiser, Coors, Winston, Castrol, and the likes, I don't think this scruffy kid from Australia fit the mold those professional teams were looking for.

I could have left, and maybe I should have left that night. But the reality was, I didn't have any place to go, or be. So again, I spent the night in the parking lot munching on the last of the crackers. I woke up to the Qualifying session, which meant paid admission. The problem was I didn't have money for admission. I did what I could to be as close I could.

I sat on the bonnet of my car and watched as the lot filled up and the crowds streamed through the gates and disappeared into the portals of the grandstands. I sat on my bonnet as the drivers raced, and the spectators cheered. I could tell a good run by the pitch of the engine, a fact punctuated by the cheer of the crowd.

But all I saw were a few fluffy clouds drifting overhead, light and free. They rode the breeze, only to get snared in the white-capped peaks of the San Gabriel Mountains to the north. Oh, how I wanted to be inside the stadium. I yearned to be a part of the action. It was a gut-wrenching thing to have traveled a third of the world only to be denied a mere 100 yards short of the dream. All I could do was sit and listen to the sounds I loved. The roar of the engines and the rumble of the crowd rose high over the grandstands and echoed through the parking lot like thunder on the Tanami during a long-awaited wet. All the crackers were gone, so I ate the only food I had left to my name, raw Brussels sprouts. I reworked my plan.

After Pomona I went back to Phoenix, though I'm not sure why. It wasn't like I had a reason, other than it was the most familiar place in this strange land. Plus, I liked the drive through the wide-open desert. It had a homey feel to it. I parked in front of the same hostel and fell back into the routine of sleeping in my car out front and eating whatever scraps were left in the cupboard. Some days it was something, other days it was nothing.

I was broke. In fact, I'd had more money working weekends in high school than I did living in Phoenix. But I never felt broke. I just felt like I was doing what I had to do to make this journey a success. There was no way I was asking anyone back home for help, no way! That was completely out of the question. I was going to survive this no matter what. I was just doing what I had to do. Life was good, man! I was in America! And I was loving it!

I woke the kids as we crossed Hoover Dam. I was taken by its sheer size and magnitude; we even took time to walk about a bit. We eventually rolled into Las Vegas somewhere around midday. At the gas station, I heard someone say something about all the mining going on up in Elko and how they couldn't find enough help. I consulted my map and found that Elko wasn't too far off the path to Alaska, so I turned right in Vegas. That one turn changed not only the direction of the car, but our lives.

It wasn't too long before Susan and the kids drifted back off to sleep and I drifted off in thought back to the crazy night that set my path toward that long drive north through the open sage-covered valleys of the Great Basin.

It was the Valentine's Day after Pomona, and it was quite the party. I only remember a few things from that night. First was seeing *her* from across the bar. Second was how quickly my heart fell in rhythm with her gait as she strutted my way. Third was me asking if she wanted to marry an Australian. Fourth was how she looked deep into my eyes, almost as if she were examining my soul as she pondered my introductory proposal. Fifth was her response: "Maybe." She just let it sit there a while before she followed up with, "I'm Susan." Last was how she took me home and grilled up one of the best steaks I'd ever had in all my life. Not long after that, she introduced me to the two kids, and then her mother. I took to the kids and they to me straight away. Not so much with her mother.

Elko Nevada never had been a big place, and back in the spring of 1990 it was even smaller. The Barrick Goldstrike Mining Company was easy to find, and the jobs were easier. Right out in front of the building was a big board with a list of open jobs. There in bold letters was "Diesel Mechanic." So, I inquired within and was hired on the spot.

In the grand scheme of things, Elko wasn't much more than a wide patch set beside a pair of lonely crossroads in the middle of the Great Basin Desert. But by bush standards, it was quite the happening place. There was a grocery store, a couple of restaurants, a few office buildings for the mining companies, a few hotels, a set of schools for the kids of the ranchers and miners, and a few neighborhoods scattered around the edges.

It felt a lot like the bush back home. It was just as dry, the miners were just as rough, and the beer was just as cold. I guess there were a few things that were different. The ranchers and miners kept to themselves with their own brand of pubs, or bars as they called them. The mountains were a bit taller and organized in nice, neat rows. They were separated by wide, open valleys filled with low-growing sage and extended for hundreds of miles in every direction.

There was a place cut out of the sage brush on the south end of town where the mining company had planted several rows of single-wide mobile homes. They rented and sold them to the hired help. It was an incentive to convince folks to move to their corner of the open desert. Coal mining had crashed in the late '80s, so at the time it seemed all roads led to Elko.

I was at home in the bush and settled in quite nicely. The kids made friends quickly. Susan seemed pleased with the life we were building, though there was a restlessness about her she never could shake. The money was much better and went farther than anything we had in Arizona. But still, even that wasn't enough to scratch her itch.

A SHED WITH A TWIST
OF ALCOHOL

I was assigned to a mine tucked way up in the hills, about seventy miles out of town down a paved highway. I settled into work quickly. The guys all knew what they were doing and ran a professional shop. I took to it, and them, right away. It was quite a profitable mine and had top-of-the-line equipment. I got to work on the latest and greatest CATs and Dresser haul trucks, not a bad way to spend the day.

There was a watering hole in the middle of town set aside for miners. I quickly got into a rhythm of stopping off there before heading home on the weekends. Me and the boys—Andy, Jimmy, Jethro, and Kenny—hit it off instantly. Stories would fly around the table as we each took turns talking about where we were from and how we came to be here. Take Andy for example, he grew up doing all kinds of fishing, hunting, and camping with his dad and brothers in the bush of Wyoming. He chased a job down to the desert after the coal dried up.

When it was my turn, I wowed them with tales of building a dragster at age sixteen and working on the Southern Thunder. It turned out Andy and his family were into racing the short tracks; I knew there was something I liked about that guy!

We got into a routine of work, watering hole, and home. I was getting that familiar feeling again, like this was it. This was what life held for me. Life was always going to be an endless cycle of working the same job, sleeping in the same bed, and drinking at the same stool, no matter how far I went, or what job I worked.

Then, one day, I told them. I hadn't planned on telling. In fact, I promised myself I wouldn't. Not after what'd happened every other time I'd told my mates my dreams. That laughter was seared into my memory. But there was something telling me I should tell them. It may have been the beer talking, but I don't think it was. I think it was me.

"I'm going to build a Nitro Funny Car one of these days." I wished I could've taken the words back even as I spoke them. I steeled myself for their response, but got a much different reaction than I had expected.

There was a torrent of "How cool is that!!" "Are you kidding me? That's awesome!" and "That's the coolest thing I've ever heard!"

I was expecting to be laughed at for having a dream, which, in a way, would have made it easier to put off pursuing it. But then the questions started, "When are you starting?" "What's next?" "How can we help?" "How do I get a piece of the action?" I was in shock. It was a different mentality with this group. They had all moved from other places looking to improve their lives. These people had dreams of their own that had gotten them this far, and they understood others having their dreams.

I was a man possessed when I eventually made it home that night. I had a plan to rework. I didn't sleep much that weekend. I wrote down everything I could think of, starting with everything I needed, everything I wanted, and everything I hoped I could get. Then I put it in order of priority. By the time Monday rolled around, I had "THE" plan all worked out.

I told the boys at lunch. "First thing I need to do is build a shed. I hate throwing money into a building, but ya can't build a car if ya don't have a place for it to live. So, I'm going to have to build a shed, but it's gotta be on the cheap."

Jimmy said, "I know where you can get some trusses. Corky's had some sitting out back of his place for going on a year now."

"Corky, the Bail Bondsman?"

"Yeah, I guess he got paid in trusses a year ago. He'll probably give you a good deal. I'll ask if you'd like," he replied.

"Well yeah, I'm all about that. But why do you know Corky, the Bondsman?"

Jimmy just looked at me, so I left the mystery there and took the trusses.

One of the boys at Barrick had heard about the demise of the sugar beet factory up in Burley, Idaho and that they were selling all the parts and pieces for real cheap to anyone who'd go up and get them. Rumor had it they had a lot of tin siding. It was a bit rough, but the price was right! Jethro even volunteered to drive up with me to pick it up, with his truck and trailer, of course.

We were in business. I spent the next several months saving all the money I could and gathering materials for the shed. Susan was a bit taken aback by how obsessed I'd become, but she was into it. The kids treated the pile of lumber and tin as a playground.

I designated the spot for the shed myself. It was on the edge of the little lot, just south of the single-wide trailer. I'd planned on digging the foundation and footings myself, but it didn't work out that way. I never asked for help, it just kind of happened. Someone at work would ask how the shed was coming along, I'd tell them, and then help would spontaneously appear.

The weekend of walls and roof was the only exception. I made a bit of an announcement at lunch: "Well, I've got everything ready! The floor's in, the lumber, trusses, and panels are ready, so it's time for walls and trusses this weekend. It's a big job and not something a guy can do alone. I'll have beer and pizza for anyone who can help."

It was a bright Saturday morning; we had just finished the night shift. Some of the guys I knew, like Andy, Jimmy, and Jethro. But most of them, well, I didn't know who they were! They'd heard about the shed, pizza, and beer, and decided to make themselves useful, and fed. I wasn't prepared for the crowd, so Susan restocked the pizza and beer halfway through. The shed went up quickly and we spent the rest of the day basking in the company of great people, eating cold pizza and drinking warm beer.

Everything was just right! Until it wasn't.

I spent the remaining $367 to my name on raw Chromoly pipes for the chassis. Reality hit the day they arrived. I was standing alone in my empty shed, looking at this pile of pipes, and wondering out loud to myself. "How're ya gonna do this? Ya have no tools for building, no saw for cutting, no mill for notching, no welder for welding, no nothing! You've never built a car from scratch before. You wouldn't even know where to cut the pipes even if ya could. You're screwed! You have guys showing up this weekend to help, and they aren't going to know what to do!" I kept beating myself up as I circled the pile of pipes in the middle of my empty shed.

Then all of a sudden, it hit me; I had an idea. I ran out, jumped in the car, and was off. There were four stores in town: the grocery store, the hardware store, the feed store, and the parts store. With any luck, one would have it. Thinking logically, I started with the parts store, but they didn't have it. Next was the hardware store, but they didn't have it either. My heart sank. I was losing hope. I drove past the feed store, my sights set on the grocery store.

There it was! On the top shelf of the hobby aisle was a 1:25 model of a real NHRA-sanctioned Fuel Funny Car. They only had one, but that was all I needed. I swung back by the parts store for a quality pair of calipers. Then, with a bit of measuring and math, I designed my very first built-from-scratch Fuel Funny Car. Which, in reality, was nothing more than a 25:1 model of a 1:25 model of the Snake's Army Funny Car.

Things went slower than I'd hoped. I had no proper machining tools and couldn't afford any, so all the cutting, notching, and fitting were done by hand with hack saws and files. We spent the next several years in that shed building on that car. Somewhere along the way I signed up at the local community college to learn how to tig weld. I got along real nice with my teacher, and he let me borrow a welder from time to time.

That shed soon became a little hub of friends. Guys were coming and going at all times of the day and night. Most of them would work a bit and hang out for fun. Andy, Jethro, and Jimmy, they were the anchors of the core of mates that formed.

Late one afternoon, I ran to the machine shop for a job. There behind the counter was the little blonde from the dentist office. "You!" she yelled from across the counter. With a smile on her face she continued, "You! I told my husband about you! I told him about this crazy Aussie who'd rather spend his money on race car parts than on teeth. I told him how you're building a race car and he asked me, 'what kind of race car?' And I asked him, 'there's more than one kind?' And he says, 'there's lots of different kinds.' Then he asked me to ask you what kind of race car you are building the next time I saw you. So, tell me, what kind of race car are you building?"

"Well, you can tell your husband I'm building an Alcohol Funny Car. It's not much to look at, not at the moment anyways, but it'll be top notch when it's done, the real deal." I replied.

"Alcohol Funny Car. I have no idea what that means."

"Yeah? Well, it's right up there, some of the fastest cars on the planet."

That was that, until the next run to the machine shop. Again, I was greeted with, "You! Yeah, you! So, I told my husband about the Alcohol Funny Car, and he told me to tell you that if you need any help, he's a good mechanic and he'd be happy to. Happy to help that is."

I asked for his number and told her I'd give him a call when I needed help. That didn't settle with her, and she wouldn't relent until

I'd surrendered my number. I'll be damned if Ben didn't call the very next day. It turned out he was an excellent mechanic and he fit right in with the core team. Funny how some things just happen, like they were meant to be.

We spent the days working at work, and the evenings working in the shed. There was always me, Andy, Ben, Jimmy, and Jethro, and perhaps the occasional passerby. We'd be BSing about this or that, or sometimes about nothing at all, and our wives, Susan, Tina, Lisa, and Beth, would walk in. The conversation wouldn't change. Instead, they'd join right in and we'd keep going until the wee hours of the morning. It became a regular thing, and we became a real community.

It had a familiar feeling about it, like Dad's shed back home in Adelaide. There were no worries, everything just felt right. The people, the work, the goal, the smiles. At times I thought I might look up to see Mum standing in the doorway with her arms crossed, just watching. She'd sprinkle a bit of wisdom on us and leave us with an invitation to church. It was home.

Life has a way of happening whether you're mentally present or not. I became obsessed with the car. Every waking minute and most of my sleeping ones were spent either thinking about it or working on it. I'd wake up and work on the car. I'd go to work and think about the car. I'd come home and work on the car again, then I'd go to bed and think about the car some more. Susan had always been a little unsettled. The attention I was giving the car was attention not going to her, which only added to her unsettledness.

I'd been building on the car for over a year when I'd saved enough for an engine block. I was so excited when it finally came. It was winter, and the thought of that beautiful Keith Black aluminum block spending its first night out in the cold just broke my heart. So I brought it into the trailer and gave it the prime real estate right in the middle of the living room. The next day when I came home from work, she was wearing flowers in all eight cylinders.

There was a time when that would have been funny. Maybe it was, and I just missed it. But I was taking everything way too serious. Maybe I overreacted. Maybe I didn't react enough. For many years, I thought that was the beginning of the end of us. But as I look back, it's clear to see it was somewhere in the middle. By the time the summer of '92 had passed, Susan had packed up the kids and made her way back to her mother in Phoenix.

I wasn't prepared for my emotional reaction when she finally left. The silence, emptiness, and threat of perpetual loneliness wrecked me, and I grieved. Some guys would've cried, some guys would've fallen into depression, and I'm guessing some guys would've celebrated. But me, I'm not some guy. I coped by avoiding feeling all together. I doubled down on my obsessions and distractions.

I filled every minute of my life with intense focus. When I worked at work, I worked. When I worked on the car, I worked on the car. When I went to the pub, I was there for a reason. I was always focused and intense on the task at hand. The hardest parts were those alone times commuting from one distraction to the next. It didn't matter if it was to or from work, or the pub, or the parts store. Those times when the driving was slow and there was nothing but me, the open road, my own thoughts, and feelings, those were the hardest. I needed a proper distraction, so I found a reason in the pub.

One night, after a proper reasoning, I found myself lost in the rough-textured ceiling of the single wide. That familiar sinking feeling was taking hold and pulling me down. To save myself from suffocating, I escaped to the shed for a reconning.

There I was, alone, in the very place I'd been running from since Susan left. With nowhere left to run, I was forced to deal with myself and every feeling I'd avoided, suppressed, and masked for months. I broke down. I mourned the loss of Susan and the kids. I missed them; I was lonely. I screamed as I questioned my abilities as a builder and driver. I was embarrassed by my aspirations. I yelled at my failure. It had been three years and I had nothing to show for my time. I was ashamed. I cried for trading my family and every cent I'd ever earned for an idea; I was foolish. After letting it all out, I laughed at the heavens with the reply: "I was born for this; this is who I am, and it's what I do! So, let's do it!"

With that, the running was over. I was myself again. I could see everything so clearly. I grabbed a pen and paper, sat down on the old couch in the shed, and reworked the plan all night long.

I started by taking inventory of my life. First was the short list of all my assets. It consisted of half a race car, a trailer house, a shed, and a truck for getting to work.

Next was the shorter list of everything I'd done on the half-built race car. It consisted of eighty percent of a chassis and an engine block sitting on blocks. They were both short lists, but they were longer than when I'd stepped off the plane three years earlier.

I moved on to the long list of things I needed to get done on the car. The "to do" list included things like finish the chassis, finish the engine, get a body, build a clutch assembly, and install safety systems like fire suppression and kill switches and such. The list kept going on and on, and included a few other biggies like get a license and an EMT certification.

Last was the even longer list of everything I needed to buy to make the car happen. The "to buy" list included everything from the long list, plus all the parts and pieces with their corresponding costs attached. It included things like wheels, tires, a body, a super charger, belts, nuts, bolts, etc. On and on it went down the paper, and up and up the cost went.

I was determined to build the car with my own money. After studying the "to do's" and "to buys," I figured I could get it all done and paid for in three years. "That's too long! I don't have three years!" I thought. So, I reworked the plan again. I figured if every last penny outside of rent and petrol went to the car, I could get it done in two. I consulted the racing schedules and found my debut race. I wrote "Phoenix 32 Funny Car, May 1994" on a page of its own and taped it on the shed door. I stood there and said out loud, "I will be ready for the Phoenix 32 Funny Car Race in May of 1994."

The next two years were pretty cut and dry. Every hour outside of work, and every penny outside of bills, was spent on the car. To buy more parts, I worked every bit of overtime I could. Sometimes I'd work all the way through the seven-day change, which was against protocol. I was meant to be resting. But it seemed everyone at the mine knew what I was doing, and they helped any way they could.

Eating became an elective activity, and most of the time, I elected to not. I usually bought a much-needed car part instead. I learnt to hold off hunger by eating a steady diet of tomato sauce sandwiches. Occasionally, when hunger got the best of me, I'd throw in some frozen veggies for relief. Things got to the point where Jethro's wife began slipping an extra sandwich in his lunch box just for me. Soon others were doing the same. I'm not sure why they thought me worth it, but it saved me in more ways than just physically.

Time spent on the car also meant doing "research." I went to every race within a day's drive. I needed to know who was racing and what they were about. I also needed them to know me and what I was about. That's where I met Ricky Ruiz. He ran a car out of Sparks. He was a good guy and was always happy to help when I needed specialty parts, or just plain old advice.

One day I was chatting with Danny, the manager of the local Napa store, while on a parts run. I said something to the effect of, "Yeah, before long we'll be racing in all of the tracks around these parts." To which he responded with something like, "This is the only part around here, for hundreds of miles."

"Yeah, by these parts I mean Nevada as a whole, California, Oregon, and Arizona. I guess I'm talking more of a regional part than a town part," I replied. "Anyway, we're taking on sponsors, and currently we have room for you if you're interested."

"Yeah? Currently? Who else has signed on?"

"Well, right now, if you say yes, we'll officially have one."

He smiled. "Yeah? What does it take to become a sponsor?"

"Well, at this stage we'll pretty much take anything," I answered.

"All right, how about I keep you and your crew in those rags you keep buying," he said.

"I guess by anything I was hoping for something more along the lines of cash," I said.

"Yeah, that's a no to the cash. But if you accept the rags, you'll currently be the exclusive racing team of the Elko, Nevada Napa Auto Parts store." We made it official, and he was good to his word. He kept us in rags for the life of that car.

We'd built the car around two things. First was me. I'd be doing the driving, so the seat and cage were built custom. I spent a lot of time sitting in the car, from the first time the seat was installed and all through the building of the cockpit cage. It had to fit just right. It couldn't be too tight, or I wouldn't fit with a fire suit. It couldn't be too loose, or I'd get thrashed around if something went wrong. It had to fit snug, and it did.

Second was the sleek low-slung Brett Williamsons Corvette body. The moment it was delivered was like magic. We stood in silent awe as it sat on blocks in front of the shed. Loop after loop we walked, just looking, admiring, and dragging our fingertips along as we went. The jet-black body was smooth as silk. It felt like victory to me. It was beyond bad ass.

The body was a major milestone, and something we celebrated. Which eased the sting of selling my truck to make the purchase. I'd always wanted a fancy new truck. Though it wasn't new, it was close enough, and it stung when I traded in my big Ford pickup for the tired old '83 Crown Victoria. It was the cheapest car on the lot and needed a little loving care, but nothing I couldn't handle. Yes, it was a big day when the body showed up. It also meant I could sit in the car with the body attached. We had to do a little adjusting of the cage to line up my eyes with the windshield.

I'd been around Funny Cars enough to know that racing hearts and burning cars go hand in hand, you can't have one without the other. It wasn't if a fire would happen, but when. Because there's no way of knowing when, I wanted to be prepared all the time. There'd always been something down deep telling me I needed to be comfortable around fire, so I volunteered for the Rescue Team at work. I went through the Stead Industrial Fire Fighting School, which was rigorous and very hands on. They taught me about fire itself, how to prepare for it, and how to combat it. I was taking it on faith that this training would keep me from losing my mind if, and when, a fire happened on the track. I also completed my EMT training, which taught me how to deal with the human side of things, including the aftermath of a fire.

The shed was full of projects. I'd consult my "to do" list and start on a project. Along the way I'd see something else that needed to get done and so I'd start on it. Then I'd see something else and start on it, and so on. Before I knew it, I had all these projects scattered around the shed in neat little piles. All the parts and pieces were there, finished. Some were in advanced stages of completion, others, not so much. The boys were good, but nothing really got done unless I told them exactly what to do. So, we all worked on the same project at the same time, which was a lot of fun, but made for very slow going.

We were nearing late summer of '93 when I came to a realization; if I was going to make it to the 32 Funny Car Races in Phoenix by May of '94, I was going to need some additional help. And I was going to need it quick. I wasn't in Australia anymore; they weren't going to let the kid drive just because he'd built a car and showed up.

These guys had rules and regulations that needed to be followed to the T. To get my license I needed to make a total of six runs at sanctioned events. There, officials would watch and evaluate everything.

By everything, I mean everything. It would start with the inspections. The car had to be spot on with all the required safety features and equipment. Then they'd observe my crew from the moment we'd enter the staging area to the time I'd leave the track. I had to show I could handle the car at each step from staging, burnouts, back up, launches, straights, stops, and exits. They would be scrutinizing all of that, in addition to my driving. I had to be spot on from beginning to end.

With Phoenix being the first event of the following season, I needed to get my license that year, and time was running out. What I had was a great group of friends who'd do anything for me. But none were professional level crew chief material. What we needed was Adrian, so I gave him a call.

Of course, I couldn't tell him the whole story, so I figured I'd tell him the parts he needed to know, when he needed to know them. I may have exaggerated some bits, like exactly how close we were to finishing the car. And I may have let him assume others, like the shop and equipment.

Finally, I appealed to his warm heart. "Come on, it'll be like old times. You and me at the track on a maiden voyage of a new car. I've never christened a car without you, and I don't want to start now. Not with it being my first American dragster and all. Besides, I need you to be here. At least see me through to get my license." Some may have called it begging, but I called it a rather thorough convincing. Either way, he eventually relented and agreed to come for a month, "But only until ya get your license," he insisted. "Perfect," I thought.

Adrian got the rest of the story when he arrived in Elko. The gravity of the situation set in hard as a rock as I took him on the grand tour of the facilities. The truth is hard to exaggerate, assume, or gloss over when it's staring you in the face. What we had was a bare frame, a bare block, several little piles of parts and pieces scattered around a rough shed, and no tools. His accommodations were a tired old couch in a single-wide trailer, and an empty fridge. He would have left right then if he could have. That's one advantage of living three hundred miles from the nearest International Airport, I suppose.

He just needed a bit of time, and another thorough convincing or two. Eventually he came around and we put our heads together to figure out how we'd have the car ready for Winnemucca in two weeks. It really was like old times. Adrian worked full time, me, Andy, Ben, and the crew were either working at the mine, or working on one of the little project piles scattered about the shed. We had almost everything we needed; it was just a matter of putting things together. As for the few parts we didn't have, I was in America, not Australia. I could get anything quite easily.

I could put off the inevitable no longer. I'd used my focus on the car as an excuse to not think about all the other small but essential things we needed. Things like a helmet and fire suit, and such. I'd paid cash for everything up to that point, but I was out of cash and short on time. So, I broke out the plastic and started charging. It's amazing how fast those little odds and ends add up.

Andy was our resident artist. He painted everyone's helmet out at the mine. Once he'd get to know a guy, he'd freehand some custom painting, tag line, or saying on their helmet to make it personalized. So, when it came time for putting our sponsor's logo on the car, he was our go-to guy.

He did a good job, considering the fact that I could be intense. But my brother Adrian, he took intense to another level. Plus, he had a tendency to hover, intensely. It's a thing of beauty really. He'd stand back on his left leg with his right foot perpendicular and out a little, to give him a bit of a bend. His right arm was in a folded position, with his left elbow resting on his right wrist and left hand holding his chin. It was as if his hand would direct the intensity of his laser-focused eyes. He'd hover over any project to make sure it was done to his standards, and his standards were very high, which was exactly what we needed. It's what made him so good at whatever he did.

For some reason, the logo painting warranted a hovering. The intensity of that hovering must have thrown Andy off his game. We stood there, just looking at the car, instinctively tilting our heads back and forth and side to side in an effort to make it fit. I finally said, "it seems so right, yet so wrong at the same time." To which Andy replied nervously, glancing between me and Adrian, "the safety helmets at the mines are so small, and curved, and the car is so big, and flat." Andy wasn't courteous out of kindness; it was in fear of Adrian's intensity that he took the fall that day. I'll just say it did resemble the actual Napa logo and leave it at that.

AN AMERICAN FUNNY CAR

Then, one day, it happened. I walked into the shed after work and Adrian said, "Well, it's done! We have a race car!" I could hardly believe it; I had an American Funny Car! I wanted to celebrate, but I knew what was coming next, so I couldn't really enjoy the moment.

Adrian went on to ask, "So, have you thought about how we're going to start it?"

"Yeah, I've thought about it. I've thought about it a lot. I don't have the $1500 for a starter, and I don't have the credit for it either," I replied.

"So, we have a car but no way of starting it. You know, that's not a small detail, it's like a major thing! How're we gonna . . . I mean, what're we . . . I mean, hell! It's a starter! How do we start without a starter?" he ranted.

"Yeah, about that. Like I said, I've thought a lot about it, and I have a plan," I answered.

"Do you now?"

"Yes, I do, and I'll tell you it in two words: Ricky Ruiz." I answered.

"Ricky Ruiz?"

"Yeah, Ricky Ruiz. He's a racer out of Sparks. He's been helping with parts and advice for the last couple of years. He'll let me borrow a starter." I said.

"Really? Well, that's nice of him. How far is Sparks, and how do we get it from him?" Adrian asked.

"About that . . . by borrow a starter, I mean it's more like a "Ricky will let us use it at his place" kind of situation. All we have to do is get the car to his shop."

"Okay, how are we going to get the car to Sparks?" he asked.

"I have a plan for that too." I answered.

"Do you now?"

"Yes, yes I do, and I can tell you it in two words: Al Murdock."

"Al Murdock?"

"Yeah, Al Murdock has agreed to let us borrow his trailer," I said confidently, knowing what was coming next.

"Okay, so that's great. Is there a trailer hitch on the Crown Vic?" he asked impatiently.

"Yeah nah yeah, I've thought about that too, and I have a plan for that," I answered.

"Really?" he asked.

"Yes, yes I do, and I can tell you it in one word: Jethro."

"Jethro?"

"Yeah, Jethro. He's a mate from the night shift. He just bought a brand-new Dodge pickup. It's a beauty. It's shiny blue with a Cummings engine and everything." I answered.

"Jethro's just gonna let you borrow his brand-new fancy pickup?" he asked.

"Well, it's not so much him letting us borrow the truck as it is a "him letting us use it as long as he's the one doing the driving" kind of situation. Anyway, I've already got it worked out. He's agreed to tow the car from here to Sparks then back to Winnemucca for the license runs."

I was proud of myself for thinking that far ahead. But then again, with all of the moving parts and pieces, I was only hoping they would all come together as planned. Maybe then I could find a moment to enjoy.

Bright and early Friday morning, as the sun crept up and the day crew crept in, we wrapped up the night shift and headed west for the four-hour trip to Sparks. Jethro stayed true to his word and let us borrow his truck, and he did the driving. Al's trailer was loaded with the car and the toolbox holding the few tools I had to my name. It was a tight fit with Jethro, me, Adrian, and all of Jethro's farming tools and horse equipment, but there was nothing we couldn't handle.

It was late morning when we rolled into Ricky's place. He was waiting with a spot set aside for us in his shop. It didn't take long to set up. Ricky was willing and ready to do anything to get this Australian kid's Funny Car up and running. He took his time looking over the car and was impressed with how well she was put together.

"Let's do this; let's start her up!" he exclaimed.

"Yeah!" we answered in unison with big smiles and high fives. But no one did anything. We all just kind of waited for someone to get into the car. I guess everyone assumed someone else would do the honor. For me, I thought Adrian should have the honors for coming half-way around the world and working so hard. Or maybe Ricky should do it for helping with the final touches. Besides, it was his shop.

Finally, Ricky piped up and said, pointing at me, "There's only one person who should be sitting in this car, and that's you!" So, I jumped in and settled down into the cage. She fit perfect. Ricky and Adrian connected the starter, and with a thumbs up and the flick of a switch she roared to life. I could feel the power bundled up inside just waiting to be released. Ricky and Adrian hovered over her as if suspended in air. They zipped back and forth with a tweak here, and an adjustment there, while alcohol fumes filled the shop.

I gripped the steering wheel with both hands and felt connected to the sheer power within. It was like I was plugged in; I felt the energy coursing through my entire body. It started at my hands and feet, and it worked its way up my arms and legs and converged at my heart. That's when it hit me, all of it, at that very instant. It was as if all the joy of chasing a dream, coming to America, getting married, working at the mine, building a shed of dreams, and then sitting in that dream had been mixed and bottled with the agony of the Southern Thunder burn, leaving my family and everyone I knew in Australia, the rejection at Pomona, and the divorce. The cork had popped and all the emotions I'd been storing up inside for the past five years were released at once. Tears flowed and there was nothing I could do about it.

I was prepared to deny it if anyone asked. I was ready to blame it on the fumes. But no one asked.

I wasn't sure when Jethro disappeared; it was probably during the fine tuning after the initial start. But I wasn't too concerned until it was time to load up. He was a big guy, as strong as a buffalo, and we needed his help. I found him stretched out fast asleep in his big blue truck. He was all tucked in nice and snug, using his jacket for a blanket. I was still riding high on adrenaline and emotion and may have been overly enthusiastic with how quickly I opened the door, with the force I used to grab his feet and shake him awake, and the volume of my voice as I yelled, "Come on, let's go!" Because all hell broke loose.

Jethro's entire body rose a foot off the seat, he let out a yelp heard across town, his eyes swelled to the size of saucers, and a gun flew from under his jacket and was pointing right in my face, all before he landed! I flinched in panic, but quickly recovered. "Wait, man! It's just me! What are you doing? Calm down!" I hollered.

"I'm protecting myself. You never know!" he yelled back.

"You never know what?" I replied.

"You never know who's out doing what and where! Especially when you're sleeping. I don't know these parts!" he said.

"Well, calm down and put that thing away. It's time to load up and hit the road," was all I could mutter. They say the third time is a charm, but there was still nothing charming about looking down the barrel of a gun.

To save us from running back and forth we spent the night in the open bush on the outskirts of Winnemucca. It was a modest camp and a moonless night. We slept under the countless stars of the Milky Way and basked in the emotional high of the day. Life was good.

Bright and early the next morning we met up with the rest of the crew at the Winnemucca Regional Airport. Winnemucca wasn't a regular thing. It was hosted by a group raising interest, and funds, to build a racetrack in Fallon. Lucky for us, somehow, they'd arranged to use the airstrip for the day.

We were riding high from the happenings of the day before, until we entered the staging area that is. I felt we were on parade as Jethro drove to our slot on the far end of the lot. One by one we passed the who's who of the California Independent Funny Car Association (CIFCA) with their big trucks, fancy trailers, traveling shops, and professional crews. My confidence waned with each passing crew.

What we had was a big, blue, borrowed truck loaded heavy with farming equipment and horse gear, a mismatched trailer we'd borrowed from old Al Murdock, the starter motor Ricky actually let me borrow, a small box with a few tools, a bag of rags from the Elko Napa Store, and absolutely no spare parts. If our truck and trailer wasn't enough to catch their attention, our appearance was. There was nothing uniform about us. Jimmy was never seen without his signature cowboy hat. Jethro was in his blue bib overalls. Ben lived in his machine shop clothes. Randy was dressed up like he was going to church. And Adrian was sporting his faded blue one-piece overalls. We were a motley looking crew for sure.

My confidence hit bottom during a moment of silence just before our run. I was standing next to the car looking out at the stands full of people and I had this strange feeling. I felt like the entire crowd was there to watch me screw it up. I knew we were nobodies trying to run a car that was way above our skill level, and I felt they knew it too. It's funny how those thoughts of doubt will creep in right at the wrong times.

The next thing I knew we were on deck. All doubt dissipated as I nestled into the cage. Adrian and Ben fired her up and she roared to life. Again, I felt the power coursing through me. I swore I was going to drive the car blindfolded if I had to, and I almost got my chance.

I'd spent a lot of time in the car throughout the build. I'd sat in the bare frame without my fire suit, both strapped in and not. I'd sat in the bare frame with my fire suit on, both strapped in and not. I'd even sat in it without my fire suit, both strapped in and not, with the body. But I'd never sat in it with my fire suit on, strapped in, with the body on! I didn't think it would be a problem, until it was.

The boys strapped me down tight for safety's sake, but when they lowered the body, I couldn't see a bloody thing! Let me rephrase that. I couldn't see a bloody thing that mattered. I could see blue sky, and a couple of fluffy clouds, and Adrian and Ben hovering near by, but I couldn't see the track. So I pushed up hard against the straps and stretched my neck out as long as I could, and off in the distance I could see a big pine tree to my left and a power pole to the right.

Like I said, I was bound and determined to make this race happen, so I said nothing. They rolled me up to position, and there, just over the body, silhouetted against a background of blue, were the starting lights. Finally, something that mattered! I reassured myself by saying out loud, "It's a straight track; just go straight." With that, I lit her up for the burnout, then backed her up for our first run.

"It's a straight track; just go straight," I repeated to myself. With that, I cautiously gave her almost everything she had and launched her 100 feet down the track before letting up. What looked like an uneventful run to the crowd was the adventure of a lifetime for me, and a quick lesson in driving blind! The only way I knew I was on the track was by the rumble of the gravel, and the rocks flicking off the tires and pinging the tinwork of the body. If the rumble and pings were on the left, I nudged her back to the right, and vice versa. Thank goodness for the finish line poles or I would've never known when to stop!

We took her back to the pits, and with a bit of modification to the seat, I was seeing just fine. We did three more runs that day in Winnemucca.

The boys brought their families along for the big show, so we had our own cheering section. Well, it would have been a cheering section if they would have cheered. The ladies were all bored to tears and swatting flies. Mark, Bryan, and the rest of the kids were looking for a swimming pool.

Jethro's truck and Al's trailer got us to Boise, where I completed the final two runs for my license. Just like that, I was a licensed drag racer in America! It was a bittersweet time. The sweetness was two-fold. First, I watched Adrian make a true pit crew out of our ragged group of friends. Second, I was a licensed Funny Car driver in America. I'd done it. In five short years, I'd managed to get to America and build a dragster from nothing. My crazy dream was becoming a reality. The bitter part was that Adrian had lived up to his end of the bargain, which meant he was ready to head back home to Australia, and he did.

OFF TO THE RACES

The Phoenix 32 was quickly approaching and I knew one thing for certain: I needed Adrian. He had a way about him that gave both me and the crew the confidence to do anything. It took everything I had to make the call. I was right in thinking the license runs had a lasting effect on him, but it was in a good way. It turns out he'd been prepping Donna, his wife, for several months for the opportunity to go racing in America. So, three weeks before the big race in Phoenix, Adrian, Donna, and Jessie, their six-month-old baby, arrived in Elko. There was no denying that he'd caught the bug, and I was reaping the benefits.

I could tell right off that Adrian had prepped Donna the same way I'd prepped him for his first visit. He'd told her only what she needed to know, and he let her assume the rest. But just like before, the truth is hard to avoid when it's staring you in the face. To say she was disappointed with the sparse accommodations and lack of amenities was an understatement. She felt things like groceries and such were more necessities than luxuries. I tried getting her to see the positive, "Look, there's plenty of room in the cupboards and fridge to put anything you'd like." It was clear I was only making things worse, so I left Adrian to deal with that and made myself scarce. Besides, I had racing on my brain and work to do.

I couldn't just keep borrowing trucks and trailers out on the racing circuit. For a few years, on the way to and from the mine, I'd been noticing a big old orange GMC Dually sitting out back of Fred's place. I finally inquired within. I went into hock, but was soon the proud new owner of an old orange GMC Dually with a 454 big block. With a little loving care, she was running just fine. That truck came to be known affectionately as The Great Pumpkin.

I found a real racing trailer for real cheap; the only problem was, it was in Indianapolis. A week or so before Phoenix I asked Adrian if he wouldn't mind making a run to Indiana to collect it. He was a bit hesitant as I was already on thin ice with Donna. She wasn't too thrilled about the living conditions of the single-wide and let everyone know about it, all the time. But when I offered up my credit card and told them to make a mini holiday out of it, they agreed.

I'd given him my work number in the case of an emergency, but I didn't think he'd actually use it. He used it. The conversation went something like, "Hello."

"Hey, it's me, Adrian."

"Yeah, how's it going?" No reply. "How's the trip?" No reply. "Do you have the trailer?" No reply. It was a bit unnerving to say the least, as Adrian never said nothing. But all I heard, for a long time, was him breathing. Finally, he spoke, "Do you want the good news first, or the bad?"

I said nothing. All he heard for a long time was me breathing as I thought over and over to myself, *Oh no, there's bad news. Oh no, there's bad news.* Finally, I spoke, "Good news? Maybe, yeah, good news."

"All right, well, good news it is. The trip went great, until the first blow out. Which happened just your side of Wendover."

"First blow out?" I interrupted.

"Hey, yeah, just shut up and listen, I'm the guy talking. I'm the guy telling the good news here," he interrupted my interruption.

I thought to myself, *This is going to be really bad if he's this feisty with the good news.* So, I shut up and listened.

"We hadn't been on the road more than ninety minutes before the first blow out. The next tire blew outside of Salt Lake, and they kept blowing on a regular basis. Then the hoses started blowing. First to go was the radiator. Lucky for us, we were in Evanston at the time. It was somewhere on the far side of Rock Springs when the muffler blew up."

I had the urge to interrupt and ask what he meant because mufflers don't blow up, they just kind of slowly rust out and die. But I resisted and let him continue.

"Apparently the carburetor had been leaking fuel. Somehow it made its way into the exhaust and filled the muffler with gas. The explosion blew the truck damn near two feet off the ground. I thought I was dead for sure! The tin of the muffler blew off with such force it formed to the bottom of the truck! Some of it is still there. I couldn't get it off! Donna still hasn't completely recovered from that one. By the time we made it to Indianapolis we were running on six new tires, she had all new hoses, belts, and a muffler!" Adrian exclaimed.

I said nothing. I just wondered what state of denial I was in when I sent them off in the first place. There was no saying how long that truck had been sitting and rotting out back of old Freddie's place. Replacing all those rubber parts at once was too painful for me and my bank account, so I fixed what I had to and hoped for the best.

Adrian went on, "And are you aware of the gas mileage a truck like this gets?" I said nothing, wondering how bad it could be.

"Eight miles to the gallon running empty, five miles with the trailer," he said. Then for emphasis and an extra jab he added. "That's what an old Dually with a 454 big block gets. Oh, and did I mention it's all on your credit card?" He knew how to hurt me.

"Ouch," I groaned while doing the math in my head. "Yeah," he agreed.

I came to my senses and asked, "Wait, this is all good news?"

"Yeah! Are ya ready for the bad?" he asked.

"I'm not sure," I heard myself say.

"Ready or not," he said. "It was somewhere out of Omaha on the trip back when the transmission started acting up. Nothing too bad, just a slip here and a chug there. But just this side of Lincoln it finally gave out. And by gave out, I mean, it fell out."

"Wait, fell out? What do you mean, fell out?" I asked. I'd heard of transmissions giving out, but never falling out.

"I mean the transmission fell out of the truck! It was strung out all over the highway! The patrolman said the only way he'd help was if I cleaned up the mess, so I did! I was picking up parts and pieces for nearly 300 yards. He eventually pulled me off the freeway and left me here!"

"Here?" I repeated as a question.

"I don't quite know for sure. We're sitting in some car park at some petrol station somewhere just west of Omaha with what's left of the transmission in the back of the Dually!"

I wasn't too excited to go to the rescue. I was ok with Adrian's intensity; I'd lived with it my entire life. It was the wrath of Donna I was worried about. I figured the only thing worse than enduring her wrath was to leave them there. So, I got busy tracking down a replacement transmission. The closest one I could find was over in Winnemucca, and I used the term "find" rather loosely. It was the closest transmission I could borrow.

I borrowed a car from Ben, and I left work early to rescue Adrian and his little family. I went up to Winnemucca to grab the transmission, stopped by my shed to collect my little box of tools, and drove to Omaha, Nebraska. It's 1,200 miles one way from Elko to Omaha. That's right near halfway across the entire country. I did it nonstop, and in record time.

There, in the Chevron car park, just west of Lincoln City, Adrian and I swapped out the transmission of the Pumpkin. He broke the news as we worked together under the old orange truck. "You remember that deal we'd made? The one about staying all season?"

"Yeah," I answered.

"Yeah, well, if things keep going like this, that ain't going to happen. Donna's had about enough. She's talking about leaving, with or without me."

"But we're just getting started," I replied.

"I'll be with you for Phoenix for sure, but it'll be case by case after that. And Robert, for your own good, I'd steer clear of Donna if I were you."

"Yeah, gotcha," I replied, glancing her way. I was greeted by a stare that almost cut me clean through. Yeah, she was so pissed she couldn't speak to me that day. Now that I think about it, she hasn't really talked to me since!

The Great Pumpkin was okay in the end. All she needed was that tranny, a carburetor, a muffler, and new rubber everything. Oh, she'd get a bit temperamental in the heat, but other than that, she wasn't so bad. She got us to Phoenix in time for the 32 Funny Car Event.

Adrian was there leading our colorful crew of eager misfits with precision. We didn't do too bad in Phoenix. We placed somewhere around the middle of the pack, just high enough to fund another race. Which was also just high enough to keep Adrian's attention and keep him in the country for another race, then another, and another.

We were hitting most of the weekend races on the CIFCA circuit. My week went something like this: I'd get into work late Sunday night and leave sometime just after sunup. I'd head home for a bit of sleep, get up midafternoon and help Adrian work on the car, mostly just fine tuning and little odds and ends. Then I'd grab a bite to eat and head off back to the mine for another shift. I'd repeat that routine on Tuesday and Wednesday.

Thursday afternoons were spent loading up the truck and trailer. Then Friday, sometime just after sunup, I'd rush home, jump in the Great Pumpkin, and head on out to the next race. There was no time for sleep. We'd drive all day if needed, and sometimes even into the night to get to the tracks. Many times, we'd roll in real late and set up in the dark.

Saturdays were the qualification rounds. We got two runs against the clock to show what we were made of. The top time was used for Sunday's staged races, which were head-to-head tournament style races where only the winners moved on to the next round. The faster the time we made on Saturday, the better placement we got on Sunday. We always managed a solid middle of the pack performance on Saturday, which left us in the middle of the line up on Sunday. We typically went several rounds before being eliminated. But as soon as we were, we'd load the trailer and head back home and straight to work, just in time to do the whole thing over again. It was like a dream come true.

Me and the crew, we were racing out of pure love of the sport, but we had fulltime jobs, too. No matter how many rounds we won on Sunday, we still had to load the trailer and head out with the hopes of making it to work on time. Ironically, the better we raced, the less likely we were to make it to work on time.

I'd always prided myself on being a professional mechanic, and part of that pride meant I'd never missed, or been late for, a day of work in my life. Until the day we qualified in the top four. We made it all the way to the semifinals, which left us racing real late, too late to make it back to work on time. My boss and I quickly came to an understanding. There was only one reason to be late for work, and it wasn't illness or death. The only reason for being late was a good race day, the type where we made it deep into the tournament.

Racing quickly became a multi-family affair. It's funny how as observers, the families could hardly stand going to the track. But as soon as they had some responsibility or job to do, well, it changed everything. So, we found jobs for everyone, young and old.

Ben and Lisa were die-hards. They never missed a race and quickly became the core of the crew. Ben was a top-notch mechanic and machinist; he became Adrian's go-to guy for anything mechanical. Lisa naturally fell into the role of crew mom. She didn't have an official role or title, but she sure did a lot! She'd clean anything and everything, she'd feed anyone and everyone, but most importantly, she wouldn't take crap from anyone!

As for Andy and Tina, Andy was a better friend than anything. He knew his way around a shop and would do whatever I asked. He came as much as he could, which was about half of the races. Even the kids got into the action by cleaning parts, trailers, and pits.

It was always interesting to see who'd show up on Friday mornings for a weekend of racing. We always found room for whoever showed. We'd fill up the truck and pile people in the trailer. Couples had to get there early for prime trailer seating. It was nothing but good times.

We got a late start on our first trip to Los Angeles. I was driving and the conversation centered around the best route. Andy suggested west to Sacramento, then south. Ben was for south to Vegas, then west. I sided with Ben. Dusk had faded to dark, and everyone had faded into sleep as we sputtered into Beatty for gas. There was a slight chill in the air, and I shivered as I studied the map under the dim light of the tiny gas station. "That road will keep us out of Vegas and take at least an hour off the drive," I said to myself as the pump clicked off. I consulted no one and headed west.

I noticed two things right away. First was the amazing time I was making. I hadn't gone that fast, for that long, since Truckee to Sacramento. Second was the heat. The chill faded, and before long I had the windows rolled down for circulation. I remember thinking, *I've haven't seen it this hot with it being this dark since the Kimberly.* That's when I passed the "Death Valley National Park" sign. *Ha! Awesome. I've never been here!* I thought.

Things went well until we reached the far end of the park. The road going out was steeper than expected, and things quickly ground to a halt. Maybe not a complete halt, but it was pretty close. I gave the old Dually everything she had, but she topped out at eight miles an hour, give or take, but mostly take and before long we were cruising along at 7 miles an hour. Then 6, then 5. I remembered hearing someone say we should steer clear of Death Valley before the trip, and now I understood why.

The last thing I needed was for someone to wake up to this mess. I'd never hear the end of it. So, I kept silent, kept the pedal to the metal, and kept creeping along at 4 miles an hour, then 3 miles, then 2. I had hopes of getting away with it all the way up until zero. Finally, the pumpkin just stopped right there in the middle of the road. The engine ran, but she did not, so I turned her off.

There I sat, motionless, in a truck full of sleeping people at two a.m. on the uphill side of Death Valley, hoping no one would notice. It was the stillness that woke them. Adrian was first to stir, wiping the sleep from his eyes he asked, "what's going on?"

"Oh, just lettin' 'er catch her breath," I replied.

"How long we been sittin' here?"

"Oh, a bit. Can't say for certain," I replied, knowing quite well it'd been well over ten minutes. Ben was next, then Lisa, Andy, and so on. Before I knew it, they were all awake and mumbling about the heat and how we weren't going nowhere. Finally, Andy asked, "So, where are we?" I'd been dreading that question.

"Yeah, about that. We're just climbing out of Death Valley," I confessed.

Ben piped up, "Death Valley! We're not going through Death Valley; we're going through Vegas!"

"Yeah, about that, no. We're going through Death Valley, and to prove it, here we are." I caught crap from the whole lot of them.

Adrian finally said, "we can stay here all night complaining, but it's not gonna get us where we're going. So, let's get going." With that I fired the pumpkin back up, dropped her into gear, pushed the peddle to the metal, and stayed motionless in the middle of the road.

"There's not enough power to get moving up the hill," I said.

Adrian fell into work mode and started barking orders. "Here's what we're gonna do. Everyone out! We need the load as light as possible and we're going to have to push." And we did. By we I mean everyone else but me, I was driving.

They got out and began pushing the pumpkin up the hill. Slowly she picked up speed, and before long they were running alongside. Finally, Adrian hollered, "Okay, jump in." And one by one they did. Almost everyone jumped in. Lisa ran her best race, but even with all of us cheering her on, she was losing ground. We had to make a decision, the truck or Lisa.

After making Lisa the driver, we began the process all over again and the great pumpkin slowly sputtered up the hill as we pushed with all our might. The sun was reheating the eastern sky when we finally crawled out of the valley of death. That detour was supposed to cut an hour off the drive, but it ended up stretching it out by three. I almost learned my lesson on that trip.

I drove through Death Valley one more time, it was a few years later, but with much the same result.

Again, it was dark, they were asleep, and I was driving. The old truck could be a bit temperamental in the heat. Eventually, the heat got the better of her and she vapor locked and died in the middle of the road.

It was the silence that woke them. Mathew, the crew chief at the time, was first to stir and asked, "What's going on?" Before I knew it, I was caught up in a case of deja-vu as they were all mumbling about the heat and how we weren't going nowhere. It quickly escalated into multiple obscene exchanges about Death Valley and how we weren't supposed to be there.

Mathew brought us back down as he said, "we can stay here all night arguing, but it's not gonna get us where we're going. So, let's get going." With that, he popped the hood and after some twiddling and tinkering announced, "She's vapor locked." He stepped back, thought for a moment then jumped into action, "Here's what we're gonna do. Andy, grab the race car starter bottle," which was nothing more than a plastic bottle with a flip cap on one end, "I'm going to be our fuel injector."

A few moments later he'd perched himself on the front bumper, popped the air filter cover, and was spraying fuel right into the open carburetor. "Fire her up," he yelled from behind the hood. We hadn't pulled that maneuver together before, but you'd have never known. We were in perfect synch. Mathew sprayed fuel into the open carburetor as I cranked the starter. She coughed, sputtered, and died. Mathew kept the fuel streaming while motioning to try her again and again. She finally sputtered to life. I dropped her down into gear and the Great Pumpkin slowly began creeping up the hill. We continued that way for the next 3 miles. Eventually we made it to flatter ground and the truck's fuel system took back over.

After that, I wasn't allowed to drive alone anywhere near the southern California and Nevada border. I couldn't be trusted. We all have weaknesses, and Death Valley is mine. Whenever we were near the area, someone was assigned to stay up to make sure I didn't take any short cuts. No more Death Valley for Robert!

Adrian was there for each race, but he was only committed to one race at a time, and there was no guarantee he'd be there for the next. A fact he reminded us of often. But we always seemed to place just high enough to both almost break even and keep Adrian's interest. When all was said and done, we did ten races with CIFCA and five Match Races that year.

Unlike the CIFCA races, where you're competing for cash prizes, Match Races come with a guaranteed check. You're racing head-to-head, but there's no prize for the winner. The entire purpose is the show. The crowds love the roar of the engines, and the smell of the fumes and burning rubber. They love the clouds of smoke rising from the track from the screaming burnouts. I could put on one hell of a show. I could burn out with the best of them, and I did, every chance I got.

Match Races were more than a guaranteed paycheck; we were literally getting paid to practice. We were getting paid to fine tune the car. With each race and each match, we were getting faster and faster.

So fast, in fact, we had to slow down toward the end of the season, because with speed comes regulations. We were going fast enough to stay in the game, but slow enough to not be required to upgrade the safety equipment. The truth was, I didn't want to upgrade. We'd placed in the money enough to keep us going, but I was still in hock up to my ears. I'd put much of my life on credit, and it was chasing me down fast. The last thing I could afford was a full fire suppression system. So, we kept things slow. That's when two great things happened.

First, on July 4, 1994, I was sworn in as a U.S. citizen. I'd never been so proud. I was proud of who I was and where I came from, but I was also proud of who I had become and where my life was going. I took the oath seriously and with great responsibility.

Second, I took an expat assignment to Papua with the mine. It was a great opportunity and came with hazard pay, which looked to be enough to get me caught up on my credit cards, and then some.

BACK TO PHOENIX

apua was a place of extremes and contradicting absolutes. The mine was perched high in the central mountains near the ridges at the end of the Impossible Road. It was much like all the others I'd worked. There were designated areas for living, dining, play, and work. The difference was that it was an active military zone. We were flanked on one side by a modern military with uniforms, helmets, and M16s. On the other side were the native tribes, wearing nothing but wooden piercings, holding tight to their spears and machetes. I wasn't sure what to think about all of that. But then again, I wasn't there to think about all of that, I had a fleet of Caterpillar equipment which took all my thought, time, and energy. I quickly immersed myself in the challenges of tuning the fleet for extreme conditions, tt seemed that's all I ever thought about.

My shift at the mine was six weeks on and two weeks off. Lucky for me, the Phoenix 32 Funny Car was at the front end of a two-week rotation. The first real time I had to think about racing was on the plane to Phoenix, and then the reality of what I'd done with the team hit me at once.

I knew Adrian wouldn't be back, and I needed a Crew Chief. Ben and Lisa were the backbone of the team. Ben was a good mechanic, but he had his own shop to run. In fact, at any given time he employed at least one of our crew. Lisa was team mom; she just did whatever needed done. She even took charge of the racing team finances, which meant she was running my finances. They were integral to the team, but neither were Crew Chief material.

Lucky for me, I was referred to Mathew, an ace mechanic from Australia looking to make it in the U.S. So I hired him without ever meeting in person, just a couple of phone calls. Before I knew it, he was in Elko prepping the car for the season. It kind of made me nervous, having a crew chief I'd never met, it seemed everything I had was riding on a stranger.

The dry Phoenix air was somewhere between comfortably warm and pleasantly hot, depending on where you were standing, sun or shade. I chose the sun; I've always liked the heat. It was Andy who finally picked me up at Sky Harbor Airport.

That Mathew; he's something," he said, sparking the conversation that lasted the entire ride to the track.

"Yeah? Like how do you mean?"

"Well, I can't quite put my finger on it. He's got a level of intense professionalism about him, and he's always tinkering with, well, everything!"

"In a bad way?" I asked.

"No, it's not in a bad way. He's almost as intense as you and Adrian. In a good way, I mean. He's only been here a month and he knows everything about the car. He says it's primed and ready for this weekend."

"Yeah? Well, he came highly recommended. I can't wait to meet him," I added. Before long, I was surrounded by the crew and the sights, sounds and smells of racing. I was home.

"Oh, man! It feels good to be back at the line," I said to myself as the body was lowered and locked into position. And just like that the outside world went away. It was more than just my body being shut off from the outside world, it was like my brain shut off as well. Leading up to a race there's a million things to think about, the tune, the timing, the clutch, the crew, the crowd, the driver next to me. I'm not sure how it works, but when that body is lowered and locked into position, it all just goes away. I'm left alone with nothing, not even a thought. It's just me, completely present with the car, the lights, and the moment, and we were one.

The lights flashed, the engine roared, the g-forces locked me in tight against the seat, it was like a dream.

"Man, that was fast! What were you thinking!" I yelled at Mathew as I rolled into the pit.

"What do you mean? That was awesome!" he yelled back.

"Yes, it was awesome! Fantastic in fact! But . . ." I paused.

"But what?" he questioned.

"But we're not ready for that fast," I said.

"What do you mean? Fast is why we're here," he said.

"Right, we do want fast, but not too fast. Not that fast."

"I don't understand," he replied with a questioning gaze.

"Look, we get a lot of leeway because we're good, but not that good. Once you go over 225 mph, we're bumped into a whole other league. You got all sorts of additional rules and regulations to abide by. We're not equipped to race at these speeds, yet here we are, racing at these speeds!" I exclaimed.

"You mean you've been holding back?" he asked.

"No, not exactly holding her back. No, I wouldn't say that. We've just been progressing at a very slow, controlled, and steady pace. Now you've gone and worked your car magic and blown us right past the mark. This changes things. This changes everything," I answered.

"What does that mean, changes everything?" he questioned.

"It means we need a fire suppression system, and we don't have a fire suppression system," I replied.

"Yeah, I knew something was missing."

"Yeah? Well, we won't be running again until we have one. Let's hope that run holds, because we're not running any more today," I added.

"Well, that was a hell of a run; it should hold," Mat said with a smile.

"Yeah, that was a hell of a run! But we can't really celebrate until we have fire systems, and we'll need it by tomorrow if we're going to run the rounds," I insisted with a smile.

"What was I thinking?" Mat muttered.

I replied with, "You were just thinking fast. Nothing wrong with thinking fast. You take care of the engine and car. I'll take on the fire system. We're all in on this, and we ain't backing down."

"Andy!" I yelled.

"Yes sir!" came his reply from across the pit.

"Quick, we need you and your tin snipping skills!"

Andy's eyes grew big with excitement as this was the first thing outside of painting, cleaning, and scrubbing I'd asked of him. "Yes, I'm in. What needs snipping?" came his reply.

"We need a fire suppression system, and I need you to build it for us! And we need it by tomorrow," I said.

The excitement vanished as quickly as it came. "Okay. Yeah. Well. What do you mean, fire suppression systems? What is that? I don't know what that is. I don't know how to build that."

"No worries. You and me, we're on this. We'll do it together, but mostly you. I'll tell you what and how. Now, get in the truck, we have equipment to buy," I said as I hopped in the truck and hoped my credit card, and my sanity, would withstand the pressure. It was times like this; when things were on the edge of chaos, and people were looking to me for what's next, and I wasn't sure what to do, or if I could hold it together, that I discovered a secret weapon. My race face. It was my best attempt at a casual and pleasant smile with a tone of "Yeah, everything's just fine" woven throughout. I didn't matter what I was feeling inside, my race face let everyone around me know that everything was just right.

We arrived back at the pits with the raw parts about the time the afternoon qualification runs wrapped up.

Ben greeted us with, "We're in! That run held. And get this, we've qualified at number three. The officials will be by at eight a.m. for final inspection."

"Well, that gives us about fourteen hours to build a fire suppression system from scratch," I replied. Andy and I worked all night.

It was right about five a.m. when I passed out in the cab of the truck. That was usually when I started race days. There was something exhilarating about a race day morning. It was excitement, anticipation, nerves, and panic all wrapped into one. I loved riding the crew as we prepped, checked, and rechecked every detail. But the jetlag, combined with staying up all night, just kind of all hit me at once.

Mathew woke me about thirty minutes before the first elimination round. "Hey, we're all set. You ready for this?" he asked.

"As ready as I'll ever be," I replied. "Hey, I've been thinking about the crew, about how we look on the starting line. What would ya think if we had the crew line up in a nice, neat row behind the car at launch?"

"Seems a bit intense, maybe even bordering on the fringe of obsessive. I like it!" he said with a smile. "Now, who's gonna to tell them?"

"Isn't that a bit obsessive?" Andy asked as I explained the new starting line procedure.

"No, it's not obsessive at all. A little intense maybe. But it'll show the other teams how united we are, and it may even intimidate them a little. Besides, it'll look really cool on television. Who's in?" I wasn't sure if it was out of respect, fear, or camaraderie, but they all agreed.

"Oh, and one other thing. When we're out there, we're sending a message in everything we do. From the way we look, to the way we stand, and the way we watch the race. I want us to look like business the entire time. If we lose a round, no hanging your heads or moping; keep them high like you're proud to be here. We take our losses and learn from them. If we win, don't jump up and down. Don't celebrate there on the track. Remember, we are business. I don't want people to look at us celebrating and think that's our moment. I want them to see us win, nod, and go on with business as usual. I want them to think we're used to winning, like that's what we do. That'll intimidate the hell out of them all!"

Mat leaned over and whispered, "I think you may have just crossed the line there. But ya know, I didn't care. We're going to show them all who we are."

The boys rolled me to the starting line. Mat fired up the engine and lined up with Andy and the crew behind me. The burn out was flawless. Lisa guided me back into position and joined the others, completing a solid line across the track behind the car. I was intensely calm.

I said out loud, "Okay, focus. Drain the mind. Be one with the car. Be one with the lights. Be present." I could feel the lights as they hovered overhead. I could feel the car which encased me. Together, we were one.

Life can be chaotic, just as chaotic as the cars I love. Life is made of a million bits and pieces all moving at once, each in its own way, doing its own thing. Then, every once in a while, it all comes together. All the bits and pieces move at the same time, in the same direction, and in perfect rhythm.

It was as if the chaos of life, and the chaos of the race, had fallen into perfect rhythm. Me and the crew, we were one with the car. Me and the car, we were one with the lights, and the balance brought peace to the track. We sailed through round one, then round two. Everything was in. The crew knew me well enough not to celebrate after each win; we needed to earn the right to celebrate.

Then came round three. I'd never made it past round three before, but I did that day. Everything was in balance, and before I knew it, we were lined up as one for the final round of the Phoenix 32. All was as it should be.

"Okay, focus. Drain the mind. Be one with the car. Be one with the lights. Be one. Be present."

I came to at the end of the line to a crowd of cheering fans and excited press. We had done it! We won the Phoenix 32! Any pent-up celebration was released that night. We partied like we meant it, which of course, we did. All night and into the wee hours it went. It was a blur of bars, hot tubs, hotel rooms, and more bars.

As an expat, tax laws dictated I couldn't spend more than a week in country while on assignment. So, Ben and Lisa, Andy and Tina, and Holly, my current girlfriend and I all went to Mexico for a week to continue the celebration. What a week it was!

We met up with the rest of the crew the following weekend in Vegas for another round of winning. We didn't take first, but it was close. Soon enough I was back in Papua to finish my tour, and the crew was back in Elko to get along with life.

CHAOS AND ORDER

Everything in my life was in order, which must have knocked the universe off kilter; something had to give. It was Ben and Lisa who paid the price. All the crew and I could do was watch as their lives went spinning off into utter chaos. Lisa'd had a feeling something wasn't right in Phoenix, and it worsened in Mexico. It was much more than a nagging feeling; it was a nagging intuition. It kept nagging long after the trip, and it filled her with fear.

She feared she could be wrong, which would threaten her devoted trust. Or worse, she feared she could be right, which would mean . . . well, it would mean unthinkable things. Things she couldn't bear to think, but things she couldn't stop thinking. She questioned her own sanity. Was she crazy? Was she obsessing over nothing? Was she wrong? Was she right?

Finally, she gathered the courage to confront Ben. "It feels like there's more than the two of us in this relationship. Am I right?" she asked fearfully. He answered with a single word, no explanations, no justifications, no accusations, just a single word: "Yes."

It wasn't so much the single word that broke her, but what it meant. It meant that somewhere, sometime, Ben had betrayed her unfettered trust. It meant she had given him her life and he had given it away like it was loose change. "Who?" she begged. He wouldn't say. She invited him to leave that day, and he did.

Andy rearranged some of his kids' bedrooms and offered Ben a place to stay, and he took it.

Complete and utter chaos. That's how things were when I arrived back in Elko. The divorce was in full motion. Lisa was in trouble; it seemed a little more of her died each day. Her world was falling apart around her and all she could do was hold the broken pieces of her heart, wishing them back together. She didn't look the same. It was more than being sad. She looked, well, she looked like hell. It was like she was dying inside. She was making it to work, but that was about it. The boys were stepping up as much as they could with chores and such. But they had their own wounds to bind.

Time wasn't working for Lisa; she continued to struggle. Ben left her with nothing, and when the machine shop closed for good; well, it left her with less than nothing. She worked part time at the dental office, but that wasn't enough for the mortgage, let alone for food and clothes. It wasn't long before she had to sell the house. It was a friend from work who offered a camp trailer and a place to park it. She said they could run a cord for power, but it would be best to use the facilities in the house when needed.

The boys were strong, broken, but strong. They were coping the best they could. They were her only support and sole purpose for holding on. All I could do was watch, and hurt for them, and with them.

The plan had always been to build a Nitro Funny Car. The Alcohol car was just a way of testing and tuning, like the first pancake on a hot griddle. It was to make sure things were right. That first year of racing in the U.S. helped me to see that things were just right. I could change continents, change careers, build a car, and race. In short, I could chase this dream.

I began collecting parts and pieces for the Nitro car of my dreams in the spring of '95. I started with a frame and kept gathering as time went on. The mechanics was the easy part, paying for it, that was the hard part, so it took years.

We were on the circuit and having the time of our lives traversing the west. We hit every racetrack within a twelve-hour drive. From Denver to LA, and Phoenix to Seattle, we hit 'em all. It was toward the end of the '96 season when everything fell into order. It was a beautiful fall evening at the Bonneville Raceway in Salt Lake City.

The weather was perfect. The sky was lined with scanty thin clouds, the kind you'd never notice if you weren't looking. The lazy evening sun sank low in the western sky, leaving the track in the shadow of the mountains and the sky on fire. The raceway was active as crowds cheered and crews scurried. Every now and then a couple of cars would roar to life and streak down the track. The air was thick with the smells of popcorn, beer, oil, gasoline, and alcohol fuel. I found myself just back of the starting line as every sight, sound, and smell settled in on me. Life was good.

I felt the presence of someone stroll up beside me. Assuming it was one of the crew, I said, "I love times like this."

"Me too," came the voice. I knew that voice. It wasn't one of my crew, it was Jay, the track manager. He continued to say most everything I was feeling. "It doesn't get much better than this. The crowds, the noise, the smells. I can close my eyes and tell what race is what. Sometimes I can even tell which cars are racing, just by the sound. And sometimes, depending on which way the wind is blowing, I can tell by the smell."

I replied, "It's a thing of beauty. I can't seem to get enough."

"Yeah, me too. It's strange though, to think this is the last time we'll be here like this," he added.

"Yeah, I heard. This is the last race here at this track, right?"

"Yep. We're tearing her down next week. We'll rebuild in the same spot and should be back up by mid next year in a state-of-the-art facility. It'll be called Rocky Mountain Raceway."

"That'll be something. You know, there is one sound and smell that's missing here," I said.

"Yeah?"

"Yeah. Nitro," I replied.

"Oh man, that would be something. I've tried to stage match races, but working out two schedules is near impossible. I've tried pulling exhibitions in from Vegas, Phoenix, and Denver, but no one will come, not without someone to race against," he responded.

"What if there was someone to race against? What if there was a Nitro car here in Salt Lake?" I replied.

"That would be something I could work with. But it hasn't happened yet," came his reply.

He'd caught me in a vulnerable moment. We'd just finished our last run, at the last race at Bonneville Raceway, and I was feeling really sentimental. It may have been the emotions left over from the win, it may have been the alcohol fumes, or maybe it was the alcohol itself. Whatever it was, it slipped out just the same. "Well, what if it did happen. You know, I've always dreamed of building and running a Nitro Funny Car. I know how to do it. I was Lead on the Southern Thunder back in Adelaide. In fact, that's why I'm here in America. I came to run my own. I have most of the parts and pieces sitting in my shed back home."

I regretted it as soon as I said it. I felt so exposed. I couldn't believe I told someone like him my dreams. My mind flashed back to the pubs in Australia, and I braced myself for a laugh or a jab at my sanity. But what he said was, "I think that's brilliant! Where's home?"

"Elko," I answered.

"Elko? There're no drag strips in Elko, not like what this'll be any way. If you're going to run Nitro, you'll need a local track that'll handle it. Tell you what. If you do ever get all those parts and pieces put together, you let me know. I think a Nitro Funny Car would be something people would come out to see. Yeah, the Rocky Mountain Raceway could use a dose of Nitro."

"You know, one of the things holding me back is track time. Nitros are touchy beasts; they need to be worked and reworked. Just the tuning itself is a piece of mechanical artwork. Some call it voodoo sh . . ." I stopped to edit my language. He was a Mormon and in all my trips to that track I'd never heard him drop an "f" bomb, or any other bomb for that matter. I continued. "Some call it voodoo, but I call it art. You can piece it together with all the patience in the world, but you never really know what's what until you run it down the track. And track time is, well, it's expensive," I said.

I may have caught him in a vulnerable moment. He'd been watching the last event at the Bonneville Raceway and maybe he was feeling sentimental, too. It may have been pure emotion, it may have been the fumes. I know it wasn't the alcohol since he was Mormon, and in all my trips to that track I never saw him with a beer in hand. Whatever it was, it slipped out just the same.

"Tell you what, you let me know if you ever build that Nitro Funny Car. We may be able to work out some kind of partnership, something that'll get you the track time you need, to do the testing you need."

Those word kept echoing through my mind, "some kind of partnership, something that'll get you the track time you need." It was all I could think about the entire drive back to Elko, at work, in the shed, and everywhere in between. I'd become obsessed again.

I reworked the plan. I'd sell the alcohol car, trailer, and shed, put that money with the Papua money, move to Salt Lake, and build my Nitro Funny Car. Everything was in order. What could go wrong?

SECTION 3

NEW

BACK IN THE HOSPITAL, AGAIN

Lisa needed air. She needed to stretch, and breathe. Yet she couldn't leave. She needed to be close, just in case. So, she walked the halls but never strayed too far from Robert's room. Every now and then she'd take a sip from the water cooler by the nurse's station. On one such trip, she stepped back from the cooler, fell against the wall, slid to the floor, buried her face in her hands, and cried.

She drifted back to the time he brought her home. *I had nothing! I was shattered in pieces and scattered all around. Ben had taken everything! He broke me and left me in pieces. I truly thought he was my one and only. For eight years he was my other half. I lived in complete trust, and as it turned out, compete ignorance. And with Tina! Of all people, why her?*

I had nothing. My entire inheritance was invested in the machine shop, and Ben screwed that up while he was doing the same to me and Tina. He may have been a good machinist and mechanic, but he was not a good businessman, or, as it turned out, a good husband either.

I kept everything. But 100 percent of nothing is still nothing. I kept the house, but couldn't afford the mortgage. I kept the boys, but couldn't afford to feed them. I was about to move into the borrowed camp trailer. But it was Robert who showed up on the darkest of days. He didn't ask what I wanted or needed. He didn't pity or coddle me. He just kicked me in the ass and said, "Look Lisa, you gotta get your life together. Those boys, they need you. They need a mother."

I cried, "I can't! I can't eat, I can't sleep, I can't focus, I can't think! I can't even feel anything. I can't feel my heart most of the time. It's broken! That bastard broke it!" I went on and on.

Robert was stunned; the poor guy didn't know what hit him. Finally he stammered back with, "Look, I ain't any good at this, especially with all the feelings and all. But I do know one thing. Those boys need you. Like it or not, you are more than their mum right now. You're their everything; you're all they have left."

"It's too much, I've got nothing left to give. My heart is gone. The money, my inheritance, is gone. He spent it on that lousy excuse of a business! Everything is gone!" I continued to cry.

"You are not gone! You are still here. I've watched you for years and I know you. You are strong! It's in you! If you can't pull it together for yourself, you pull it together for the boys. If you can't love right now, just lean on them, let them love for you, because they will. They need you!" It was like he believed in me more than I believed in myself. For the briefest of moments, I believed, and for the briefest of moments, I felt, and for the briefest of moments, the tears stopped.

"By the way, grab your stuff, all of you," he hollered out to the boys. "You're coming with me."

"No, we're not going with you," I said.

To which he replied, "Well, you aren't staying here. It's like you said, you've got nothing."

"I can't. I can't go with you! The last thing I need is a man." I cried again.

"Look, Lisa, I don't want anything from you. You and me, we are not a thing. This is completely platonic; I just want you and the boys to have a safe place. I want you to be there for these guys. I want you to work on you. Besides, I've got my own life going on. I've got work and places to be. If it helps, think of this as a selfish thing on my part. I still need you at the track. You're the best team mom out there. You, you keep us going.

But you and me, we aren't a thing. But I do need you at the track and I need you to be there for the boys."

His words pierced the hard pieces of my broken heart, and I believed him, 100 percent. He'd never lied before and besides, I knew Robert. I knew he was making the most of life as a single race car driver. He was living in the fast lane. He liked his women as fast as his cars. I knew who he was, and he saved my life.

"Mom! Come on!" Bryan called. "He's awake!" Lisa pulled herself together and made her way into the room to assume her position at Robert's side. The others huddled around. Bryan held the board as she gently placed the marker in Robert's hand, but before she could, he grabbed her hand and squeezed tight. Silence surrounded the hand clasp. They needed time, and the family gave it to them. It was Bryan who finally broke the silence, "Come on! What's next? So far, we have, ORDER A," he hollered, as if waiting for a game to begin.

"I think it's an H," Bryan yelled.

"Not me, I think it's an N," said Neal.

"I don't know, I'm going to wait to see what's next and what makes sense," said Mark.

"Three?" yelled Bryan.

"No, that's not a three, that's an E," Mark replied.

"I'm with you on that one," said Lisa.

"That's gotta be a W!" yelled Bryan.

"Yes," the rest replied in unison.

"NEW," said Neal.

"ORDER A NEW," said Mark.

"What do you think? 'Cause I just don't know," said Lisa.

"You got me," replied Neal.

"Maybe he only wants a new Big Mac," quipped Mark. Bryan giggled.

Robert grabbed Lisa's hand, and she, his. Together, they held tight. Everything about Robert was tight. He shifted, squirmed, and twitched, so Lisa squeezed tighter. Neal and the boys headed home.

Slowly, Robert relaxed, and the tightness subsided. Gently, he drifted off again. Lisa continued to hold tight. She leaned over and whispered in his ear, "Sleep for now, but please don't leave. You can't leave. I need you." With that she curled up on the little cot next to his bed and tried to get some sleep for herself.

NEW START

4 MONTHS EARLIER IN MAGNA, UTAH.

"What's that noise?" I asked myself. "I have no idea," I replied. "And why do I always talk to myself when I'm waking up?" "I don't know, but that noise, it sounds awfully buzzy." "Oh jeez, it's the alarm!" "Quick, hurry! Kill it off before it wakes her up!" Instantly my hand flailed down over the alarm in a buzz-defying, and self-talk ending, crash.

"Really, an alarm?" Lisa whined from under a mountain of blankets.

"Yeah, it's time," I replied.

"On New Year's Day? You set an alarm on New Year's Day at eight a.m.?" she moaned.

"Yeah, but this isn't just any New Year's Day. This is THE New Year's Day. This is January 1st, 1999. This is THE first day of THE year it all happens!" I cheerfully replied.

"You know you're crazy!" Lisa moaned, snuggling deeper into her burrow.

"You're not the first to accuse me of that. But you are the prettiest!" She loves it when I say that. "Breakfast in 30 minutes!" I announced, slipping out of bed.

"Don't wake the boys. Give them today to sleep in. Please . . ." she begged from the depths of comfort.

"Maybe, we'll see. Oh, and Lisa?" I paused at the door. "I'm glad you're here." With that, I turned and wandered into the kitchen to cook pancakes and start all over again. It seems that's all life is: one new beginning after another, all strung along one after the other. There I was, staring another beginning right in the face.

That day marked the end of a year and a half of the transition from Elko to Salt Lake. Lisa and the boys couldn't have slept in even if they wanted to. I wasn't exactly quiet in the kitchen; I wanted the whole house to know this was the long-awaited day.

Brandon was the first to arrive, but before long, Mathew, Andy, and the rest of the crew let themselves in. They weren't exactly quiet either, so it wasn't long before Bryan and Mark wandered in, followed a few minutes later by Lisa.

"Get 'em while they're hot! Plates there, pancakes there, syrup there, dig in!" I announced. There was no "yes sir," no "thank you," just an ungrateful rumble rising from the crowd. "Where's the bacon?" "Wait, what, no bacon?" "We gotta have bacon!"

I glared from behind the piping hot griddle and replied, "Bacon? No, there is no bacon. Do you know how many racecar parts I could buy for what it would take to feed you all bacon? Pancakes is what we got, and pancakes is what you get. Now eat up, you ingrates!" And they did, loading their plates and spreading out. Some sat at the table, some at the bar, others spilled into the living room.

I was so excited and inspired, I wanted them to be excited and inspired too, so I just started talking. "This is it boys! This is the day we start assembling all the bits and pieces I've been collecting over the years. We have a lot of work to do to get race ready. It's not just a matter of building the beast, it's a matter of tuning it, and it's a matter of learning our jobs and practicing them. We'll assemble, disassemble, then reassemble it over and over, again and again. We'll make our jobs automatic so we can do them with our eyes shut. This is the day we make this dream a reality."

Brandon piped up, "Hey, ah, I have a question. Why Utah? I mean, why or how did you end up here?"

"A few years back I made a deal with the boys down at the track. We are now the resident Nitro Funny Car of the Rocky Mountain Raceway. We'll put on exhibition shows and match races and such," I proudly replied.

"Cool, and they pay you for that?" came a follow up question.

I answered slowly, "Well, pay comes in many forms. We'll get some match races, and they pay cash—enough to cover fuel and a few parts and such. But mostly we get track time, which includes fuel and insurance, which is as good as cash. Each time I don't have to pay to go down the track is like money in my pocket. Besides, it's one thing to build a car, but tuning, that's an entirely separate thing. And it's all about the tune. Building is bringing all the parts and pieces together in the same place. Tuning is getting each of those pieces to do what they do at precisely the right time and in synch with the system."

"How badass is that!" exclaimed Andy. The others agreed.

"So, you have everything you need?" asked Mathew.

"Pretty much," I replied. "Been collecting for the past few years now. It's all out in the shed just waiting to be assembled. Today marks the beginning of the build, and we have till April to make it happen."

I noticed Andy nudging Brandon, like he was urging him on to something. Finally, Brandon spoke, "Is it true? Did you really build your own control panel?"

I smiled and replied, "Yep, sure did!"

"Really? That's even badasser! For real! Who does that?" Brandon stammered, looking around the room.

"I do," I replied, continuing with the story. "After making the deal with Rocky Mountain, I hatched me a plan to get here. I sold the alcohol car at the end of the '96 season and immediately began looking for work. It took some doing, with lots of driving back and forth, but eventually I found it at Wheeler. Which, I might add, is an amazingly top-rate company, filled with top-rate mechanics. Namely, you all!"

With those words, a hearty cheer of approval filled the house. I continued.

"Yeah, so, I sold everything else worth selling and showed up here in July of '97. I started out living with an old crew member, my good buddy Jimmy. He was single and had this big house all to himself, so he filled it up with more single guys. The place was rocking with parties every night. It was quite the bachelor pad. But not me, I had things to do. I slept on a mattress in a corner of the unfinished basement. I built me a makeshift work bench out of bricks and an old door. It wasn't much, but it did the job.

"I knew two things. First, I knew I didn't have the money to buy the panels the other guys were using on their fancy cars. Second, I knew I could build one. I'd been reading, watching, and learning to understand the technology in these cars for years. All I had to do was find them."

"Find what?" asked Bryan.

"Parts. I had to find generic parts to build the panel. I started at the regular parts store, but they had no clue what I was talking about, though the guy thought it was cool. So, I went to the hardware store hoping for the best. They didn't have anything, but the guy told me maybe a specialty plumbing supply store might have what I needed. They didn't, but they told me about an industrial parts supplier across town.

So, I go there, and while talking to them, another customer overheard the conversation and said he's a maintenance mechanic at a food processing plant, and they have all types of pneumatic equipment for their machinery. And he said they get their parts from another industrial supply place on the other end of town. So, I go there and finally, I'm finding what I needed!

"I bought all the bits and pieces, tubing, and fittings I needed, and got to work. Before long I had it all laid out on my work bench. The central control panel's lying in the middle with tubes running off to different parts of the door. I had it all hooked up to the actual parts they'd be controlling. The slide valve here, the ignition retard system there, the clutch cannon over there. I've got this big CO2 bottle hooked up and I'm running actual tests down there."

"You're kidding!" pipes in Andy.

"No, I'm serious! Raging parties rocking overhead and I'm down there in my unfinished basement sitting at my makeshift bench. I've got this whole system built and I'm simulating runs. I could play with different variables; like, pressure levels, altitudes, and different oil viscosities. I was studying and learning how the guts of these cars work from the inside out. And I did it all for a couple hundred bucks."

"That's so cool," Brandon said.

Andy added, "that's like, the badass-est!" which was met with a cheer of agreement as we all raised our forks like we were toasting pancakes.

A few minutes later, Brandon broke through the idle chatter and asked, "So where was Lisa?"

"What?" I asked.

"You were living in a basement by yourself and building a control panel. Lisa, where were you for all of this?" he asked, turning to her.

All eyes fell on Lisa and stayed there as they waited for an answer. "Well, I was in Elko. You see, me and him. We weren't a thing yet," she replied with a sheepish grin and a nod toward me.

I added, "No, we weren't a thing until, well, later. But I kept thinking about Lisa and how we weren't a thing. I found myself thinking about it, and her, and us a lot. I thought about how I'd never run a race in America without her, and how I wasn't sure I wanted to start now. Yeah, I thought about her a lot. But I wasn't sure what she was thinking, or even if she was thinking of me.

"I'd had my share of women after the divorce. It was kind of a defense mechanism in a way. I figured if I kept my mind and body busy with racing, working, and women, I wouldn't have to think about the pain of being left behind. It helped, but it didn't.

I watched, from the front row, as Lisa's heart, and life, were shattered into a million pieces. I watched as she meticulously picked up every last piece and put herself back together, bit by bit. She emerged a changed woman. She was strong, and by far the fiercest mother I'd ever seen. I watched in amazement as she built the best life she could for those boys and surrounded them with love. You don't see that kind of strong very often, and when you do, you better take a chance on it. But like the fool I am, I'd left her in Elko.

It was about a year ago I made the trip. I wanted to have the conversation in person. She arrived right on time, as usual, looking as good as usual. About the time the drinks came is when I finally got the nerve to start talking about what was on my mind. Then I just rambled. On and on I went, it was something like; 'Lisa, I've been thinking a lot lately, mostly about you. And I've been thinking a lot about you and me, and how we aren't a thing. I've been thinking about how maybe we could be a thing, and even more important, about how maybe we should be a thing.' Then as quickly as I started rambling, I stopped, and I let it all just sit there on the table. And boy, did she let it sit.

I'd just found the courage of a lifetime to open my heart, and she let it sit there on the table for what seemed like a lifetime. Then, right about the time I was thinking I'd made a mistake and opened myself to something that wasn't to be . . ."

Lisa interrupted my story mid-sentence. "That's when I finally found some words of my own. They came out in a ramble sounding something like, 'I can't believe you! Who are you to come here and say that? You've given me everything. You picked me up when I couldn't stand. You brought me light when there was none. You gave me room, and time, and space to be me. You gave me and the boys, well, a place! A place to live, a place to grow, and a place to heal. Now you come here asking if maybe we might be a thing?'

All he could do was stammer, "Yeah, no, yeah, well," so I continued, "I thought I was ready to stand on my own when you left. I was right. I was, and I did. But there was a part of me that kept thinking about you and me, and how we were never a thing. I wondered if you ever thought about me, and us, and if we could have ever been a thing. You see, I thought I had my heart put back together, but it turns out you'd taken a piece with you when you left. I need it back, and I think the only way to get it is to take the rest of you with it."

I broke in. "So then I said, 'well, I'm yours.' And just like that, we were a thing, and the crowd cheered.

"She stayed in Elko with the boys to finish the school year. Figuring I'd need a place for all of us, I bought this place. It was a repo, a great deal, but it wasn't fit for regular living. It was fine with me; I'm a bushman at heart and don't really need too much. I gutted the entire thing and lived out in the shed. I moved inside when winter got bad. But then again, I didn't have a water heater or even a regular heater, so it was still pretty much like camping. I worked at Wheeler during the day and on the house at night. I had a couple of rooms ready by the time Lisa and the boys arrived."

Bryan interrupted, "Yeah, but we still had to run to the gas station to use the bathroom." Everyone laughed, including me.

I continued, "Yeah, but it was summer, and camping in the summer is much easier than winter. I had the water and electricity going before the cold set in, and look at us now! The house is done, we're all settled in, we're eating pancakes, and building a race car!"

For the next three months you could find me either at work or in the shed assembling all the bits and pieces. It was happening! The Nitro was becoming a reality, but without Adrian. Not even my best convincing, pleading, or guilting could get him back. I tried it all, but he just kept droning on about family and responsibility. I was able to get some help from Australia though. Mathew agreed to come back, and Neal, my nephew, jumped at the chance to see America. A few guys from Wheeler, including Brandon and Jason, volunteered to help. Just like that, the old shed out back of the little bungalow in Magna, Utah became a hub of building and tuning.

The simple complexity of nitro cars is both beautiful and perplexing. The core systems are the frame, body, wheels, engine, blower, clutch, and control panel. The auxiliary systems are safety systems, brakes, and parachute, if you can call safety and stopping auxiliary. Yes, on its own, each part is incredibly simple. But each is so much more than an individual part; each is a vital piece of the whole. When brought together in the same place, in the right order, at the same time, they become greater than their parts. Together they become a chaotic, living, breathing system.

Like a fire-breathing dragon, each part has a purpose. The frame is the bones, giving it structure. The body is the skin, giving it form and grace. The wheels are the legs and feet, giving it gait and traction, and the engine is the heart and source of its power. The blower is the lungs, bringing the breath of life. The clutch is the muscle, flexing in perfect time. The nitro is the blood pulsing through the lungs and heart, exploding in time and powering the entire system. Then, with the force of thunder, it's spewed from the headers high into the sky. Like the breath of a dragon, the nitro burns hot and loud, with enough ferocity to light up the night sky and shake the insides of every living thing within a half mile. The management panel is the nervous system controlling it all, though it is nothing more than a bunch of pneumatic solenoids strapped to a board with tubing strung to the muscles like nerves.

The tune up, well, that's the brains of the operation. It's the voodoo shit. After a thousand bits and pieces have been gathered in one place, then assembled in order, the tune up is the magic of getting each of those parts to do what they do to their optimal potential at precisely the right moment. Each bit relies on the next, and each is affected by every other piece in the system, so a slight adjustment to one means a slight adjustment to them all, or not. Just like the fire-breathing dragons, they are magic. They are the things which dreams, and nightmares, are made of.

Just as in seasons gone by, I had my sights on the Phoenix 32 in May, which meant I was on a tight timeline. I had to finish the car, test it, tune it, license up, and get myself to Phoenix by the first weekend in May. I was focused on that weekend. Others called me intense if they were trying to be nice, possessed if they weren't.

But I had reason. This was not only my dream, but my future. I'd put everything I had into that machine; it had to be perfect. I was present for the placement of every nut and bolt. I checked and rechecked each and every piece as it took its place in the system.

I relished every first as it came. The first time I sat in the seat was like a surprise birthday party. The first time we put the body on was like Christmas all over again. She was a thing of beauty with a smooth-as-glass custom paint job. It was pure white, with the Southern Cross crashing through the hood, and thunderous bolts of blue night sky. I even donned the matching helmet even though I had no intention of using it. The new helmet with the fresh air connection had arrived the day before; I'd be wearing that for safety's sake. And, for the record, when it came time for the fine tuning I strapped myself in the seat with my driving suit, helmet, and the body in position! I'd had my share of driving blind!

Then, one day right about mid-March, it happened. I was so excited I started yelling from the shed. "Lisa, we're ready! Come quick, Lisa! Lisa! Lisa!" Over and over, I yelled her name. Finally, she rushed into the shed wearing nothing but a robe and a scowl.

"Quiet! You'll wake the neighbors!" she growled.

"We're ready! We're ready to start her up for the first time! I wanted you to be here for it!" I said, knowing how proud she'd be.

She wasn't. She looked at us like we were crazy and said, "Are you serious? It's midnight! No, you're not starting it up now. We'll have to wait for tomorrow, when it's day and I can warn the neighbors! Now shut this thing down and come to bed!"

I may have been possessed.

It about killed me, but I worked the entire shift at Wheeler and got home as quickly as possible. True to her word, Lisa warned the neighborhood. She had a little spiel she told each one. "Hello, my name is Lisa. I live just over there; we're building a race car and we'll be starting it up here in a few minutes. It'll be quite loud. I just wanted to warn you."

To our amazement, many of them followed her home. I guess they took it as more of an invitation than warning. That was fine by me. I'd been so focused on work, house, and car I hadn't the time to meet any of them before. By the time Lisa made it home we had quite a little crowd gathered in the driveway.

"I wish Adrian was here for this," I mumbled aloud as I eased myself into the belly of the beast. Lisa smiled as Brandon connected the starter. Mathew turned to the little crowd and said with a smile, "All right, you're going to want to cover your ears for this. It's about to get loud."

I glanced at Brandon with a thumbs up and, with a flick of a switch, she roared to life. I could feel the power bundled up inside just waiting to be released. Mathew and Brandon hovered as if suspended in air, then they zipped back and forth like bees with a tweak here, and an adjustment there. Thunder rolled from the beast while a thick blue cloud of nitro methane fumes filled the shop and billowed over the drive.

There was something familiar about the whole thing, like I'd been there before. In a way I guess I had with every other race car I'd started for the first time. It began with the white vacuum painted car and the Wobit's Wail back on Baker Street, then again with the alcohol car in Sparks.

But this was something different. It was as if I held a lifetime of dreams right there in my hands. I felt lucky, blessed, and grateful all at the same time. I knew in my heart how few people truly attempt to chase their dreams. Some are held back by the cost or the sacrifice, others are held back by how big the dream seems, or how small they feel. Whatever the reason, few people get to hold their dreams as I did in that moment. I cried. I wasn't ashamed and I didn't even try to hide the tears. I just let them flow. But then again, so did Mat, Brandon, Gary, Lisa, and the rest of the crowd for that matter. Those nitro fumes will do that to you.

The next few weeks were filled with a lot more starting, testing, tuning, and tinkering. Out of respect, Lisa made the rounds through the neighborhood each time we fired her up. Sometimes a crowd would gather, sometimes not. It was always loud.

April was a big month; it was the month for upgrading both my ride and license. I picked up the brand new truck of my dreams on April first. I felt like a king! I received word the same day that my brand new, state-of-the-art racing trailer would be ready for delivery after the fifteenth. The problem was that it was in Atlanta. That made for some creative scheduling as I needed to "license up" my Alcohol license to a Nitro license, which required three runs on at least two separate days.

I crafted a plan to make the first two runs on the tenth, then I'd send the Australians off to pick up the trailer soon after. They would have well over a week to make the run to Atlanta, giving us plenty of time to settle into the trailer before the final run on the twenty fourth.

I set the tune myself a few days before the first run. But it was an educated guess really, like throwing a dart while blindfolded. It was nothing but a place to start, knowing that every run after would be used to dial it in closer to perfection. This is where the search for the line of chaos begins, the one you don't know you've found until it's too late.

Nitro cars are in a completely different league than any other drag-ster. Nitro burns hotter and slower than alcohol, and to maximize horsepower you're pushing through so much fuel it's still burning as it leaves the headers. This accounts for both the dancing flames and 10,000 horsepower with the rev of the throttle.

Nitro cars just want to run fast. So much so that when the throt-tle's wide open they'll rip themselves apart from the inside looking for more power to give. The stress on the engine is so much that it's not long before things start breaking or exploding. One has about four seconds of full throttle, sometimes more, sometimes less, before it's given its all and the engine is left in shreds.

Sticking to the plan, I rolled into the Rocky Mountain Raceway on the tenth with a borrowed trailer. I knew two things for certain that day. First, I was going to run my very first nitro car and there wasn't anything anyone could do about it! Second, that was the last time I'd arrive in a borrowed trailer!

Mathew and the crew were spot on. They checked and rechecked every nut and bolt, making small tweaks to this and that along the way. The next thing I knew I was strapped into the belly of the dragon and sitting at the start line. I'd never driven a nitro car before. I'd built them, tuned them, taken them apart, and put them back together, but never driven one. I might have been a bit nervous, hes-itant even, as Mathew went to poking and prodding, preparing to wake the beast. Then, with the flick of the switch, she roared to life!

It was at that moment the reality of what was about to happen hit me. I knew what to do; I'd rehearsed it a thousand times in my head. But for an instant, I forgot everything. It wasn't anything I hadn't done a thousand times before. Yet it was like nothing I had ever done before. The power and energy were at a whole other level. I just sat there, strapped in tight, with the pure energy of the fiery engine coursing through my veins, wondering what the hell I was doing.

That all went away when Lisa signaled for the burnout. I was completely present.

Many folks think those burnouts are for show, with the gut-rumbling noise, and the pillars of fire lighting up the night sky. But they serve a functional purpose. Drag tracks are special; they're treated with a special low viscous tar. The friction of the burnout heats the rubber of the tires, making them sticky, and the tar of the track, making it tacky. In short, they prime both for optimal traction.

I rolled through the wet, and with a simple nudge of the foot, the dragon let out a deafening roar and spit dual pillars of fire as the rear tires spun to life. In half a second, I was fifty feet down the track in a cloud of smoke! I stopped, and Lisa guided me back to the start. Mathew and Brandon popped the body, tweaked this and that, and closed her back up. Lisa casually tapped the hood, looked me in the eyes, gave me a thumbs up, signaled the "all clear," and walked off.

"Here I am, clear the mind. Focus. Be one with the lights," I said to myself. I knew it wasn't a real race, but there's something to be said for ritual. Besides, needed this run to qualify for a real race.

The lights flashed and I kicked the dragon with all my might. I'd felt power before, but not like that. It was as if time slowed down just for me. With that simple kick, I felt the blower breathe in fresh air, I felt the pump eject a gallon of nitro all at once, and I felt the engine consume it all in one fiery gulp. I sank low to the track as the tires buckled under the raw power of the centrifugal clutch. I was thrown back into the cage as the tires sprang to life.

I was fifty feet down the track in .9 seconds. The g-forces trapped me to the back of the cage; it was all I could do to keep my hands on the wheel. In 1.2 seconds, I was 100 feet down the track. The g-forces kept coming, more and more! My cheeks pushed backward, but the helmet was tight. With nowhere else to go, they flattened out across the helmet padding.

In 2.5 seconds I was halfway down the 1,000-foot track. Fire streamed endlessly from the headers and the gut-wrenching roar filled the track. The g-forces pushed out what little air remained in my lungs. Another 1.5 seconds later I crossed the line, pulled the parachutes, braked to a stop, killed the engine, took in a deep breath, and sat in deafening silence as I marveled at what I'd done. That was it; I was a real nitro driver, with my own Nitro Funny Car!

I emerged victoriously from the belly of the beast, and just like the dragon, I let out a deafening roar for all to hear. I danced around the track hitting high fives with everyone as pure adrenalin pumped through my veins. I was the official king of the world and I wanted everyone to know as I yelled, "That was nothing! What are we going to do to make it interesting, light it on fire?"

I don't know why I said that. Adrenaline can make us do and say crazy things, I guess.

As the crew rebuilt the engine, I reviewed the data. I'd gone 210 Mph in 5.6 seconds in my own Nitro Funny Car! That time was not a record in the Book of Racing by any means, but it was a record in my Book of Life. It marked the realization of a dream I'd been chasing for ten years. We still had a lot of work to do to get her competition ready, but that was the first run of a hand-crafted Funny Car. There were no glitches, no mistakes, and no problems to note. It was a near perfect run and a success in any book.

The second run, not so much.

I cleared my mind and was one with the lights, but then a bad thing happened. I had a thought, *maybe I can break my own record.* My focus went from the lights to the clock, and I slow off the line. It got worse. I wasn't accustomed to so much power, and the machine took over. I pumped the throttle, trying to wrestle for control, but I was too late. I'd drifted into the other lane and lost the second contest. As per NHRA rules, that run was disqualified. I was two runs in, but only one counted. I needed two successful runs on the twenty fourth.

On the thirteenth, I packed up my brand-new truck with my brand-new cell phone and both Aussies and sent them off to fetch my brand-new trailer in Atlanta. "Where's Atlanta?" Neal asked.

"It's that way. Just head off that way and figure the rest out as you go," I said, pointing east toward the big mountains, and they did. I had no clue where Atlanta was!

A week later, I officially left Wheeler to race my Nitro Dragster full time. The boys in the shop knew me well and gave me quite the sendoff. They celebrated how all my plans, work, and sacrifice had come together to make it happen. It was surreal, and one of the proudest moments of my life.

I was still on top of the world when I received the call. "He's gone, the bastard's gone!" Mathew bellowed from the other end.

"What do you mean gone," I asked.

"Gone! As in not here. He just up and left! The bastard! He said something about seeing New York City last night, and this morning he's gone!" Mathew vented.

"Well, where are you now?" I inquired.

"Atlanta. Just picking up the trailer now," he said.

"What have you been doing? It doesn't take a week to get to Atlanta! Does it?"

"No, not really, we kinda took a scenic route," came his reply.

"You better get a move on or we're not going to make the twenty fourth! Don't take any more scenic routes and call me every couple of hours to let me know you're okay." And he did. That was the thing about Mathew. He lived for racing, and he'd do anything to get the job done. The fact is, he drove the whole way from Atlanta to Salt Lake by himself, only stopping for fuel and caffeine.

It was then I had time to think about how maybe sending those two might not have been the best leadership decision I'd ever made. They'd been bickering back and forth since arriving in the country, and there I went and sent them off across it. Yeah, that was my bad.

Like clockwork, Mathew called every two hours, and I'd chat him up to keep him awake. He was somewhere around the Colorado-Utah line when I decided to go meet him to take over the driving. Andy and I headed off late in the afternoon but lost cell signal in the mountains. Andy kept his eyes on the road, and I kept mine on the oncoming traffic.

"There he is," I exclaimed!

"Yeah, I see him," Andy replied, flashing his lights and slowing down. Mathew rushed right on by.

"What the!" I mumbled.

"I think he's kind of out of it. He's been driving for nearly thirty hours now," Andy replied. We chased him down pretty quick and drove up right on his bumper. Andy honked the horn and flashed his headlights, but nothing. Mathew just kept driving, so we kept on chasing. He seemed surprised to see me as I knocked on the driver's window at the first red light in town.

"Slide on over buddy, I'm taking over from here." He was sleeping soundly before the light turned green.

We had a day to move into the trailer. I spent all evening and well into the wee morning hours settling in. I loved everything about it. I love how compartmentalized trailers are. I love how every tool and spare part has its own drawer, or cubby, or closet. They are sanctuaries of professionalism and order. There's a place for everything, and everything goes in its place. I love the smell. It's a beautiful cocktail of fuel, oil, and solvent; shaken, not stirred.

SECOND RUN

On April 24th, 1999, the crew assembled bright and early for another big bacon-less breakfast bash. The mood was light and happy as we talked through the plan of the day. We had to make two successful runs, separated by a complete rebuild. Everyone was in and the energy was good. But the mood took a sharp turn to quiet when Lisa turned, paused, looked me straight in the eyes and said, "Robert, we have to talk. You can't put the crew in white uniforms. It doesn't make sense."

Who's the sell out? Who's been talking to Lisa! is what I thought as I scanned the table. Lisa was the only one making eye contact. The boys dug into the food, making like there was nothing else going on. What I said was, "Why? It would be classy. We gotta be top rate. We've gotta do something to stand out. We can't just blend in with the crowd."

"What does that have to do with white uniforms," she asked.

"No one else is doing it. We'd look so sharp out there," I responded. I finally noticed—they weren't digging into their food, they were fiddling with it.

"Do you know why no one else is doing it? Can you imagine trying to clean a white pit uniform? Come on, that's just crazy talk," she said, which ruffled my feathers.

"Crazy talk?" I questioned loudly, looking directly at Andy. It was him. It had to be. He was putting up the most resistance the night before. He looked up from his food fiddling and said, "Yep. Pure crazy talk." The silence was deafening. No one dared chew. He sat there, half scared and half brave. It was the first time he'd made such a stand.

"You know, this is my car. This is my crew. This is my deal and I have the final say," I said, looking at him straight on.

"Pure crazy talk," he responded, without missing a beat.

I sat there, half in shock and half angry that he had the courage to call me out. Silence lingered as the reality of what I was fighting for sank in. I broke the silence with a smile as I laughed. "Yeah, I think you're right! Pure crazy talk!" Lisa was next to laugh, giving the entire table permission to join in.

"You gotta admit though, it would be cool to see an entire crew in white all lined up on the black track at launch. The roar of the engine, flames shooting out the sides," I said with a smile.

"Right, that would be something," Andy replied. "Would, not will. Right?"

I never did answer.

We rolled into the track in style. I was driving my own brand-new truck, pulling my own brand-new trailer, hauling my own brand-new Nitro Funny Car. I had never been more ready, or more proud. It was my day, and I knew it!

With two weeks to kill, we had taken our time with the rebuild. Every nut and bolt on the car had been checked and rechecked. Everything we needed for the on-track rebuild was in the trailer. If I was a big operation, I'd have had a second engine for the second run. But not on my budget. We would make the run, strip her down, rebuild the engine, and put her back together between runs. Trying to be inspirational, I mumbled something like, "We need to be fast and efficient boys. Look at this as a practice for the big times. We need to be fast and perfect out on the racing circuit."

I tested the nitro; it was perfect. I walked the track; it was perfect. It was, for all intents and purposes, the perfect spring day for going fast. The pitch-black track was skirted in green spring grass. White snow held tight to the mountain peaks above. The sky was the perfect shade of azure blue, not a cloud could be found.

The burnout was flawless. The roar of the engine echoed across the track; flames shot high, bright, and hot into the crisp spring air. The screaming tires primed the track with a fresh layer of hot rubber, leaving a blue haze lingering above the car on the breezeless day.

"Clear the mind. Focus! Be one with the lights. This is the first of two runs today. I don't need to set any records. I just need to get the car down the track to get a license. I've got this. Focus and be one with the lights." With that last bit of self-advice, I kicked the dragon and she kicked me back tight into the cradle of the cage with the crushing weight of multiple Gs. My fingertips gripped tight to the edge of chaos. At .75 seconds I hit 80 miles an hour, at 1 second, I . . .

I . . .

I . . .

I can't breathe. Why can't I breathe? I thought to myself. "It must be the helmet," I answered.

I came to in a frantic fight for air, yelling as loud as I could, "Take it off! I can't breathe! Take off the fucking helmet!"

"No, don't! There might be a spinal injury," came a familiar voice. It was Midgley, the track's Rescue Chief. "Stay down, stay calm! Help is on its way!" he said with a calm intensity.

"Get the helmet off my head! I can't breathe!" I yelled again in a full fight for air.

"Robert! Stay calm! The helicopter is on its way; it'll be here soon," he said again. I cussed some more as I frantically pulled, pushed and yanked at the helmet. Finally, Midgley relented and eased the helmet off; it didn't help. I continued gasping frantically until it all went away.

"Lisa, is that you?" I wasn't sure if I was asking out loud or to myself, but she answered just the same. I squeezed back tightly on the hand gripping mine.

"Robert! I love you!" she yelled over the whirling of the helicopter. "They won't let me ride with you, but I'll meet you at the hospital as soon as I can!"

"Ma'am, I need you to step back; we have to go," yelled the Life Flight paramedic. "Ma'am, now!"

"See you soon!" she yelled, releasing her grip.

I heard voices yelling back and forth over the rumble of the helicopter. "His O2 is very low!" "We need to intubate right now!" "Robert! You need help breathing! We're going to put a tube down your throat!" "To do this, we're going to put you to sleep!"

SECTION 4
BODY

BACK IN THE HOSPITAL,
AGAIN AND AGAIN

"**H**ello. Yes. This is Lisa. Yes, Lisa," she said into the phone at the nurse's station. Warily, she looked around as if someone might hear. In hopes of privacy, she stretched the cord to its limits and huddled against the far wall. "Yes, Lisa. This is Coralie, Robert's mum. It's good to meet you," Lisa continued. "Yes, me and Robert, we've known each other for several years, and we've been together for some time. Really? Never mentioned me. Yes. We moved here together from Nevada."

It felt strange to have such an intimate conversation in such a public place, especially considering the topic. It was a delicate situation. Everyone at the hospital knew Lisa; she'd been by Robert's side every minute of every day for the past week. She'd been there for the entirety of the induced coma. She was by his side through every bandage change. She watched as they laid him on the sterile steel table and dipped him into the tepid water. The gentle soakings separated the bandages from the charred and crusted burns. She watched as the skilled nurses scraped away the dead and damaged skin over half of his body. She held his good hand as the same nurses spread the antiseptic cream in thick layers like frosting across the open wounds.

She watched as they wrapped him like a mummy in layers of gauze and cotton mesh. All the while, he lay motionless as the ventilator did the breathing for him.

Yes, the hospital staff knew Lisa, but they knew her as Mrs. Schwab. She'd never given that name, and they never asked. She just introduced herself as Lisa and that she was with Robert. She let their imaginations, assumptions, and fancy illegible signatures do the rest. Of course, she didn't correct them when they ran with it.

It was, in fact, a big deal. If the hospital had known they weren't officially married, well, that would mean they weren't officially "family." In accordance with the new health privacy laws and corresponding hospital policies, legally, they would be forced to deny her access. And that couldn't happen. She needed him, she needed to be there, and he needed her. Their bond was stronger than most who came through with proper paperwork to prove the relation.

"What, me? Blonde . . . I don't know, average, I guess . . . Wait, this isn't about me, it's about Robert. He's on a ventilator . . . No, he hasn't been able to breathe on his own since the accident . . . Yes. He's been in an induced coma for a week. They started bringing him out of the coma this morning, slowly, to see how he responds. So far, it's been positive . . . He's woken up three times this morning. He can't talk, though . . . No, it's because of the ventilator tube, but he seemed aware both times . . . Yes, he's burned over fifty percent of his body . . . the entire left side. He has all his fingers and toes . . .

"His face, forehead, and eyes are bad, but how bad, we don't know. His eyes are swollen shut and he's been unconscious, so there's been no way of telling. The doctor Isn't saying anything until the swelling goes down and he's awake. Some of the nurses have braced us for the worst case scenario that he may never see again. But that's not the biggest concern. His throat and lungs are burned really bad. I understand they got the tube down his throat just in time, just before the swelling closed it off. We almost lost him that day, and it's still of most concern to the doctors . . .

"I don't know. I've told you everything they've told me. As you can tell, that's not much . . . Yes, he's sleeping now. He's heavily sedated. No. No, there's no need to come, there's not much we can do. Besides, Neal is here and he's a tremendous help." She said those words knowing it was more of a financial decision than anything, which put yet another crack in her already broken heart.

"Mom, Mom! Come on, he's waking up!" Bryan yelled down the hall with his head poking out the doorway.

"Mrs. Schwab, he's waking up again, I need to run . . . Yes, he is strong . . . he's a fighter. We'll know more soon. Mrs. Schwab, it really is good to meet you. I wish it was under better circumstances . . . Yes. I promise, I'll let you know what happens, as soon as it happens . . . Yes, you too. Bye."

With that, Lisa hung up the phone and raced back to Robert's side. Mark brought the board and Bryan handed over the marker, saying, "OK, so far we have, ORDER A NEW."

"Let's see what we're ordering," said Lisa.

By that point, the entire room was in on the game, including the nurses. They all joined in. Everyone was guessing and calling out letters as they appeared. "Is it a P?" "An 8?" "I think it's a B!" "B, yes B!"

"Zero!" "O, it's an O!"

"Is that another O?" "No, that's gotta be a D!" "I think you're right, that is a D!"

"Y, that's a Y!" "No, that's a T!" "No, I'm sure that's definitely a Y!"

"You're right! BODY! ORDER THE NEW BODY," Mark hollered above the rest with his fists raised in victory. With those words, a reverent and confused silence fell over the room as each scanned the eyes of the others in search of meaning.

A tear formed in the corner of Lisa's eye as she choked down a sob in a moment of doubt. *This is so unlike him, he's a fighter*, she thought.

Mark broke the silence with a calm, "Look, there's more. His hand is moving again. It's an N! No wait! A W! No, an M, it's an M!"

The rest cautiously joined in. "H!" "No, it's an A!" "Yes, an A!"

"I!" "No, it's a T!" "Yes, that's a T!"

"MAT. Are you kidding me?" Bryan said softly, followed quickly with a loud, "He wants us to tell Mathew to order the new body!"

Mark said directly to Robert. "You want us to tell Mathew to order the new body for the car?" Robert made a check on the board and a thumbs up sign.

The entire room froze in silence, processing what he'd said. In an instant, the tears in Lisa's eyes changed from those of despair to ones of joy. In her heart, she knew this meant two things. First, God wasn't finished with Robert just yet. Second, Robert wasn't finished with life just yet. She didn't know how, but she knew he was going to be okay. She felt it with everything she had.

In unison, each family member sprang to life, cheering and hugging anyone and everyone in sight. He was going to be fine! The nurses stood in confusion, but eventually joined in the celebration as the family explained the significance of what had just happened. "He's ordering race car parts. The body is a new race car body! He's not finished racing; he's going to be fine."

Bryan relayed the message to Mathew to order the new Funny Car body, and with that, they went to work.

RECOVERY

Dr. Steffes took the family's enthusiasm in stride as he donned his bravest bedside manner. His mind was weighed down with experience; he knew they were all victims. He knew the road ahead, and it wouldn't be easy. He'd seen families band together, just like this. He'd watched as they smiled and cheered with the first sign of progress. He'd watched as they mapped recovery plans and scheduled coverage calendars, vowing never to leave a loved one alone.

But he'd learned that the emotional torture of helplessly watching loved ones in pain burns the soul, leaving similar scars on the inside of bystanders as to those worn by the patients themselves. Some families crumbled quickly as the reality of a burn recovery set in. In an attempt at self-preservation, some families left the patients alone to fend for themselves, while others faded slowly away under the strain.

Yet he'd seen other families come together, struggle together, and carefully distribute the emotional weight between them, emerging stronger than they'd ever been. He didn't know Robert, Lisa, or the boys, or the crew for that matter. He didn't know where they would be next week, next month, or next year. Would they be broken? Would they be whole? He only knew it would be difficult. He needed to set realistic expectations for them, complete with facts and milestones.

He kept his heart guarded and hoped for the best as he turned to

Lisa and said, "He hasn't taken a breath on his own for seven days now. The first step is for him to breathe on his own. Once he's completely out of the induced coma, we can get to work on that. Then, once the swelling in his esophagus has receded, we will remove the breathing tubes."

"Okay, doctor, so the first goal is to breathe on his own, then it's to remove the tubes from his throat. Then?" Lisa questioned.

"Then, assuming everything goes well, and there are no infections, we'll look at skin grafting. The entire left side of his body may need grafting, especially the deep burns on his leg, torso, arm, and forehead. He's lucky; the right side of his body is relatively unharmed so there's plenty of skin to harvest. But let's take this one step at a time. For now, let's concentrate on breathing."

"Okay, we'll focus on breathing for now," Lisa said as the doctor turned for the door.

Her eyes fixed on the tubes protruding from Robert's gaping mouth. One fed him life-giving oxygen, the other, the suction tube, pulled all sorts of hell from the depths of Robert's charred lungs. She traced that tube to the clear plastic tub filled with black goo and chunks of blackened flesh. There was no way of telling how many times the nurses had emptied that tub, but it had been working non-stop for a week and showed no signs of slowing. "Excuse me, doctor. How long are we thinking? Till we get to that point, that is?" she asked as he approached the door.

"There's no way of saying for sure," Dr. Steffes responded, "it could be a couple of days, a week, or maybe longer. There's no telling what his lungs are doing."

Twenty four hours later, the breathing and suction tubes were gone. He was supposed to be resting, but Robert called out in a quiet, raspy whisper. "Lisa. Is that you? Are you there?"

"Yes, I'm here," came her gentle reply.

"You've been here all along? Where are the boys?" he squeaked.

"It's okay, Neal's with them," she replied.

"Neal? I thought he was in New York," said Robert.

"Yeah, he was, for a bit. Turns out he went on a little east coast adventure before heading home. He was in LAX when the accident happened. We were able to page him there an hour before his flight to Australia. So, he's here now; well, at home with boys."

"The accident. What happened? What have I done?" Robert rasped.

"It's okay, we're not going to worry about that now," came Lisa's gentle reply.

"But really, what happened?" Robert questioned again.

"All we know is you hit the wall right after launch, burst into flames, and you were on fire the entire length of the track," Lisa replied. "They had to cut you out and Life Flight you up here to the hospital."

"I don't remember much. Only bits and pieces here and there," Robert said.

"Excuse me," came a thick European accent. "Hello, Robert. I am Katja, your nurse. It's time for changing bandages. This is first time for changing since waking up; it is extremely painful process. Here are your meds for coping with pain."

"Meds, what meds?" asked Robert.

"Morphine," replied Katja.

"Morphine? I don't think we'll be needing that," Robert whispered.

"I suggest you take it and see how goes," Katja warned.

"No, it's okay. We'll see how things go and I'll take it if needed," came Robert's whisper.

"Okay, suit yourself," she replied in defeat, then added, "Doctor will be in soon. He will remove eye bandages."

A few minutes later the doctor announced himself as he entered the room. "Hello, Robert. I'm Dr. Steffes. How are we doing this morning?"

"Hanging in there, Doc," came Robert's raspy whisper.

"Well, I'd say you're doing fantastic considering everything. You're breathing on your own, and you just talked to me. That is fantastic!" said the doctor.

"All right then, I'm fantastic," whispered Robert. Lisa smiled.

"Okay, Robert, I'm going to remove the bandages from your eyes here before your complete bandage change. It's been just over a week since the accident and the swelling has subsided enough that we may be able to open your eyes enough to see," he paused. "Well, to see what the damage is, or isn't." With that, he motioned to Katja. She closed the blinds, turned off the lights, and pulled the door almost closed. A single sliver of light from the hall cut the room in two, casting faint shadows through the darkest corners of the sterile room.

Lisa paced the room as Dr. Steffes leaned over the head of Robert's bed and talked him through each step. "Okay, Robert, I'm cutting the mesh sleeve. Now I'm cutting through the gauze. I'll let the saline soke for a bit before we remove it." He dabbed the bandages with a moist sponge from the instrument tray.

Silence as thick as the dark filled the room, casting shadows of doubt on the hearts of all present. Finally, Dr. Steffes broke the silence. "Okay, Robert, I'm removing the gauze from your eyes. Katja stopped Lisa mid pace with the clasp of her hand and motioned to Robert. Together, they stepped up to the bed. Lisa took Robert's good hand and squeezed tight. He reciprocated.

Robert twinged and groaned in pain as threads of gauze ripped and tugged at the raw flesh of his naked eyelids. "Sorry about that; I'm trying to be careful. This is the worst part here," said the doctor as he lifted the last of the gauze and wiped away the protective cream from Robert's swollen face and eyelids. "I'm amazed! Your eyelids are intact, though you'll probably never have eyelashes or eyebrows again. Can you open your eyes?"

"I'm trying, Doc."

"Let me give you a little boost there," the doctor said as he gently peeled open Robert's crusted eyes.

Robert flinched at the light as his baby blue eyes danced back and forth across his half open eyelids. "Hello, Doc," Robert said, as his eyes fixed on Dr. Steffes' face.

"Look at that! You have eyes, and they're intact, and they are reacting to light! That's a very good sign." Lisa's hand squeezed tighter with excitement. His eyes instantly zigged over and locked on hers.

"Lisa, it's good to see you!" he rasped. Lisa responded in kind as tears streamed down her face.

The doctor continued, "Well, there you have it. I'm not sure I understand it, but there you have it. You can see. I'm amazed that your eyes are intact with your forehead and cheeks being so burned. Someone must be watching over you, Mr. Schwab. That's all I can say, someone is watching over you."

"Yeah, someone," Robert responded, hand in hand with Lisa, as the doctor continued his inspection.

Once the doctor was finished, Katja unlocked the bed wheels and pushed Robert into the light of the hall. "Okay, let's change rest of the bandages," Katja said. Hand in hand, Lisa floated effortlessly alongside Robert.

"Lisa, you can wait in his room, or maybe go to cafeteria for something to eat," Katja said as they rolled to a stop outside the changing room.

"No, it's okay, I'll stay with him," Lisa calmly responded.

"You may want to rethink this. Changings are very difficult," replied Katja.

"I've been with him for every cleaning. I'd like to continue if that's okay," Lisa pleaded.

"Yes, it's okay, but this is going to be different. He's never been awake for cleaning. It can be difficult for family."

"I'm not leaving his side," she said defiantly.

"Don't worry, I'm not leaving your side," she said reassuringly to Robert.

Katja surrendered. "Okay, I see, I can't win with you two. If you're staying, be prepared; we'll put you to work. There's something about human touch. He will need you to hold him. Hold his hand and shoulder if you can. Squeeze. It helps."

The room was white, bare, and sterile. The steel table was cold and hard. The water and nurses were warm and soft. The nurses talked them through every step in calm, soothing voices. "The creams and ointments dry and crust up through the day, adhering the bandages to the wounds ." Nurse Katja tested the temperature of the water on her hand before turning the hose on Robert. "The water dissolves the crust and loosens everything up. We need to work slowly to give the water time to soak in. Your body is working hard to form new skin. If we were to take the bandages off dry, it would take all that new growth with it." They continued running lukewarm water over every inch of burned flesh, cutting, pulling, and unwrapping soggy layers of bloody gauze as they went.

Robert flinched in pain whenever a strand of thread stuck, or a loose gob of soggy gauze fell on a patch of raw skin. Lisa squeezed his right hand and said nothing as squeaks of pain escaped his lips.

Soon the last wad of soggy gauze fell into the waste basket. "Well, now. That wasn't so bad," Robert whispered naively.

"Oh, Robert, we haven't started cleaning," replied Nurse Jane.

"What was that?" Robert asked, bewildered.

"That was us removing the old bandages," Jane replied. "This is where it gets interesting. Now we'll clean the wounds. We'll be wiping away the old ointments and creams, plus any flesh that's ready."

"Ready? Ready for what?" he rasped in pain.

"Ready to come off. The sooner the dead skin is gone, the sooner new skin can grow, so we will take off any that's ready to go. It may not feel like it, but we'll use the softest towels we have. We'll be touching your open wounds to get everything off. It's going to hurt." With that warning, both nurses began the arduous process of cleaning the raw and tender flesh. With small and deliberate strokes, they slowly and meticulously scraped his open wounds. They continued the process across every inch of tender red skin, raw nerves, exposed muscle, and bare bone.

"AAAAAAHHHH! NOOOOOO!" Robert screamed uncontrollably with each gouging stroke.

Tears puddled in the corners of Lisa's eyes. She fought hard and swallowed her cries.

"It's okay, Robert! It's okay to yell. Please do. Get it out. This has to be done or infection will set in," said Jane. "It's okay, Lisa. You can cry. You can scream with him if it helps. In fact, it usually does."

With the newly granted permission, Lisa lost control of her tears and voice as she screamed in unison with Robert. Each gentle and gouging stroke ushered in another round of excruciating pain and its accompanying cries for relief. With hands clasped tightly, each drew strength from the other as they screamed for the world to hear.

Over and over, stroke after stroke, scrape after scrape, the nurses covered every inch of burned flesh. They started with his left leg, where the muscles and tendons were laid bare. They moved up to his hip and buttocks, then on to his tender torso. Next was his left arm and shoulder, then up his neck to his cheeks and nose. They finished with his eyes and forehead. Out of reflex, Lisa grasped his shoulder and squeezed as hard as she could, pure love and energy flowing freely between the two of them. She screamed with him and for him. She screamed for herself. It helped.

"Okay. That's it. All clean," Katja announced.

"Oh, thank you, God," Robert moaned in relief as the tension drained out of his shoulders and onto the steel table.

Thank God it's over. I've never heard sounds like that come from Robert before. Come to think of it, I've never heard those sounds come out of me before, Lisa thought.

"Now we dry, sanitize, prep, and wrap the new bandages. But we'll let you air dry a little and catch your breath before we begin," said Katja.

"Oh no, there's more," Robert lamented. Hand in hand, they let the silence play as the nurses scurried about opening tubs of creams, boxes of ointments, and snipping gauze to size.

"Okay, Robert, now we'll apply the antiseptic cream," Jane said, dipping her gloved hand into an open tub of Sulfadiazine. Scooping a heaping handful of the soft cream, she rotated her wrist back and forth ever so gently, balancing the towering gob, making sure none dripped off. Lightly, she touched the dollop to the outside edge of Robert's charred chest. Gently, she waved her hand outward across to the raw flesh of his left pectoral and shoulder, leaving a thick layer of white fluff in its wake. Robert winced and his hand clamped down on Lisa's.

"I call this frosting; that's what it reminds me of. I feel like I'm frosting a cake." And frost they did. Thick layers of fluffy cream across half of his body. Robert let out uncontrolled "OOWWWs" or "AAAAHHHHs" as they glazed the deepest burns and most tender regions.

Next, pulling from the pile of gauze they had so skillfully cut, they placed layer upon layer of soft cloth over the freshly frosted flesh. Like a jigsaw puzzle, they placed one piece at a time, carefully following the contours of the burn and around every joint; a shoulder, an elbow, a hip, a knee, each finger of the left hand. Slowly the white frosting faded to white gauze. The wrapping began at the lower extremities and ended at the top with his face, eyes, and forehead. Finally, the ordeal ended with a layer of flexible netting to hold it all in place.

"Okay, that's it! You're done, Robert. Let's get you back to your room," Katja announced, unlocking the wheels as she rolled Robert out into the hall.

Hand in hand, Lisa trudged woefully next to Robert under the weight of what was to come.

Katja parked Robert's bed in the dim light of his quiet room and quickly vanished, leaving them alone in silence, and in shock.

"That was hell. That's all, pure living hell," Robert whispered.

Exhausted, Lisa plopped into the bedside chair and mustered the strength to answer, "that went much smoother when you were asleep."

"Yeah, next time I'll take the morphine," Robert said softly as they both drifted off to sleep.

"Good evening, time for your cleaning," Katja announced through the open door.

"Didn't we just do that?" Robert questioned.

"That was morning; it's now time for evening cleaning," she replied.

"Oh, hell no!" Robert exclaimed.

"Yes. To prevent infection and for proper healing we must clean two times a day," Katja replied.

"Yeah, it's been twice a day since you arrived," Lisa added. "You've just been asleep for it."

"Is that offer for morphine still good?" he asked hopefully.

"I have it here for you," Katja replied, draping the bag of clear liquid over the saline on the IV stand. Moments later the tubes were connected, and relief coursed through his veins. Soon enough he found himself once again lying on his back, completely naked, on the cold, hard steel of what he affectionately came to call the torture table. Once again he cried out in pain, and once again, Lisa cried with him and for him.

"Why does it hurt so bad? The morphine isn't working. I need more!" he cried as the nurses scraped away the last of the morning's creams.

"Morphine doesn't actually kill the pain, it just blocks it at the brain," Jane replied. "Some say it helps so you don't remember it." And he didn't. As soon as they frosted him with the fresh layer of cream, his entire body relaxed and he slept through the last of the wrapping.

And that's how it went, every day, twice a day, for the next four days; drugs, change, recover, repeat. All the while, he was living in his own personal hell. There was no comfortable position to lay in. No matter how he tried, he was either pressing a burn or bumping one. Any movement shot pain through his extremities. It hurt to breathe, it hurt to move, it hurt to lay still. It just hurt all the time. But not once did he let on to anyone, for he had a secret weapon—his race face—and he wore it often.

There were times between changings when the drugs waned and he thought clearly through the pain. Those were the happy times spent with family, friends, and crew. Even in his state he found reason for real smiles that broke through his race face.

"Hello," Dr. Steffes said from the door.

"Doc!" Robert squawked from his bed, attempting a happy greeting. "How's it going?"

"I'm doing well, but I'm not the one in question here. How are you?"

"Oh, I'm feeling like a million bucks!" Robert replied.

"Well, that's great to hear," Dr Steffes said with an air of surprise, "I must say, I'm amazed. I'd mentioned to Lisa only yesterday that we might be ready for the next steps soon. But I didn't expect soon to be this soon."

"'This soon.' That sounds like a good thing, Doc," said Lisa.

"It is! It's a very good thing. But there is some bad news as well. What would you like first?" he asked.

"Oh, geez Doc, I'm not much for dancing around the hard parts. Just tell me how it is so we can get going with life. I've got things to do. I've got a car to build," Robert rasped.

"Slow down there. You're looking stronger than I could have

hoped at this stage. But there's still a lot to be concerned about. Your esophagus and lungs, for one. You're talking, that's a good thing, but I take it this is not your normal voice."

"Nah, you got me there, Doc. I'm squawking pretty hard, and it hurts like hell."

"As is to be expected with internal injuries like yours. Also, your oxygen levels are on the low side. I think you must have breathed in quite a few flames, probably all the way to your lungs, causing some significant damage, but there's really no way to tell for sure. All we can do is monitor. Don't push things too hard. You'll probably find you'll get winded very easily. But you're breathing, so, you know. You've got that going for you," the doctor said with a smile.

Robert laughed and moaned with a smile, "Ouch, that hurts."

"Seriously, Robert, you're looking stronger than expected. If you keep this up, we'll be ready for grafting soon. Real soon."

"Yeah, well, that's the plan, Doc. Let's get this thing done! I've got other things to do, and they ain't getting done here," replied Robert.

Dr. Steffes went on to explain the graphic details of skin grafting. He explained how they slice off a few thin layers of skin from one part of the body and lay it down on the deepest burns, the ones where the skin is either gone, or too damaged to heal on its own. "The place where we take the skin, that's the harvest, or donor, site. Lucky for you, the right side of your body is in good shape. We'll harvest from your right thigh, buttocks, back, and torso."

He went on to explain how painful it would be. "You've probably noticed how the third-degree burns, those places where there's no skin left at all, the places that look the worst where the muscle or bones are exposed, they hurt less than the skin burns."

"Yeah, sure," Robert replied.

"That's because there's no nerve endings left in those places, they've all been burned off, meaning you can't feel there."

"Well, that explains some of what I have, or haven't, been feeling," Robert replied.

The Dr. continued, "It's ironic. To heal the open and exposed wounds, we create more open and exposed wounds. When we cut the skin from the doner sites, you'll be left with a layer of raw nerves. Those wounds carry the same risk of infection, and they will hurt as much, if not more than the other second-degree burns you have now. They'll be treated the same, too."

On when race face. "All right, I'll leave all of that to you, Doc. You're the one driving here. I'll do what you say, and together we'll get this done," came Robert's reply.

"Really? That's it? No complaints or buts? No why me?" Dr. Steffes replied in shock.

"No, that's for me to figure. Besides, it's like I said, I have things to do. Did I tell you? I'm a race car driver. I've got a Nitro Funny Car to build, and I can't do that here!" Robert said. Then he asked, "Doc, I have a question for you. Of the news you just gave me, what was the good news?"

Dr. Steffes smiled. "That is a great question. I guess all of the news was hard. But the fact that you're ready for skin grafting already, well, that's definitely very good news."

"Perfect, so you're going to skin me alive and call it good! I love it! When can we get this thing done?" Robert replied with a smile.

Dr. Steffes turned to Lisa and asked, "Is he always like this? Really?"

"Like what?" Lisa asked.

"This positive ball of energy?" he replied.

Lisa smiled and paused. Burned up or not, this positive ball of energy was the only Robert she knew. He'd always filled his life with so many projects, places, things, and people, he didn't have time to whine or feel sorry for himself. He simply loved life. There was always so much to do, and he was going to do it. What needed to get done now was some serious healing, and he was going to do it. Slowly, she looked up at Dr. Steffes, and with a confirmative smile, answered with a single word. No explanations, no justifications, just a single word: "Yes."

Any doubt Dr. Steffes harbored about the strength and will of the Schwab crew was completely dispelled by the conviction in that simple "yes."

And that's how it went with everyone who happened across Robert in the hospital. From nurses and techs to janitors and doctors, they were drawn to him. No one could resist his positive energy. From time to time, crowds would assemble in and around his room as he told stories of growing up in Southern Australia and about drag racing across two continents. He'd talk about nitromethane like it was alive. He'd tell how Nitro engines generate over 10,000 horsepower, and how they'll burn themselves to complete failure in a matter of seconds if given the chance. It was almost as if his hospital room had become his latest shed. The only difference was that he was the one on jacks.

GRAFTING

"**G**ood news! It's time for cleaning, and time for operations," Katja said as she entered Robert's room.

"That's good news?" he rasped.

"Good news is you will be asleep for both," she replied.

Robert breathed a sigh of relief. "That is good news. Goodness knows I can use the rest."

Rest he did as Dr. Steffes grasped a razor-sharp instrument and shaved a broad sheet of skin several layers deep from Robert's right calf. He then sent it through the skin stretcher, which is similar to a pasta machine, complete with rollers, gears, and shredders. A sheet of skin is fed into one end, where it's tugged, pulled, and stretched to its limit. Then a delicate sheet of skin, doubled in size, yet half the thickness, comes out the other. He then carefully laid the delicate sheet of skin over the exposed muscle and tendons on the back of Robert's left leg. Piece by piece, section by section, Dr. Steffes systematically worked his way up Robert's body. He started with his calves, then his knees, thighs, buttocks, torso, shoulder, arm, neck, and forehead.

In the end, Robert's tender body was a patchwork of give and take. The right half was covered in bright red squares of raw flesh contrasted against a background of pale white skin. The left half was a solid field of charred flesh draped in a carefully collected collage of transplanted skin. The nurses frosted and bandaged the left side as usual, then continued with the right.

Robert came to a few hours later, completely bound in bandages from head to foot. "Ouch, oh. Ouch," was all he could muster.

"Would you like something for the pain?" Lisa asked. Robert nodded. She quickly disappeared into the hall only to reappear a few moments later with Jane who activated the morphine drip. Relief. Soon he drifted off in a fog of morphine.

That evening's cleaning began with the familiar trip to hell as they scoured the left side. Then he was introduced to a whole new level pain as they moved on to the right. Each bright red patch of freshly exposed flesh featured a network of completely healthy, and completely exposed, nerve endings. Each patch was meticulously scraped clean of any residue, and each scrape ushered in an entirely new experience in pain. Robert cried out, begging them to stop. He begged for mercy, he begged for morphine. Lisa held on to what she could. It hurt her to be there. It hurt her to see him hurt. It just hurt.

The following morning's cleaning was much the same. As was the next, and the one after that. After one morning cleaning, Robert looked over at Lisa with a broken race face and cried, "It hurts! The donor sites hurt worse than the burns." He squirmed for comfort where there was none. His entire body was raw, both inside and out. Lisa had no words. All she could do was hold his hand, so she did.

It was somewhere in the hollow moments, those boring stints of nothingness between the madness of the bandages, creams, and cleanings on the torture table and the morphine fogs, when Andy showed up. "A bit late for a visit, isn't it, Andy?" asked Lisa.

"Yeah, well, you know, I was just in the neighborhood," he replied.

"Hey Andy. How's it going? Thanks for the visit," Robert said.

"Yeah, sure. How are you doing?" Andy asked, but continued before Robert had a chance to reply. "Hey, have you seen your nurse, Katja?"

"Yeah, I've caught a glimpse or two. She's only been caring for me for a couple of weeks now," replied Robert.

"Yeah, well, so you know she's hot. Right?" he asked.

"You don't have to answer," interrupted Lisa.

Andy continued, "Well, did you know she was on the Slovenian ski team?"

Just then, Mathew's voice rang from the door, "Hey, how are things?"

"Hey Mathew! Things are going. It's nice of you to visit, but isn't it a bit late?" said Lisa.

"Yeah, well, I was just in the neighborhood."

"What do you mean, in the neighborhood? Neither of you have any reason to be in the neighborhood, other than to visit," replied Robert. "

Yeah, well. Have you seen your nurse?" Mathew asked.

"Katja? Yeah, we've met," replied Robert.

"Well then, you know she's hot, right? Did you know she was on the Slovenian ski team?"

"Yes, I've heard," Lisa and Robert said in unison.

"Right," said Mathew.

"So, you're both here to see Katja?" Lisa questioned.

"No, no," Andy replied. "We're here to see you, too, I guess. I mean, we are in the neighborhood, and, well. Katja's wrapping up her shift here shortly, and apparently she has a friend she wants to introduce to Mathew here. And so, you know, we're all going out. And, since we were in the neighborhood, we thought we'd swing by for a quick hello."

"They weren't lying! They were literally in the neighborhood and thought they'd just swing by to say hi," Robert said to Lisa with a laugh.

The next couple of weeks were a rhythm of morphine fogs, cleanings, sleep, and a steady stream of visitors. The crew spent more and more time at the hospital. Mathew and Andy seemed to hover.

"Evidently the neighborhood's being good to you," said Robert. "I understand I'm not the object of your affection, and I'm okay with that. I'm just glad I was able to get you up here, even if it's the nurses who're convincing you to stay." Robert smiled.

One day, after the morning torture session, Robert moaned in his broken, raspy voice, "Oooohhh, that sucks."

"Yes. Yes, it does," Lisa agreed, clasping his good hand. Robert tightened his grasp and turned to her. The mid-morning sun filled the room and filtered like a halo through her long blond curls. As he stared into her sky-blue eyes, the expression on his face faded from hard pain to soft bliss.

"Wow, you're beautiful. You look like an angel!" he exclaimed.

"Where did that come from?" Lisa smiled.

"Marry me!" he blurted.

"What are you talking about? You are as high as a kite right now," she blushed.

"No, no, I'm not. I mean it! What have I been thinking? I've gotta be nuts not to have asked before. Come on. Marry me," he begged.

She smiled and said, "That's the morphine talking! If you're serious, you ask me again sometime. Ask me when you're not high as a kite." Outside she blushed, inside she smiled and thought to herself, "There's no way of telling. If you do ask, I just might say yes."

Bright and early the next morning, Katja walked in and announced, "it's time to order your compression suit!"

"What's a compression suit?" Robert asked.

"It's a heavy-duty stretchy sock that goes over your wounds. Compression helps the healing process. You're healing up rapidly. There's already a healthy new frosting of young skin, and the grafting looks good. Once a few more layers of skin form, you'll be ready for the suit. So, we must order now."

"All right. Order it then," he said with authority.

"There's a thing about it, though. Each suit is custom for the one wearing it. You get to choose the colors. These are the most popular colors," she said, pointing to the fleshly beige and tan samples.

"What about those? Let me see those," Robert said, pointing to the bright, flashy colors.

"Those are kind of bold. Most people don't want to bring attention to themselves," Katja replied.

Lisa laughed, "That sounds about right. Go big or go home. That's how we roll."

"Oh, there's nothing to be ashamed of. I want a bright one. What do you think, red or blue?" Robert asked enthusiastically.

"Well, you don't have to choose just one. Remember, this is custom, they can combine colors," Katja said with a smile.

"Now you're talking! Why choose one when you can have them both? Let's go with red and blue, just like the fire suite we burned up! Can we put a cape on that?" he exclaimed with a smile. They all laughed as Katja nodded yes.

Then Katja's smile faded with a flicker of seriousness. "I hope I'm not intruding, but I've been watching you for weeks now and I have to ask. Are you always this happy?" Leaving no time for answers, she turned to Lisa, "Is he always this happy? I mean, for real. I asked Andy and he seems to think so. But really?"

"Oh, this is Robert. What you see is what you get. There's no hiding that fact," Lisa responded.

"I've been asked that from time to time, "said Robert. "To be honest, I don't know what people mean by it. I'm not bubbly happy all the time."

"No, it's not about that," said Katja. "I mean, you're always so upbeat and positive, even when going through the hell of cleanings and everything."

"I wouldn't say I'm all that positive and upbeat. I'm just doing what needs to get done," he said.

Katja continued, "Not once have you complained or pitied yourself. Not once have you asked 'why me?'"

"That's not going to do me any good. I've got a lot to get done. I can't build my car in here. I've gotta get well so I can get on with life," Robert replied.

"You see? That! That right there's what I'm talking about," said Katja.

"He doesn't see it, but I do," Lisa said. "That's why I'm here, and why I'll always be. That's why people gather wherever he goes. That's why he's not alone when he builds his race cars, and why he's not alone when he races. People are drawn to him, and he doesn't know why."

"That's amazing," Katja said to Lisa.

"Now, don't go talking like I'm not here," replied Robert.

Katja went on, "Most patients here have had terrible disfiguring accidents, usually from doing things they shouldn't have been doing. Like the dope-pushing chemist whose home-cooked meth blew up in his face. Many have attempted suicide by setting themselves on fire, or blowing themselves up with propane, but failed. Some just had a bit too much to drink around the campfire, and fell in." Lisa and Robert listened in silence.

"I watch them wade through the agony of recovery," Katja said. "I see them slowly realize how their lives are forever changed. They slip into deep depressions. They cry for hours on end about their raw deal, how they'll never be the same, and how it's not their fault. And then here you are. Even your cries of pain are different. There's no self-pity in your cries on the table. It's like you're just releasing pure physical pain and nothing else."

"It hurts every minute of every day, in case you were wondering," he said, trying to sound miserable.

"I wonder if it has to do with what you were doing that got you here in the first place. You were doing what you loved, right? Racing cars?" asked Katja.

"Yeah, a brand-new car. Only the third time down the track," Lisa replied.

"We have other patients, too," Katja continued. "They're not all meth addicts or suicide attempts. The innocent ones are the kids. I call them innocent, though most were doing things they shouldn't. Like the boys who showed up earlier this week. They were doing what a million kids before have done with no consequence at all.

It's just their little fire happened to take hold and catch them both. It's strange how an innocent mistake can be so permanent. The truly innocent are the ones whose accidents are no fault of their own. Worse yet are the abused or victims of others. They are the purely innocent."

"That's terrible," Lisa and Robert said as tears welled.

"Now, look at me, I'm so sorry. I look forward to coming for your positive energy, and I make you cry. I'll get this ordered; you should have it in a few days," Katja said, gathering her samples.

"It's okay, thank you for sharing," Robert said as she vanished into the hall.

The next morning Robert woke to the soft sound of sniffles. Lisa stood alone, gazing out the west window. Lost in thought, she clutched her tissue, wiping her tears and nose without losing focus on the mountain shadows retreating across the wide valley. "Lisa? Is that you?" asked Robert with concern.

"Yeah, I'm here," she replied with another sniffle.

"What's wrong? What's going on?" he inquired.

"Oh, God. This is just so hard. It's another day, the sun's rising, and the valley is waking up. Someone's climbing out of bed without a care in the world, not knowing that, before the day's over, they'll be here, in this place, living in their own personal hell."

Robert quickly put his brave face on. "Oh, it's okay. It's not that bad. I'm doing well; we'll be out of here soon."

"Oh, it's not you. It's strange. Its just . . . Did you know there's a boy here who just turned sixteen? He got his driver's license as soon as he could, two weeks after his birthday. Two days later, he was hit by a drunk driver. His car burned, and he burned. He wasn't doing anything to deserve this; he was getting groceries for his mom. He was innocent and now he's burned over his entire body. There's one little patch on his back, the size of a football, that's not burned. They're harvesting skin from that little patch every week as they graft his entire body," she said in a rush of sniffles and tears. All Robert could do was hold out his hand for her. She grabbed it and together they shared tears for the boy down the hall they'd never met but hurt for just the same.

Their silent tears were broken as Katja entered the room with the magic cocktail. "It's time for morning cleaning," she said in a cheerful voice. Concerns for the boy quickly evaporated as Robert fell into a cloud of confusion. Should he mourn the unknown boy down the hall? Should he reply with a cheerful greeting? Should he cry for the personal hell he'd been living, or for the impending torture? The thought of another session on the torture table triggered a flood of anxiety. Every muscle clenched, leaving him on the edge of panic.

"Here you go," Katja said as she reached for the clamp on the morphine tube. There was something calming in that gesture; it was the promise of relief. His anxiety levels spiked with the thought of a cleaning, and the closest thing to comfort he found was in the familiar drip, drip, drop of each drop of morphine as it rolled down the tube. Solace was found in the following fog.

THE GREAT ESCAPE

The compression suit arrived a few days later. It was as loud and bold as they had imagined. The body was a bright brilliant blue, the sleeves, legs, and yes, even the custom cape was a vibrant red.

"I think you look like Superman!" exclaimed Mark.

"No, I think you look like Spiderman," replied Bryan.

"I think you look like Super Spider Man, said Dr. Steffes from the door.

"Doc!" Robert greeted him with his usual cheer. "When can I get out of this place? I've got stuff to do you know."

"That is the million-dollar question," replied the doctor. "You're a very interesting case. The burns and donor sites are healing as they should. The young skin is coming in strong, and there are no infections. The grafts are taking hold, almost."

"Almost?" The entire family turned with a questioning look.

"Perhaps it's best if I have some time with the two of you," he said, nodding to Robert and Lisa.

"Neal, would you mind taking the boys for a bit?" asked Lisa.

"Yeah, not a problem. Come on, guys," he said, motioning them to the door.

Dr. Steffes started, "I'm concerned about a couple of things, Robert. The first one being your face."

"Well, I'm not sure how to take that, Doc," Robert quickly retorted with a half-smile. "I mean, you're not a real looker yourself, but then, I wouldn't go telling you that to your face." It was Robert's way of bracing himself for what was next.

"Yeah, I set myself up for that. It would have been a shame to just leave it there. Thanks for keeping things light as I'm about to go heavy," the doctor replied.

"Just doing my part," Robert added.

Lisa looked at them both with disapproval and begged, "just let him talk."

"I'm not sure how your eyes survived, but they did," the doctor said, "and you seem to have full vision, which is, in itself, a miracle. The bad news is, the graft on your brow and forehead is not taking, that happens sometime. The burn is deep. I think what little skin you had left after the fire must have come off with the helmet because there was no skin there when you arrived. This can be a complicated thing. The wound will remain open and will need to heal on its own. It'll take time, the skin will grow from the outside edges in. Infection is a risk and will be for quite some time. You'll need to take extra care to keep it clean."

"You're sounding like it'll be on my own. Will I be going home?" Robert asked.

"Normally at about this time I'd say yes. As I said, for the most part, things are going well. The worst of the surgeries are over. You've learned how to clean and bandage yourself. But there's something more than the forehead going on here."

"More? Like what?" Robert interrupted.

"Just let him talk, will you?" said Lisa.

"We'll get to that once we're done talking about your beautiful face. Skin does interesting things as it heals. With a wound as large and deep as your forehead, there will be a lot of scarring. As it heals, the skin will change shape. It'll shrink and stiffen and distort as the scar tissue builds. There's no telling for sure what effect this will have until it happens, so we'll need to watch it closely," the doctor said.

"Until it happens? Until what happens?" Lisa asked.

"It's the skin around your eyes I'm most concerned about. We will most likely need to do some reconstructive surgery to correct any skin distortions. This could range from the dramatic to not much at all. My guess is something in-between. As it stands now, your tear ducts are gone. We'll need to build you some new ones. And maybe we'll do something cosmetic too. We'll just have to watch and manage what comes." He paused.

Lisa and Robert squeezed each other's hands so tight, their fingernail beds went white.

Dr. Steffes continued, "But that's not what's keeping you here. It's your vitals."

"My vitals?" Robert questioned.

"Yes. Your heart rate, blood pressure, and oxygen levels are all out of whack. That explains why you keep fainting during physical therapy. Your body is working way too hard for the oxygen it's getting, and it's putting a strain on your heart. Any extra strain on the heart and lungs just puts you right out. My guess is it's related to those chunks of burnt flesh you've been coughing up. I suspect those are parts of your throat, esophagus, and even bits of lung. There's no telling how bad the damage is down there. I have to say it again; it's a miracle you're here based on that alone. We need to get your vitals stable before you can go home."

"How do we do that?" Lisa and Robert asked in unison.

"I'm not completely sure," the doctor said. "We'll run some tests on you during tomorrow's therapy session. I'll review the results and keep working on things from my end. Meanwhile, you do your part and keep healing like you've been. You keep that up and you'll be fine."

"All right, Doc," Robert replied with resolve. He looked at the entire healing process as the challenge at hand. It was a problem to solve. When looked at in its basic parts, it was simple. It was just a set of tasks waiting to get done, and he was going to do them. Nothing more, nothing less. "I've got this!"

"You know the news I just gave you was split, Robert. It's not all great news. There are some challenges and questions left unanswered," said Dr. Steffes.

"Yeah. I'm good. We'll get it figured out and deal with it as it comes," he replied.

The doctor looked at Robert. "I know I've asked this before, but I have to ask again. Are you always like this? Are you always this happy? I've been watching you all this time and nothing gets you down."

"Oh, don't let this cheerful disposition fool you, Doc. I'm down. Believe me. I've worked my entire life to get my own Nitro Funny Car. It's been the driving force behind everything I've done for the last decade. I've given it everything I have, and you know what? I got it. I said I was going to do it, and I did it. I built my own Nitro Funny Car.

"The best moment of my life was when all the work came together at the same time and same place, and we launched her for the first time. It was like magic! The g-forces pinned me up against the seat and stretched my cheeks up against the helmet, but no g-forces could pull the smile from my face!

"I had it all right there. I had it for a grand total of two weeks. And now? Well, here I am. My entire life's work went up in smoke in half a second, and it took me with it. So, yeah, I'm down. It's just, I need it back. It's like air. I don't know what I'd do without racing. It's a part of me, it's who I am.

"So that's my plan, to get it all back. I can see what needs to get done and I can't help but do it. Complaining and whining about it is pointless; it doesn't help. It's not going to get my car back. I know what it's going to take, and it ain't complaining."

"As I live! That IS you. Through and through a hundred percent you," the doctor said, and with that, he stood, turned, and left the room in amazement.

Neal and the boys drifted back into the room a few minutes later. Robert was getting stronger, but even so, almost any movement left him winded, tired, and gasping for air.

"I've gotta get outta here," Robert said in frustration. "I'm going stir crazy, being cooped up in here all the time. I'm busting loose. Who's with me?" he asked, looking at the boys with a labored smile. Mark and Bryan both piped up in unison, "Me!"

"Good, because I need your help getting out of this bed. Mark, you grab the chair. Bryan, you help me up," he said, reaching with his good hand. Bryan grabbed hold and pulled with all his might as Robert strained to his feet, turned slowly, and plopped into the wheelchair.

"Who's going to drive the bat-chair?" Robert asked with a smile. "Me," they yelled in unison. Mark quickly backed up the chair. Just as they reached the foot of the bed, Robert let out a blood-curdling scream, "AARRRGGGGGGHHHH! Stop! Stop! Stop! Please! Stop!"

Everyone froze but Lisa. "What is it? What's wrong?" she yelled as she sprang into action.

"Catheter! Catheter! Catheter! The catheter, it's still in. The bags on the bed!" He yelled in pain. Still frozen, everyone looked. Sure enough, there it was, a tightly strung tube stretching from Robert's nether region to a half-full bag hooked to the side of the bed. Quickly Mark pushed the chair forward, relieving the pressure as every male in the room winced and clinched in an empathetic cringe.

"Oh! That hurts!" Robert moaned as he searched for breath and a comfortable position in the chair. "Ohhh, aaahhhh. Yeah, ouch." Everyone in the room remained uneasily silent, legs clenched tight, waiting for his reaction. After catching his breath, he paused and scanned the empathetic eyes for what seemed like forever. Finally, he burst into laughter, giving everyone else permission to do the same.

"Okay. I'm still breaking out of here. Let's do this!" Robert announced as Lisa attached the catheter bag to the wheelchair.

"Quick, to the bat chair," Bryan exclaimed.

"You know, he looks nothing like Batman. He's more like Superman or Spiderman," said Mark.

"Yeah, well, maybe. But neither of them have cars," replied Bryan.

"The doc had it right. He's Super Spider Man," said Mark.

"Yeah, and Super Spider Man has a bat chair," replied Bryan.

"Where's my cape? I can't be a real superhero busting out if I don't have a cape," Robert said. So, Lisa tied on the matching cape and draped it down the back of the wheelchair. "Let's do this!" With that command, the boys wheeled him out the door, leaving Neal and Lisa behind.

"Mark, I need you to do exactly as I say. Run on up ahead and push the down button on the elevator," Robert said.

"What? But we're not supposed to leave the floor," Bryan replied.

"Yeah, it's like I said, we're busting out of here!" said Robert.

"For real?" both boys questioned.

"Yeah, for real! Now go on, we'll be right behind you," Robert encouraged.

Mark scurried on ahead. Bryan and Robert moseyed down the hall, arriving just as the elevator bell rang. Everything went according to plan.

They were off. They stopped at every floor and explored every corridor that wasn't locked. They walked hallways that stretched for miles. They ventured farther and farther from the room and the torture table. Eventually, they found the cafeteria. That's where Robert sweet-talked the attendant into giving him the ice-cream treats on an IOU. It may have been the raspy Australian accent that eventually closed the ice-cream deal. But then again, it may have been the bandages, or the superhero suit, or the innocent smiles the boys flashed on command. It's hard to say; it was probably a combination of those factors that made the little crew irresistible.

They ate their ice creams on the front sidewalk, laughing, talking, and joking as the late afternoon sun faded to evening. "You can see everything from here," Bryan said, gazing across the open valley.

"There's the Great Salt Lake," said Mark.

"I wonder if you can see the track and our house?" asked Bryan.

It was about then that Robert noticed the shaking in his good hand. An unexplainable wave of anxiety swept over his body, leaving him tight, tense, and agitated. "I think it's time to get heading back. It's about time for the evening cleaning."

"But the sunset, it's just getting good," replied Bryan.

"Now!" Robert barked in an uncharacteristic demand.

The boys jumped in surprise at the sharpness of his command. They'd never seen him like that. Immediately, they set course for the burn unit. No matter how far, fast, or slow they went, a haze of anxiety hovered overhead. It was like it was physically attached to the chair. It followed them down every hall, it turned as they turned, it stopped when they stopped. It followed them into the room where Robert sat alone, surrounded by people, shaking in his chair and waiting for the next change.

He figured the anxiety might be related to the upcoming change, and it was. But not how he expected. "Here you go," Katja said, opening the morphine drip. The promise of relief calmed the shakes as the clear liquid made its way down the tube, into his arm, through his heart and eventually to his brain.

RECOVERY CONTINUED

The familiar haze of anxiety hovered above his bed the next morning. Like before, it dissipated with the magic drip. It was in that little window of clarity between the haze of anxiety and the fog of morphine when it hit him. "Oh no," he said, floating down the hall to the torture chamber.

"Oh, no what?" Katja questioned.

"Oh, nothing. It's just, um, how long do people usually need morphine for these changes?" he questioned. She may have answered, but maybe not. By then, he was lost in the fog of morphine and he didn't know or care.

Much of physical therapy in the burn unit is spent educating the patients on the proper care of burns and scar tissue. One day, they'd talk in depth about how skin shrinks, stretches, and stiffens as it heals, then they'd learn how to combat those effects with lotions, massage, and stretching techniques. Another day, they'd talk about nutrition and how the body's working extra hard to repair itself. "Diets and burn recovery don't mix. You need the calories! Calories heal," they said. No matter the topic they always ended with a walk or some type of physical exercise. No matter the exercise, Robert always ended it with a light head and shortness of breath, and sometimes he even fainted.

"This is new," Robert said as Carly, the physical therapist, attached sensors to his arm and chest.

"Yeah, the doctor would like see some biofeedback. He's hoping this will tell us what's going on," she replied.

"I'll tell you what's going on. I get lightheaded when I walk," Robert said with a smile.

"Ha, right. I think we got that part. We're hoping this will tell us why," she added with the same smile.

"Okay, let's see how we do," Robert said as the treadmill belt slowly began to turn. The heavy breathing came quickly. He knew the workout was being recorded, and he was not going to show any sign of weakness. "Keep it up, keep going, march on. You got this," he kept telling himself over and over.

He woke a few moments later, draped across his wheelchair. "That came on quick. It was all I could do to guide your fall back to your chair, but I did it," she said with a proud smile.

"Yeah, well. That was something. You sure that's the best way to find out why I'm fainting?" Robert replied, straightening himself in the chair.

"What?" asked Carly.

"Is there a better way to figure out why I'm fainting than by watching me faint? There's got to be a better way."

"That is a great question . . . for the doctor. I just perform the tests," she replied.

The room was calm and still when Robert quietly woke from his afternoon nap. He didn't say a word. He just looked up into Lisa's blue eyes as she read her latest novel. It was almost as if he was looking into forever, and he lost himself in the softness of her skin, the warmth of her heart, and the gentle beauty of her soul. He marveled at the hardness of her will and the fierceness of her loyalty. He felt he could tell her anything, so he gathered his courage and broke the silence.

"Lisa, I gotta get outta here."

"Oh, hey there. The boys are at school. They'll be up later," she said with a smile, lowering her book.

"No, I mean it. I gotta get out of here, for good. I . . . I . . . I'm scared," he sheepishly confessed.

"Scared? What do you mean?" she gently probed.

"I'm afraid. I'm not used to being afraid and I don't like it," he replied.

"What are you afraid of? Whatever it is, it's okay. I'm here. You're not alone," she assured him.

"It's the morphine. It turns out, I like it. I like it a lot. But I don't need that in my life. I'm not taking it anymore," he insisted.

"Is that what you were talking about during last night's changing?" she asked.

"Yeah, that's when I got scared. That's when I realized, well, you know," came his reply.

"Well, you need it for the pain, especially for the changes," she said reassuringly.

"Yeah, but it's not so much that I like it. It's that I can't not have it," he said with an urgency in his voice that was foreign to Lisa.

"What?" she asked.

"It's like my life starts falling apart when it wears off. I get anxious and unfocused. Everything and everyone just pisses me off, and the only thing that sets it right is the morphine before the changes. It's not so much that I want it, it's that I don't want to not have it. I think it's only gonna get worse if I don't stop soon," he confessed.

"So . . . So, n-now, how're you feeling now?" she stuttered.

"Miserable, and it's only going to get worse, I can feel it coming on. And I've seen the whole drug thing before. I've seen people living for the next hit or drink and doing whatever it takes to get it. I'm not that. I can't be that! It's not me. Is it? Am I that?" he pleaded, gazing into her eyes.

"No. No, you're not that," she assured him, taking his hand.

He felt the strength of her spirit and the warmth of her soul with the touch of her hand. It galvanized his will and he replied, "I can't be that. It scares me, thinking there's a chance I could be that."

"So, now you have another battle to fight in this war," she replied.

"I gotta get out of here," he repeated.

Just then, Katja walked in. "Time for changing," she said, placing two cups on the bedside tray, one with water, the other with meds. He looked at them, then up at the little bag on the IV stand and fidgeted.

"Maybe I'll start stopping tomorrow," he muttered. Just then, his eyes caught Lisa's and his heart caught hope. He repeated, "I gotta get out of here." Lisa silently slid the clamp on the morphine drip cutting him off at the source.

"Excuse me, Katja, what happens if I don't take the morphine?" Robert quietly asked, glancing at the clear bag.

"Oh, not much. Just pain," came her reply as she followed his eyes to the bag.

"Then what's the morphine for again?" Lisa asked.

"The morphine makes it so you don't care about the pain, so you can't remember the changes," she replied.

"Well, that makes no sense. No sense at all," Robert said, wondering how something could make no sense, yet so much sense at the same time. Hope faded.

"We can load you up with more Tylenol if you'd like," Katja offered.

"Yeah, sure," came Robert's reply, sending her back down the hall for a moment.

Robert looked back at the bag as hope continued to fade. Lisa took his hand again and repeated, "That's not the Robert I know. You got this. Let's try this one time without the morphine and see how it goes."

"Yeah," he agreed, relying entirely on her hope.

So began another trip to hell as Katja wheeled him to the torture chamber.

Over the next several days Robert battled the excruciating pain of young skin growing over bare flesh. He endured the unexplainable weakness of low oxygen which kept him fainting in therapy. He survived coughing fits where he hacked up chunks of raw flesh from deep down inside his lungs. All while experiencing full blown morphine withdrawals, complete with uncontrolled sweats, tremors, and shakes. He forged ahead, driven by his will for home, and sustained by Lisa's constant loving presence by his side.

Yet even in the darkest hours of the fierce personal battles, something deep down inside took over whenever anyone entered the room. It was a brave and happy face beaming with light and energy. It masked the pain and suffering well. He couldn't explain it; he himself wondered what it was. He eventually settled on the theory that he was feeding off the positive energy of others, who, in turn, fed off his.

He even put it to the test. From time to time he'd greet a visitor with a melancholy grunt, and he received the same in reply, which was draining. The next visitor he'd greet with his good energy. He'd receive the same greeting in reply, filling his heart with hope. *You always seem to get what you give, and it's funny how it can come back so quickly,* he thought.

Dr. Steffes told him he could go home when he made it through therapy without fainting, so that quickly became his only goal. "Keep it together, breathe deep, and focus. There are no limits!" he rehearsed before each session. But every day Carly would find those limits, and it didn't take much. Usually a simple walk around the room or picking up a ball would send him spinning off in a dizzy haze. Sometimes he'd catch himself before he went out, other times he'd wake up draped across his chair. Every time his vitals were low, and every time his spirits were high.

His spirits were high because that is where he kept them. His entire life he'd held on to an unshakable optimism. His optimism was built on the tried and tested knowledge that good things come to those who are brave enough to dream and find joy in the work required to make those dreams a reality. This explained why he always seemed busy. His joy and work were contagious.

One day, on the way back from therapy, Katja asked, "Robert, you remember the boys I told you about, the ones who were playing with matches? They are having a rough time of it right now. The next time you feel like busting out of here, would you mind swinging by their room and checking in? I think they could use a bit of, well, you."

"Yeah, sure!" he responded out of reflex.

"Great! They're right down there. Just drop by sometime when you have time," she replied.

Robert thought he was ready for the boys, but quickly reconsidered as he rolled into their room. Neither spoke. They just lay there, covered in standard gauze bandages with mesh wrappings, hiding under the dark clouds of physical pain, self-pity, depression, and morphine.

"Hello, my name's Robert," he said with his signature race face, but neither responded Robert suddenly realized that he had no clue what to say or do. He'd built a life on following his passion and it had all become habit. It was just what he did, and for some unexplainable reason, people followed. He never truly understood why people followed him. He just knew if he talked from the heart and lived up to the talk, the people followed, and things got done. So, he reverted to what had worked before. He started talking from the heart about what he was doing at the time of his accident.

"I'm a race car driver from South Australia," he said. He went on to tell them stories of racing, how he built his very own Nitro Funny Car, and how he crashed it. He talked about the fire and how bad the burns hurt. He talked about what he was doing next and how he was already ordering parts for the new car. He told them how excited he was to get home so he could build a new car, and how he couldn't wait to race again.

That's when one of the boys spoke. "You're going to race again? Even though that's what got you here?"

Robert paused; the question threw him off balance. He'd never thought of it like that. That question opened the door of vulnerability. When he collected his thoughts, they had a real conversation. For the next hour the boys talked, and Robert listened. They talked about their accident, and their burns. They talked about sadness, fear, regret, disappointment of family, and the pain woven through it all.

Robert and the boys questioned the very nature of accidents by asking, "are they accidents if you were purposefully doing the thing that caused it in the first place? Is it an accident to race a car or burn a match?" They talked about control, when we have it, when we don't, and ultimately how we are left to deal with the consequences regardless. They talked about happiness and hard work, discipline and will, love of family, and the joy woven through it all. They talked, and together they healed.

THE GREATEST ESCAPE

"Robert, how much have you been drinking?" Katja asked.

"Not a drop since I've been here. Why? You have a Coors on hand?" he replied with a smile.

"No. God, no! I mean, how much water have you been drinking?"

"Oh, yeah, enough, I guess. I'm not thirsty if that's what you're asking," he replied.

"No, that's not what I'm asking. I have a hunch," she said, filling his plastic mug with fresh ice water. "Drink," she ordered.

"No, I'm not thirsty," came his reply.

"I didn't ask if you were thirsty, I said drink," she demanded. He complied with a sip. "I need you to drink twice as much water as you want. Drink and then drink some more." He complied with many sips.

Two days later, Lisa slowed the Crown Victoria to a stop at the main hospital doors where Robert and his entourage waited in anticipation of their final and greatest escape. "Dehydration. I can't believe it. It's been my life's mission to get out of here, and all this time it was a glass of water holding me back."

"Well, there were so many things going on with the changings, grafting, and such. It's just one of those things, I guess," Katja said, wheeling him up to the Crown Vic.

"You look absolutely terrifying! Like something out of a horror film," Lisa said, opening the car door. Robert was wrapped and compressed in red and blue from head to foot, with the centerpiece being the large plastic facemask built to distribute the compression evenly across his face.

"Yeah, well. I try," Robert rasped through the tiny square mouth opening. But secretly he thought the very same thing. Though he was looking forward to being home, he was not looking forward to the ride home. Lisa drove too fast and stopped too late, and he wasn't sure his extremely sore and tender parts could take it. He hoped for the best, but braced himself for the worse.

Katja met Lisa at the trunk, "Here, I've packed everything you'll need. There're all the scrubs, gloves, towels, ointments, creams, bandages, and wraps you'll need. Just do the same as we've been doing, and you'll be fine," she said, heaving the forest green trash bag into the open trunk.

"Thanks, that's quite the load there," replied Lisa.

"And if you run out, just let me know, I'll get you what you need," Katja added.

A few moments later the escape was complete as they wove their way down through the university away from the hospital. Bryan hollered from the back, "You look like Freddie Kruger's brother. At the next light, you've got to turn slowly and wave. Please?" The boys in back laughed in approval and pleaded for a wave. So, at the next light, Robert slowly turned his tender body to the right and waved. The poor driver next to him jumped in fright and quickly looked away. But his eyes were drawn back to the horror as he awkwardly refused to acknowledge the terrifying figure waving his way. Finally, out of desperation, on went the blinker, and the car next to them quickly turned to safety, leaving the boys laughing uncontrollably and cheering for more in the back seat.

"Lisa, what do you think about stopping by the track on the way home," Robert asked timidly. She cringed, but said nothing.

Assuming she hadn't heard him from deep within his cocoon of bandages and compression mask, he laboriously turned to her and asked again. Refusing to cringe under his gaze she gently replied, "Yeah, sure. We can do that. What do you think, guys?" she asked, eying the boys in the rearview mirror. "Sure," came the collectively doubtful reply. The conversation, laughing, and cheering was over.

They entered the Rocky Mountain Raceway and wove their way to the track in silence. No one dared say a word as they crossed the start line. Slowly they rolled past the buckled retaining wall marking the point of impact on that fateful day. They drove the entire length of the track, then continued out into the overflow, slowly rolling to rest at the burned patch at the edge of the sand trap.

Quietly spilling from the car, they instinctively gathered on the rough black scar. They huddled in silence. No one dared say a word, or stray from the confines of the rough black edges. Out of curiosity, Mark kicked and scraped the burned and buckled scar with his sneakers; it didn't move.

Robert finally broke the silence. "Well, this is it. This the place where my lifelong dream went up in smoke."

"Yeah, this is the place," they all repeated from the confines of the scar.

"Oh, that was a bad day," said Lisa.

"Terrible! The worst day of my life! I was so scared," came the rumblings of the little crowd.

"I thought I lost you," Lisa said with welling tears. The tears spread quickly and before long, there wasn't a dry eye on the scar. Together they mourned under the hot summer sun.

Robert broke through the tears with a sound in his voice no one had heard before. It was the sound of defeat. "I know I've been talking it up in the hospital. Talking about ordering new parts and all. But really. Starting all over again? It's a lot to ask, and I've asked too much already. Honestly, I can't ask for more."

"Robert, what are you saying?" asked Lisa.

Mark piped up, "Are you saying no more racing? No more race cars?"

"I don't know. I think so. I really think this is it," said Robert.

"Oh, come on," Lisa replied. "The dream's not over. It's not over until you quit, and you are not quitting."

"But it's a huge commitment. It's so much to ask," replied Robert.

"You're not asking. We're telling you. The dream does not die here. This may be the place it happened, but it's not the place where the dream dies. This, this is just a resting place. This isn't where it ends. We can't let it end this way! Besides, God's not finished with you. You are here. You are alive for a reason," Lisa cried with the boys circling in support.

Robert's raspy voice cracked, then broke out of joy and gratitude for being surrounded by real love. "Well then, are we all in agreement? Are we all in?"

"Yes!" came the unanimous roar from the little crowd.

"All right! We're all in! Let's rebuild this thing," Robert agreed from the confines of the black scar on the far end of the raceway, beside the green mountain, under the blue summer sky. A pure sense of unity and joy of family held them firmly in place. The feelings of unity continued all the way home, and Lisa's driving was exceptional. She took extra care to make it a pleasant ride for Robert. Not once did she drive too fast or stop too late. Even corners were taken with care.

The first week at home had the same rhythm and feel as the hospital. The kitchen was transformed into a torture chamber, doubled as a rehab center, and tripled as a place to prepare meals, while the couch became the sanctuary of recovery. It was all Robert could do to gingerly wobble the ten steps between the two.

That first week, Lisa did it all, every changing, every rehab, and every meal. But she was carrying much more. She was also raising the boys, cleaning the house, paying the bills, and going to work, and she wasn't sure how long she could keep it all up. It's one thing to be needed when you can give what's required, but quite another if you can't, and Lisa knew she couldn't. So, she devised a plan to get Robert the care he needed, the boys the love they deserved, and her back to work. It was quite brilliant, and quite simple: She enlisted the help of the crew.

By week two, the racing crew were trained in the fine arts of cleaning burned flesh, cream and ointment application, and bandage wrapping. Mathew, Andy, and Brandon all took shifts. Mathew said one day with a smile, "Nowhere in the job description of "Nitro Funny Car Crew Chief" does it talk about cleaning raw flesh and applying bandages." They all smiled and agreed, no one ever thought they would be doing what they were doing when they signed up as mechanics.

Robert was determined to heal both inside and out, but he was surprised by how weak he was. Any movement hurt, and any exertion left him exhausted. Still, he pushed himself in rehab every day. He started by gingerly limping once around the kitchen island. As time went on he added another lap, and then another. Sometimes he'd make it all the way around, sometimes he'd rest on a stool. Sometimes he'd get snarled in a coughing fit and hack up chunks of burned up tissue scabs, other times not. Every time there was someone there to encourage him along, until one day there wasn't.

By the end of week three, the wounds were covered with a fresh young coat of skin. Enough to reduce the worry of infection, yet not enough to protect the exposed nerve endings from the pain of a touch. The bandages went from protecting against infection to protecting from direct contact. Except for his forehead—regular cleanings continued there. Then, Lisa and the crew agreed that Robert was strong enough to be alone between changings. So, they divided up the duties and went their ways.

Mathew finished the morning change, but then, with no nurse

as an incentive to stay, he left for work. *Together feels so much better when you're together,* Robert thought from the sanctuary of recovery. For the first time since the accident, Robert was completely alone. There was no one to put on the race face for, and it didn't take long for his mind to wander.

The car. I've gotta see the car, he thought. *No, it's too soon,* he answered. *Neal, where is Neal?* He tried changing the topic of his thoughts, but no matter what he tried, the thought kept coming back. *I've gotta see the car.* Each time he answered, *No, it's too soon!* He tried distraction after distraction. Lisa's latest novel got really mushy really quick. A slow and delicate walk around the empty house left him exhausted on the couch. On went the TV, but he'd never been exposed to daytime television before. *What is this? How can people watch such stupidity?* he thought in disgust, clicking from soap opera to talk show. No, TV never worked.

He'd always kept himself surrounded by others and so busy building things that he'd never really experienced alone before. But there it was, barely noon, and the loneliness had gotten the best of him. "I've gotta see the car," he said one last time.

Giving way to temptation and taking the keys from the hook at the back door, he slowly stepped out into the warm May sun. Covered in bandages and compression garments, he gingerly limped across the yard. For a moment he thought he caught a whiff of something ominous riding on the breeze.

Arriving at the trailer out of breath, but full of determination, he slowly opened the side door. The smell of burned carbon fiber hit him hard in the middle of the face, almost knocking him over. *So that's the smell of a burned-up race car,* he thought as every car he'd ever owned flashed through his mind's eye.

Gathering his courage, strength, and breath, he heaved himself up into the trailer. Completely winded and blinded by the darkness, he staggered inside and with one last concerted effort he plopped himself down on the first low and solid object he encountered. Heaving, wheezing, and working hard to catch his breath, he waited for his eyes to adjust to the dim light.

Slowly, like an instant Kodak picture, the tattered state of the trailer appeared before him. He was the first to enter since the accident; nothing had been touched since that day. He'd always prided himself on running a professional shop, but cleaning and neatly stowing their equipment was the last thing on the crew's minds after that last run. *I guess we can let it slide this one time,* he thought, scanning the messy trailer.

It was then he realized he was sitting on what remained of the front wheel of his pride and joy. Carefully he stood, turning to see the car for the first time. He could barely believe his eyes. The frame was rusting and warped. Everything plastic and rubber was gone. Even the aluminum housings had melted away. "What? That's 1800 degrees!" he said in disbelief.

He'd had his race face on since the accident. It had fooled everyone but himself. He knew how strong he was, and how strong he wasn't. He'd held it together through the pain of, well, everything— the burns, the bandages, the grafting, the morphine withdrawals, and the dehydration. At times just being awake was painful; other times it was sleep that eluded him.

He continued talking to himself, both inside his head and out. "It's like I've been strong for everyone else but me. It's such a lonely place, being surrounded by everyone and having to be the strong one. Especially when you're not the strong one. All I wanted was to be alone! And now! Well, here I am, completely alone, and there's no one to be strong for. Being alone can be so lonely," he continued, looking at the lifeless remains of his dream. Tears trickled, then flowed freely, as he lost all composure.

"AAARRRRRRRRGGGGGGGGGG!" he roared at the top of his broken lungs for the world to hear. Then he directed the anger at the car. Furiously, he began kicking the burned pile of parts with his good foot. "You piece of shit! Why did this happen? Why me? I worked so hard for so long! We had a deal, you and me! We agreed! I wouldn't hurt you, and you wouldn't hurt me! So, there you go, take that! And that! And that! We had a deal!" Over and over, he yelled about the deal. Over and over, he kicked, until once again he plopped himself down on what was left of the front wheel, heaving and wheezing, working hard to catch his breath.

That evening, Lisa found her bundle of wraps and bandages calmly perched in the sanctuary of recovery, the same place she'd left him that morning. "How was your first day alone?" she asked.

Quickly, without thinking, he put on his race face and replied, "Yeah, it was fine, not much to say here. Not much happened." She sensed something was up, but gave him some space and silence. Inside he thought, *being alone is so much better when you're with someone.*

Later that evening, Robert broke the silence, "Lisa, if we're going to rebuild the car, we should probably start soon. Don't ya think?"

"Really? Are you kidding me? Have you looked at yourself lately? You're literally covered in bandages from head to foot. You can barely move," she replied.

"Yeah, but I'm getting stronger by the day, and it won't be too long before my skin's thick enough and I'll be mobile," came his reply.

"Okay, but have you looked at your face? Robert, the skin graft didn't take! Your forehead is an open, gaping wound. And you're worried about the car?" she asked.

"Yeah, but I don't use my forehead to build," he said

"Robert, your eyelids are gone! You're using a wet sponge to keep your eyes from drying out," she said.

"I know, but just sitting here's the hardest part. I've gotta do something! I need to stay busy," came his reply.

"I get it, it's hard. This is the only time you're going to have to recover. In fact, you're going to need this time and more. Surgery is scheduled for next week," she said.

"Yeah, can they really do that? Can they really make eyelids out of ears?" Robert inquired.

"I'm not the doctor, but they say it's how it's done. Eyelids out of ears and plastic tear ducts. At least give it until you're on the backside of that before you go out there and start pulling things apart," she begged.

"Yeah. Okay. I promise," Robert said, keeping the day's adventures to himself.

And so went June.

WHAT HAPPENED

Somewhere in the middle of July, Mathew and Brandon stopped by for a visit. After their usual greetings, Mathew made things awkward by asking, "so, how are the new eyelids working for you?"

Unfazed, Robert volleyed back, "You'd be amazed! Working well enough to see you're packing something there."

Brandon made it even more awkward by addressing the un-addressable. With no warning, he began talking about what everyone had been avoiding for three months. "So, we have pictures and video of the whole thing. You up to looking at it?" he asked, inserting the tape before Robert could answer. "We've been studying it, trying to figure out what happened, and I think I may have something," Mathew said as Brandon pushed play on the VCR.

With the push of a button the entire event played out before Robert's eyes. He'd been replaying his own version in his head for months. Over and over, again and again, he'd strained to figure out what had happened, what had gone wrong, and what he could have done differently. But his version was short, blurry, and full of holes.

He watched the burnout, the launch, the roar of the engine, the flames, the wall, the fire. It seemed so different from this new angle. In his head, he was always in the driver seat. On video, he was removed. It was almost like an out-of-body experience, as if he was watching his own life from afar, with no control.

Mathew sat quietly as Brandon replayed the scene once, then twice, and then a third time. They sat in silence, giving Robert time to process. Breaking the silence at the end of the third viewing, Robert gave permission for the discussion to commence, "I really dumped on that parade, didn't I."

"No. No, I don't think you did. I don't think it was you at all. Take a look at this," came Brandon's reply.

"The burnout, it was flawless, it was a thing of beauty. Straight, clean, and layers of rubber," said Mathew.

"Yeah, it sounded good. It really did. The tires smoked well, and it felt good," replied Robert.

"You remember that?" Brandon questioned.

"Yeah, I remember everything right up until launch. I remember the roar of the engine, the flames, and the g-forces locking me down tight against the cage. And then, well, that's it. I got nothing after that."

"Yeah, well. That makes sense. Look here. The first forty feet off the line are perfect. Zero to eighty miles per hour in seven tenths of a second. The front tires lifted slightly off the ground. Everything was textbook, just as it should be. Then, right there, the entire car rotates about twenty degrees to the left. You'd think, twenty degrees, not a big deal, but when you're continuing to accelerate from eighty to one hundred sixty in the next seven tenths, it's a real big deal!" Brandon said.

"Any slip at speeds like that is a big deal," Mathew confirmed.

"What caused the slip?" asked Robert.

"No way of telling now. My guess is an oil leak from the diaper, or a fuel leak at launch. Somehow something got on the track between the burnout and launch. That's the only explanation. It's the only thing that could have changed," answered Mathew.

"Yeah," Robert and Brandon replied in unison.

"In any other car, at any other time, that type of spin wouldn't mean nothing. But with an open throttle on a Nitro Funny Car, that's ten thousand horsepower on a solid axle, meaning full power on both wheels. If one wheel slips, the other doesn't, and well, that's a big thing. And look at this. You reacted. See how the front wheels are turned to correct the spin?"

"Look at that, I did. I reacted. I was driving and turned to keep her on track. But with the front tires lifted at launch, I'm really just riding on the back two," said Robert.

"Right, no turning back with no traction on the front tires. You were on your game. You did what you could. You did the right thing. But, well," Brandon paused.

"Yeah. But, well. Here we are," replied Mathew.

"Yeah, here we are," they all repeated in unison.

Brandon turned to the TV again. "I figure you hit the concrete retaining wall at the seventy-foot mark, going right about one hundred miles an hour. Look at that impact. See how the wall buckles but doesn't give. I think it's because of the shallow angle of impact. Any sharper and you may have gone straight through."

"And look how you just kept going down the entire length of the track," Mathew chimed in. "See, the tires are still burning rubber. The throttle is wide open the entire way, and you're gaining speed the entire track."

"I don't remember a thing. The impact must have knocked me clean out," said Robert. "Otherwise, I'd have hit the kill switch and fire suppression."

"Yeah, that's what I'm thinking," replied Mathew.

"But if I was out, I would have been limp. My foot would have come off the pedal. I was clearly gaining speed there; that engine was definitely running at full throttle," said Robert.

"Yeah, I've been thinking about that too, and I think I have it," Mathew continued. "Hitting the wall knocked you unconscious, for sure. At the same time, it dislodged the body and shoved the hood section right up into the blower, locking the throttle in open position. Only the kill switch could have stopped you then, but you were out cold."

"Thank goodness you were," said Brandon, "because that's just the beginning. The impact curled the left headers back, directing all the exhaust and flames back into the car, bathing you in fire the entire length of the track."

Mathew interrupted, "Now, you would've thought the fire panels would've protected you, and you'd be right. But those flames burned right through the firewall."

"That's right! It did. I seen it! The aluminum panels completely melted away!" exclaimed Robert.

"Those flames were not just burning you; they were burning the car. Everything inside was burning. Everything plastic is gone. All the hoses, cable casings, ties, and even the aluminum panels were all melted away. That's one hot flame to melt that firewall," Mathew replied.

Brandon continued, "Your fire suit protected you from actually catching fire, but that suit is only so thick, and there's not much insulation. That explains the back of your left leg being half burned off like it is."

They paused and sighed in unison.

Brandon added, "And check this out. You were hugging the wall the entire way. Because there's no traction on that part of the track, the tires continue to spin all the way. You were burning rubber the entire length, man. Look at that. You crossed the finish line unconscious, engulfed in flames, and going 150 miles an hour. Who knows how fast you would've been if that edge was prepped with traction?"

"I don't think that's ever been done before, at least not that I've heard of," Robert said in awe.

"Wait, what?" Mathew asked.

"An unconscious guy, burning in flames, crossing the finish line at 150 miles an hour, with the throttle wide open and the engine blowing itself to pieces. I haven't heard of that before. Usually, they're doing something to kill the flames and stop the car, like killing the engine, hitting the brakes, releasing the chute, or flipping the fire suppression switch. Something!" Robert said.

"Yeah," they agreed.

"Where and how did I stop?" asked Robert.

Mat replied, "The trap at the end finally got you. The safety crew, they were on their way before you'd hit the end of the track. Midgley said he called for the helicopter from the ambulance as he was chasing you down the track."

"You're kidding!" Robert exclaimed.

"No joke," Mathew said. "He said it looked so bad from where he was that he went ahead and called before he even got to you. The fire burned all the zip ties, which explains why all the cables and lines had come loose. It was Roy who dove into the flames first, but somehow your feet had gotten all snared in the tangled mess of cables. He tugged and pulled for a spell, but couldn't get you out. He didn't give up. He passed out trying. Luckily, he fell back out away from the car and Midgley guided him down. Midgley went back in, tugged and pulled to no avail. You, you just sat there in the flames while the fire truck sprayed water over you and the diver. Then he turned and walked out of the flames and began yelling and waving his arms. But we couldn't tell what he was saying because he was dressed in a full fire suit. Finally, we got it, he was motioning for cutters. Just then, out of nowhere, Suzy Wells showed up with her own cutters."

Brandon piped up. "She ran from the other end of the shutdown area. For some reason, she knew, maybe out of instinct or something. I think she must have started running about the time you stopped."

Mathew took back over, "However she did it, the important thing is, she handed the cutters to Midgley just after Roy went down. Midgley then jumped into the flames and was able to cut the cables and pull you out. Who knows what would've happened if she hadn't shown up when she did? In a way, she saved your life."

"She saved me, too," Lisa said. "She was there when I got there. I was freaking out! I couldn't understand why you were still in there. You were just sitting in flames. Suzy stopped me from jumping in. I would have. I was going to jump in and pull you out myself."

Everyone paused out of respect as Lisa's voice cracked with that last assertion. "I believe you would have," added Robert. Everyone agreed.

Brandon eventually continued, "when Midgley eventually did get you out, he dragged you clear of the flames and went right to work cutting off your fire suit. I guess to cool you down and assess the burns."

"After watching the car burn like that," Lisa said in a shaky voice, "I didn't think there was any way you'd make it out alive. I knew you'd be all burned up. But when you were laid out on the track and they were cutting off your suit, I saw a flash of pink flesh on your belly. It was kind of a relief and I thought, thank God he's not all burned! I couldn't help it, but that's what I thought."

Robert took her hand and replied, "The only thing I remember was feeling like I was suffocating. I couldn't breathe. I thought it was the helmet. I was yelling for someone to take it off, but no one would."

"Yeah, they're trained not to take helmets off in case of spinal injury," said Lisa.

"Yeah, I get that, but I was suffocating. I couldn't breathe. I got the helmet off, but it didn't help," replied Robert.

"And I think you left part of your cheeks and forehead in the helmet. Some of that skin just sloughed right off," said Lisa.

Then Mathew said, "What I don't understand is how the fresh air was activated. All the other safety systems were idle, which makes sense with you being unconscious and all. But why was that one on? How?"

Robert thought for a moment before answering. "That! Yeah, I can't explain that. I was sitting there in the cockpit, and I don't know. For some reason, I looked over and saw the switch and without thinking, I just flipped the switch. I don't know why. I hadn't done it before and had no reason for doing it then. But for some reason, that time, I did."

Silence lingered until Mathew said, "Well, that flip is just one of many things that saved your life. The fresh air helmet's the reason you're still here. You were breathing fresh air as those flames shot up inside the cabin. At first, anyway. Eventually the fresh air system melted and burned. The flames eventually burned the helmet visor, which explains the burns on your face and forehead. It also explains your throat and lungs. You were breathing flames for who knows how long, burning your esophagus and lungs. You were swelling up pretty quick, the Life Flight crew intubated you shortly after takeoff."

"I remember being loaded into the helicopter, and Lisa holding my hand. She sqeezed it tight while telling me everything would be okay. The next thing I remember is waking up in the hospital," said Robert.

"Seems there were a lot of little things all coming together that saved your life," Lisa said. Everyone in the room agreed.

The conversation slowed. Brandon played the video another time or two as they thumbed through the pictures. Robert drifted off, lost in his own thoughts as he played the scene over and over in his mind, just as he'd done a thousand times a day since the accident. Only now, instead of the entire replay being from the driver seat and filled with holes and fog, it was somehow sharper and clearer. His vantage point changed from the driver's seat to the out-of-body views of the pictures and video. He saw things both in first and third person, at the same time.

He heard the roar of the engine and saw the flash of flames at launch. He saw the front tires rise and the car rotate. He felt the steering wheel as he cranked it to the right in a futile effort to stay on the track. He felt the impact leaving him unconscious. He watched the concrete wall buckle as it kept the car on the track and the spectators safe. He watched the hood slam into the blower, locking the throttle in the wide-open position. He watched the exhaust system curl, shooting burning nitromethane onto his unconscious body and setting the interior of the car aflame. He watched his own limp body continue the ride in a cloud of smoke and flames. He watched the safety crew risk their lives and work fearlessly to free him from the fiery tangled mess. He watched as Suzie came to the rescue with her cutters. He watched with just as much control as he had at the time of the accident. And he watched it over and over and over.

After what seemed like an eternity, he looked up from the TV and said, "It's time."

THE REBUILD

On Memorial Day weekend Robert and Lisa unloaded the burned-up car and set up a table near the entrance of the Rocky Mountain Raceway. There, in his superhero compression suit, complete with the pressure plate on his forehead, Robert signed autographs and talked with fans. He hesitated when first invited, but the boys at the track persisted. "Come on, it'll be great. Fans ask about you all the time. It'll give them a chance to meet you, see how you're mending, and how you're making a comeback." So, he did.

Robert and Lisa talked, laughed, and assured both friends and strangers alike they'd be back as the roar of engines and resounding cheers from the crowd echoed in the background. It was good to be home.

The accident affected each crew member differently, but they all dealt with it in only one of two ways. They either stayed or left. Some obsessed over finding out what went wrong, and were determined to fix it. Others thought it was all fun and games, until it wasn't. They couldn't distance themselves fast enough, or far enough. No one could blame them for leaving, and no one did.

This exodus left only two, Mathew and Brandon, so the rebuild got off to a slow start. There were nights were it was just the three of them out in the shed. Then Justin McCully, a buddy from Wheeler, showed up. He must have talked, because Stevey Shaw appeared shortly after. Then came Kim Brown, then Nick Davis, then finally Cody Walk. All from Wheeler. They knew Robert and his passion for racing. They'd heard about the accident and wanted to help in any way they could.

Robert never really understood what drove them to help, and he wasn't about to ask. He just accepted their help graciously. Sometimes he wondered if they came out of pity for his situation. Other times he thought it might be a bit more selfish, like for the prestige of doing something extra cool. Most times he felt they were just good-hearted people doing good-hearted things. Yeah, it had to be that, and he held it as truth.

One thing he knew for sure was that they were all highly-skilled, professional mechanics. They took the trade seriously. They knew the importance of getting things done right and they worked effortlessly and efficiently together. *It's all so natural,* he thought.

Then there was Ken, the neighbor from a few blocks over. Bryan first noticed him driving slowly past the house, again and again. He pointed him out to the rest of the family. No one was sure what to make of it. Should they be concerned by the creeper? Should they get the authorities involved?

But one day Ken poked his head inside the shed for a formal introduction. He explained how he'd heard about the accident on the news, then asked if there was anything he could do to help. He wasn't a mechanic, but he fit in with the crew and could clean parts with the best of them. Night after night, he'd show up to clean parts. No one ever did learn what his day job was, or if he had a last name. But he sure could salvage burned race car parts.

Then one day Jeremy Schwab called from Arizona with a request of his own. By then, he was an older teenager with its accompanying angst and moods. Robert and Jeremy had stayed close with constant calls and visits after the divorce. Why not? He'd raised Jeremy for several years and counted him as his own, so much so that Jeremy took his name. The request? Well, the next thing Lisa knew, she had another boy living in the house, and Robert had another crew member. Jeremy fit right in, quickly becoming part of the core team.

Then Bryan showed up with the Cypress football team. Well, not the entire team, but a pretty big chunk of them. They were young, eager, and willing to help. They brought with them a youthful zeal for life that almost matched Robert's. They fit right in. The boys in the shed even toned down the language, for a bit.

Before long, the crew had assembled. Their entire focus was salvaging as many bits and pieces as possible; Robert didn't want to buy anything he didn't have to. Each new part was purchased only after the old part was thoroughly inspected and its integrity was confirmed or rejected.

Many late-night shed conversations revolved around isolating what went wrong, and more importantly, what could be done so this never happened again. One evening Robert sparked the conversation, "When I get back into that car, it needs to be the safest car on the planet." Mathew was taken by the urgency in Robert's voice, he let the comment sit for the longest moment, as if he were marinading in it. Finally, Mathew broke the comfortable silence, "The trouble started when the car rotated after launch. There had to be something on the track to cause the slip,"

"It had to be either fuel or oil," replied Robert.

"Yeah, me too. It wasn't there after the burn out, but it was definitely there at 60 feet," said Mathew.

"The diaper must have leaked," said Robert.

"Right," Mathew responded. "That's the only explanation: the flimsy little bag leaked. So, what do we do? Make it bigger?"

"Yeah, that's an option. But I was thinking something even bigger. We know it's not a matter of if there's a leak, but when. Those flimsy bags don't catch it all, the way they swing and sway. I was thinking of something a little more sturdy. How about a complete aluminum belly pan? One we can quickly slide on and off. Something that's big enough to catch anything, liquid or solid, coming from anywhere, fuel or oil," said Robert.

"Yeah, that's brilliant," Mathew said. They got to work cutting, snipping, welding, and building the first solid drip-pan on a Nitro Funny Car.

Every few days the conversation turned to another topic of safety. One evening Mathew said, "Robert, we gotta talk about all the plastic and rubber strung everywhere."

"Yeah, I've been thinking on that too," came Robert's reply.

Mathew continued, "everything plastic and rubber burned, including the hoses and zip ties. I say nothing rubber or plastic goes in. I say we make steel fuel lines and secure the cables with metal fasteners. No flimsy zip ties."

"I like the idea of that," Robert replied, "but that's a lot of twisting and turning for a steel line."

"Yeah, well. We've never let "hard to do" stop us before," Mathew replied. So began the twisting, bending, and running of steel fuel lines.

One day Robert turned to Mathew, "It really bugs me that I drove the length of that track unconscious and on fire, and there was nothing anyone could do about it. In today's world we should have some kind of a remote kill switch that would shut down the engine and activate the fire suppression system. Something that could be activated by the crew in case of an emergency."

"Yeah, that's a great idea. We should bring that up to the officials," replied Mathew.

"I did, and do you know what they said?"

"No, what?"

"They said they would never give anyone outside of the car the ability to shut it down," Robert replied.

"That doesn't make any sense at all. And you told them about what happened to you?"

"Yeah, I told them. It makes no sense at all, that's why it bugs me so bad."

"Well, maybe someday," Mathew replied with a shrug.

Another day Mathew piped up with, "Robert, there's something else I've been thinking about. It's another big thing. You sat in that fire for a long time."

"The fire suit," Robert interrupted.

"Right," Mathew continued, "That Nomex. I guess technically it is a shield, but it doesn't breathe or insulate."

"Right, and after time it melts, shrinks and even burns. That's why my left leg was burned so badly. It shrunk and melted until there was nothing of it left and the flames were blowing right onto my leg," said Robert. "As for the rest of me, the heat went right through. Technically I wasn't burned, I was roasted."

"Well, that's not entirely true. Any sweat or other moisture was trapped inside the suit and heated up with the rest of you. So technically, it was more like you were steamed."

"There's gotta be something better," they said in unison. And so began the quest for a better fire suit. It was a nationwide quest, leading them right back to where they started: Salt Lake City. That's where they found Mike Chapman and his recent invention, a new synthetic material with several revolutionary properties. He called it CarbonX.

It was much more than just fire-resistant. It was an excellent insulator, it kept the heat out and cool in, even after long exposure to active flames. It was breathable, letting moisture out, which meant no more sweating or steaming. Plus, it was surprisingly soft and flexible, almost cozy. The company was new, and Mike was looking for innovative applications and inroads into various industries. Upon hearing Robert's story, he was more than happy to forge a partnership and donate material for the very first CarbonX fire suit.

The date, August 21, 1999, was etched into Robert's memory. He and Lisa walked the pits, chatted with the visiting fuel drivers, and basked in the sights, smells, and comradery of it all. They were so engaged with fans and racers that neither heard the dull thud. It was the collective gasp and hush of the crowd that gave the warning that something was wrong. "I hope everyone's okay," Lisa worried.

Lefty Thomas, another racer, arrived the same time as the helicopter. He broke the news, "There's been an accident. It's Suzie Wells, and it doesn't look good."

His words pushed Robert back as the rumble of the crowd faded to echoes. "Not Suzie! Please not Suzie!" he said. Lisa rushed to the track. She had to see for herself. Robert lost himself in thought as the crowd buzzed around. "She saved my life. She's the one who brought the cutters. If it wasn't for her, I wouldn't be here today. Please let her be okay."

Lisa arrived as the helicopter left. She had no words, just a sorrowful glance and a slow shake of her head. Together they cried.

The excited crew gathered in anticipation at the shop door the day the new body arrived; they could hardly wait for the grand unveiling. But the excitement faded quickly as Robert opened the garage door. Everyone was speechless, except Brandon. He said what everyone was thinking. "Where's the paint? It's so black. And dull. And black."

"Yeah, about that," Robert said. "The last car was the realization of a lifelong dream. I wanted the world to see and ogle over it, so I made it all about the show. Every nut and bolt was chromed and polished. Every surface was painted and glossed. Not this time. This time there'll be no sparkles for distractions.

"I'm putting just as much of my heart and soul into this car as the last, it's just in different places. This one's about three things. First, the car. We have a powerful engine, a solid chasse, and a fine tune.

Second is safety. She may not be much to look at, but I can tell you there is no safer dragster on any strip anywhere in the world. And finally, it's about the heart and soul of the car—you, the crew—not the polish and chrome. We'll worry about the show later." And they did. Before long, they had a new car. It was solid, sound, and safe. And dull black. Not a speck of paint, chrome, or polish could be found anywhere.

Lisa continued to warn the neighborhood whenever they started the car, and the spectators continued to gather. One night, the crew lingered long after the crowd had dissipated. Robert stepped up next to the car, cleared his raspy throat, and said, "well boys, tomorrow's a big day. We need two good runs. That's it. Two runs and you'll be the crew of an officially licensed Nitro Funny Car and driver. We are a team! You have each worked hard and I can't thank you enough. You know your jobs, you know what to do, now it's time to go and do it. This is what we've been working for."

SEPTEMBER 4, 1999.

It was the perfect day for racing. The sun was shining, not a cloud could be found. The late summer heat kept fall's nip at bay, though it was close—you could feel it in the air. It was Labor Day weekend, and the crew had been in the pits since sunup. They'd been watching the crowds flow through the open gates all morning. Streams of fans, trickles of drivers, an occasional paramedic, and a pair of fire divers strolled by to say hello and wish them luck. Most were on edge, but they hid it well. Except the track managers. They were all out of sorts and it showed. It had only been four months since Robert's fire, and three weeks since Suzy's incident.

It was just after noon, Robert's time to run.

"So, how are you feeling?" Mathew asked, hovering over the engine.

"Who, me? Yeah, I'm good," Robert replied, focused on the task at hand.

"Really? No jitters? No flashbacks, no nothing?" asked Mathew.

"No, I'm good. It's kind of strange. I wasn't sure how I'd be. But, for some reason, I'm fine."

"No kiddin'?" asked Mathew.

"I don't actually have many memories of anything bad from that day. Don't get me wrong, I never want to step in a hospital again. But here? Now? No, I'm good. I guess it was because I was completely unconscious through the entire thing," Robert replied.

"Huh, I guess I can buy that," replied Mathew.

"I do wish for one thing. I wish I was wearing that CarbonX suit right now."

"Yeah, it's too bad it wasn't certified in time," said Mathew.

"It's just a matter of time now. The wheels are in motion. Just a matter of time," replied Robert.

"All right!" Mathew continued, "Here we are! The car's ready, the crew's ready—on the edge but ready. And Lisa, well, she's dangling over the edge."

"I think I'm gonna puke," Lisa repeated as she paced in circles on the far side of the car.

"It seems everyone's on edge but you," Mathew continued.

"Hey Mathew, please tell them what I told you—that I'm all good. Maybe it'll help 'em take a step back away from the edge," Robert replied.

"Yeah, will do. Well, it seems everything and everyone's ready for this. Now, I do have one question for you. Have you put any thought into how you're going to get that helmet on?"

"Yeah, I have thought about that. Haven't done anything about it, just thought," Robert said.

"Any solutions?"

"No, just figured I'd tough it out," he replied.

And try to tough it out he did. Before long the entire crew was involved, but nothing worked. They tried pushing the helmet on slowly. They tried jerking it on quickly. They had one push the bandages in while another pulled the helmet down. They even tried wedging his head in with shims, but each attempt ended as his whimpers turned to full yells of pain and cries for mercy. Finally, Robert had the idea of strapping the bandages down with electrical tape. "Pull it tight, it's just like when I played rugby," he instructed. The combo of compressing the bandages and the slick shell of plastic tape made the act of pulling on the helmet bearable.

The crew went into full motion as he took his place in the dull black Funny Car. Back and forth they zipped like bees coming home. It's shocking how quiet it is, tucked up inside a Funny Car with your head in a helmet. There's a lull between being strapped in and the time the engine starts. That's when you're completely alone with nothing but your own thoughts.

"Oh no!" he said out loud as anxiety filled his helmet. "I was hoping I'd believe those words I said to Mathew. It's all right; everything is gonna be all right. Just clear the mind. Be one, be present. "Oh no," he continued as his breathing escalated. For a second, he thought he just might puke. "Oh God!" he exclaimed, wringing his fingers on the wheel.

With those words, it was as if time stood still, and his entire life flashed before his eyes. It started with his mum, her love for God, and her mission to save not only her family but the entire neighborhood. Then came his first driving lessons at summer camp, the first dragsters in his dad's shed, the Southern Thunder, road tripping with the boys, running from life, waking up in the Kimberly, running full speed back at life, the Tanami Track, America, Phoenix, Elko, Utah, the crash, recovery, and the rebuild. He saw it all.

"Okay, God, I know it's you. I know we haven't necessarily been on speaking terms these last few years, but I know you're there. And I know I wouldn't be here without you. I'm not sure how I got from Baker Street to here, but here I am, nonetheless. I feel you've guided me here for some reason. You're the one who gave me this love for the sport, the understanding of simple mechanical things, and a way with people. You gave me the pure will and relentless drive to make this dream a reality. You're the one who spared my life last time. This is my life, and now it's yours., With those words, all traces of anxiety drained from his body and complete focus settled in. He was present.

The dragon thundered to life. Mathew disconnected the starter and took his place opposite the lights as Brandon dropped and locked the body into place. From deep within the belly of the beast, Robert spoke again, this time to the beast itself, "All right. It's just you and me now. You may have won last time, but today is mine." With that, he kicked with all his might!

The beast kicked back, locking him tightly in the seat. There's no time for thinking when one's accelerating from 0 to 200 mph in 2.5 seconds. But that day, on that run, he did. His head locked tight against the seat under the weight of four g-forces. *Oh, that feels nice. The way my head sinks in against the padding of the helmet, it makes some extra room, relieving the pressure from the forehead.* The dragon roared, flames danced, the crowd cheered, the parachute launched, and the pressure was back on. He needed one more successful run and he'd be a licensed Nitro drag racer.

Back at the pit, the crew swarmed as the car rolled to a stop. Up on the rack she went, and they worked together in perfect rhythm with a singular focus on the task at hand. Off with the body, and then the ballistic covers, the oil pan, and the fire walls. The hot clutch dropped from the bottom as the blower popped off the top. Soon nothing was left but the bare engine block sitting alone on the chassis rails, waiting for the new parts to be massaged into place.

The rebuild was flawless and took less than ninety minutes. Again, Robert whimpered as he pulled the helmet over his tender forehead. Again, he climbed into the belly of the beast, and again he was trapped alone in the lull between strap-in and start. Only this time, in an instant, he saw the faces of everyone who'd helped him along the winding path from Adelaide to Salt Lake. There were his family and mates on Baker Street, Steve and Jill in Australia, the backpackers in Venice, Susan and the kids in Phoenix, the crews in Reno and Magna, and of course Lisa and the boys. It was like God was answering his prayer by showing him all the lives he'd touched along the way. Then, the dragon roared to life, the flames danced, the crowd cheered, he sank tight against the cage, and the pressure eased as he crossed the finish in a cloud of victory and a storm of gratitude.

WHEELER AND CAT

The pressure returned a couple of weeks later when Mathew announced he'd accepted an offer with another team. He left immediately, hooked up with the team in Phoenix, and traveled the circuit from there. Though it hurt, Robert understood and couldn't blame him. He knew Mathew needed a cash-paying job and wished him well.

Robert had been so obsessed on licensing up and building race cars, he'd lost track of everything else. He sat alone in the shed confronting the brutal facts. He had a Nitro Funny Car, a license to race a Nitro Funny Car, a crew, and that was it. He'd given everything for those cars, including his heart, soul, energy, and money. Especially money. He'd spent everything on those cars, and then some. He'd even sold his beloved truck and trailer, mortgaged his house, and still he was shy of even.

The plan had always been to build a race car and make a living on the track. But life had other ideas, so once again he was forced to rework his plan to accommodate life. Of course, it still revolved around racing, but he needed money. He figured he would get back to mechanicing at Wheeler. They said he'd always have a place there, after all. Then he could save for more car parts, a truck, and a trailer.

But first, there was one other item of business to address. Free of morphine and full of fear, he gathered every ounce of courage to his name and asked Lisa one last time. In a truly unromantic and awkward moment, he blurted, "Marry Me?" She said yes. So, on December 30, 1999, they married at sunset on a beach on the edge of Adelaide, South Australia. It was a beautiful ceremony full of friends, family, and West End Draft.

Later that winter, the dull black body made its way to Twin Falls for a coat of paint. Robert's only instructions to Eldon were, "the theme is 'Thunder from Down Under,' go ahead and do what you think is best," a stark contrast to the first car. Eldon did his thing, and the car came back a deep metallic blue with bright white lightning bolts rising from the front wheel and streaking their way up and back the entire length of the car. It was pretty badass by any standard, though those lightning bolts may or may not have been mistaken for trees from time to time, even by the most badass of observers.

Robert quickly found he needed more money than he had. He needed more time and experience to fine tune the tune-up. He needed more test runs, match races, and exhibitions. He needed the life blood of any racing team; he needed a sponsor.

He started with what he knew. *Wheeler!* he thought. *Why not? They're the local CAT guys. All they do is big machines, either building, fixing, or selling them. Surely they'll see the value in having their name associated with a Nitro Funny Car.* It turned out the guys in marketing had no idea what a Nitro Funny Car was. Plus, they'd never sponsored any type of physical thing before. All their advertising was traditional: print and radio. *No worries, I'll just wear them down,* he thought.

With Wheeler's sponsorship stalled in the early stages, and no other prospects on the horizon, Robert figured he needed professional help. He found it in the form of Tim, a flashy guy and fast talker who made everything sound right. Tim had just quit his high-profile marketing job in New York City to start his own sports marketing company. Robert was assured by Tim himself that, "this is the time to get in. Your rates are low and will stay that way as a thank you for trusting us in these early stages. We are poised to grow huge, and no doubt, our rates will grow with demand. This is the time to sign," and he did.

"So, what are we doing here?" Brandon asked again as they pulled into the Golden Spike Arena in Ogden.

"It's a promo spot," Robert replied.

"Yeah, you've mentioned that. But why are we here? This is an arena for like rodeos and stuff. Shouldn't we be doing a promo spot at a track somewhere?"

"Ya gotta think big if you're going to make it big. Ya gotta think about what's next, and according to Tim, this is the next big thing. Tim says you gotta take risks," answered Robert.

"So that's what I don't get. Why are **we** *here*?" Brandon questioned again.

Robert explained, "Tim's other big client is the Barrell Racing Association. His idea is to revolutionize their sport by combining it with ours. The horse racers will compete head-to-head just like dragsters. They'll have starting lights, and lanes, and everything. Except they'll weave through the barrels like usual."

"Okay, so that still doesn't explain why **we** are I," Brandon repeated.

"Well, we're going to barrel race with the car to show the link between barrel racing and drag racing. According to Tim, this is something so big and revolutionary, you gotta see it to understand it."

"Okay. I think I gotcha. So, you'll be doing donuts around barrels in a rodeo arena, in a dragster?" Brandon summarized with a questioning tone.

"Yeah, that's pretty much the plan," came Robert's response.

"Well, you're right. This is something I've gotta see. Just one thing, how will the car handle on dirt? Have you ever driven on dirt?" he questioned.

"Yeah. I mean, no. No, I haven't driven in dirt before. And, uh, I've been wondering about that myself. The car's never seen dirt, let alone touched it. Yeah, so, this'll be something new for everyone involved," answered Robert.

Hmm, ain't that something. She handles much better than I'd have ever thought in the dirt, Robert thought, spinning circles inside the arena. Freshly tilled dirt flung high and light with every tap of the throttle and every turn of the wheel. Before long, the entire arena was filled with dust.

Oh, and Nitro fumes, which aren't anything like gasoline fumes at all. Nitro fumes are deceptively sweet, almost like a mist of honey. But they quickly turn on you with a swift kick to the face. Before you know it, your eyes are burning and full of tears, your nose is running uncontrollably, and your esophagus clamps shut, leaving you helplessly fighting for your next breath. Which explains how Robert found himself strapped into the "Thunder from Down Under" covered in dirt, helpless, and alone in an empty rodeo arena, with several abandoned camaras rolling. "Guys? Hello? Brandon? You there? A little help here? Please?" he begged.

That was the only time GC ever yelled at him, for letting his Funny Car touch dirt. It was also the last time he saw Tim. It turns out, drag-style barrel races wasn't the next big thing. But you never know for sure, if you don't try.

Robert knew most everyone at Wheeler from the back of the shop to the front of the office. The marketing guys could hear him coming from a mile away as he chatted with reception, talked with accounting, joked with purchasing, and waved to support. Randy in Marketing drew the short straw, so they pushed him up front as their offering. The truth was, they were running out of creative ways to say no. Randy braced himself for impact, but Robert just nodded, waved a hello, and walked on by.

"What just happened?" asked an anonymous voice.

"Nothing. He just walked on by," Randy replied, blank faced.

"Where's he going?" came another voice. Randy hung his head out the open door and answered, "He's headed to Rob's office!"

"No, he's not! He's not going to the president of the company! Really, where is he going," echoed the anonymous voices.

"I kid you not, he's talking to Kim right now!"

And he was. He was talking with Kim, Rob's executive secretary. Usually, they chatted in the break room or the parking lot. But there he was, right outside of Rob Campbell's office, the president of Wheeler Machinery.

"I need a favor, Kim. Check this out," he said, handing over the daily newspaper, pointing to a big, bold headline on the front page of the sports section. "Look there, me and my car, we're front-page news."

And he was. There, on the front page of the sports section of the Salt Lake Tribune, was Robert standing with the Thunder from Down Under. He'd made quite a spectacle of himself that summer, drawing in big crowds on exhibition nights. Fans couldn't get enough of the fire-breathing dragons roaring to life and lighting up the night sky.

"And look there. It says me and the crew are from Wheeler Machinery. That there is free advertising. What do you say you put that on Rob's desk so it's the first thing he sees today?" he said.

"That's a great idea, but it's missing something," she replied. She drew a thick yellow circle around "Wheeler Machinery" with a bright yellow highlighter. "There, now he can't miss it," she smiled.

That's how Wheeler Machinery became the official sponsor of the Thunder from Down Under. It's also why Randy from Marketing made his first trip to the shop floor. "Here you go. They're the decals Kim ordered. She said they were for you."

"Nice! Are these the Wheeler Machinery and CAT stickers for the race car?" Robert asked, already knowing. He just wanted to hear Randy say it out loud.

"Yeah, I guess so. Hey, Robert. Congrats and good luck," Randy said, turning toward the door.

Excluding the boxes of rags from Napa, Wheeler was Robert's first official sponsor, and he took it seriously. Each decal and patch brought with it another level of responsibility to the brand, and he was committed. Wheeler had done good by him, and he promised the same to them.

It started small, with a few decals in exchange for a few barrels of fuel and oil. But over the next few years it grew into much more. Before long, his deep blue car made its way to CATERPILLAR yellow with a Wheeler Machinery brand. He wore the color with pride. His logo was a kangaroo driving a Nitro Funny Bulldozer. He even tied a stuffed kangaroo doll on the wheelie bar for good luck.

Soon he was making appearances at industry trade shows. He and the car had a way of bringing in potential customers by the droves. He'd dress in his finest CarbonX suit with Wheeler and CAT patches and talk cars. When a potential whale or well-known Kamatsu customer came by, he'd butter them up by popping the body and letting them sit in the hot seat. By the time he was done, the sales guys had another connection on the line ready to reel in, and they did.

Robert also worked company parties and morale events. Some things just bring people together. People are drawn to things bigger than self, and the car was one such thing. Young or old, shop or office dweller, from the janitor on the floor to the CEO in the mahogany office, the car transcended them all, bringing them together in common awe. It was truly a great connecter.

On one occasion, Robert started her up in the parking lot with none other than Rob Campbell in the driver seat. The crowd was stunned by the rumble in their gut as the dragon roared to life. Rob was stunned by the pure power coursing through his body. Robert was building more than just loyalty for the company, he was breaking down barriers between the front and back offices, and winning fans to the sport. And he loved it.

By far, Robert's favorite off-track functions were the common shows made by and for the common folks. The trade shows and employee functions were great fun. But people had to be there; they were paid to be there. But the common shows like Auto-Rama or the Transportation Association Exhibitions brought in everyday folks who wanted to be there.

He and the crew always looked for opportunities to make someone's day. Like the time he saw the tired mom pushing the little boy in the big chair. She trudged slowly along, tubes and bags hanging from the chair. Robert went out of his way to make the connection. After a few minutes, he asked the little guy if he wanted to sit in a real race car. His face lit up and with hopeful eyes he glanced at his mom for permission. She smiled and nodded.

It took the entire crew, but they managed to maneuver him into the driver seat. There he sat, in a real race car, his face lit with a smile so pure and contagious it spread through the entire event. He revved, bbbrrrred, eeeerrrrrred, and screeched his way through an imaginary race, giggling the whole way. All the while a series of tubes and wires connected him to the empty chair beside the "Thunder from Down Under."

Smiles turned to tears when his mom told his story. "He was released from the hospital just yesterday. There's nothing else the doctors can do; they give him a week, two at best. What you gave him today, well, I can't thank you enough. But to see that smile, well. Thank you!" she said as tears streamed. Not a dry eye could be found on the crew as she disappeared into the crowd. Those moments were always Robert's favorite. He wasn't just wearing a logo or representing a sponsor; he was making a difference.

THE PURSUIT OF CHAOS

Rocky Mountain Raceway, and Spencer Young, stayed true to the deal by giving Robert plenty of test time in the form of exhibition runs. Each exhibition was an investment in Robert's education. There's only one way to get experience, and that is to jump in the driver's seat and get experience. There is only one way to fine tune a dragster, and that is to race a dragster. Each run filled him with another dose of confidence and filled the stands with crowds of screaming fans.

He kept the relationships with the Australian racers and mechanics alive. Whenever he encountered a hitch, a problem, or a new situation, he'd reach out to GC, JB, or one of the others. They were always happy to help with a nugget of advice, a tip, or a trick they'd learned along the way. Of course, each nugget came with its accompanying story of how they'd learned the lesson.

Then one day the Raceway upped the ante by scheduling a match race with none other than Ray Porter. Ray was a driver out of Southern California, and a big name on the NHRA circuit. Robert was nervous; it'd been years since his last head-to-head race. But it turned out Ray was not only an excellent driver and a brilliant mechanic, but he was also an all-around great guy. They almost became friends over the next few years as Robert built his cars and crew to NHRA standards. He looked forward to their matches as Ray had a way of putting him at ease, plus he always learned something.

Robert quickly found the great divide between wanting a Nitro Funny Car and having a Nitro Funny Car. When building, you buy or custom manufacture each bit and piece once, put it in its place, and before long, you have a car. But once you have a car, those bits and pieces tend to wear out, break, or blow up. So, you must buy or manufacture another, and then another, and another.

They're not delicate machines by any means. Every bit is either cast aluminum, machined steel, or quality titanium. Every piece is solid. But when pushed to the limit, even solid things blow up. The trick is identifying why something blows so it doesn't happen again. He questioned everything. Was it a flawed part? Was there some micro fracture that developed over time? Was there a flaw or impurity present from manufacturing? Was it the tune?

Yes, it was probably the tune, because it usually is. There's either too much of this over there, or too little of that over here. The entire machine is nothing but a million little pieces all strung together, one after the another, and each bit affects the next. Fine tuning is dialing in each of the million little pieces, so they work in perfect rhythm, each carrying its own load at precisely the right moment. If it's off by a millisecond, she blows. If there's too much there, she blows. If there's not enough here, she blows.

Each run left his tune and showmanship a little finer. Half the race is delighting the crowd with a spectacular show, and the show starts at the burnout. He'd roll slowly through the patch of water, or the wet, which reduces friction so the tires spin freely down the first 100 feet of the track. The thick cloud of black rubber smoke mixes well with the pillars of fire lighting up the night sky. Some nights, when things felt right, he'd back up through the wet again, giving the crowd another spectacular burnout.

Those years also gave him experience at blowing up engines and dealing with tire shakes. Tire shakes are deceiving. They're vicious because there's not much to see in real time, just a sputtered start. But slow it down and one sees each phase of launch. The lights count down to nothing, the driver kicks the beast, simultaneously waking the super charger and fuel injector, sending shockwaves through the core and flames out the headers. Ten thousand horsepower are instantly released. The solid axle delivers the energy to the wheels, leaving the big fat tires bearing the brunt.

The inside of the tire spins first. Twisting and torquing, they buckle under the pressure, dropping the car several inches at launch. When conditions are right, the tires slip as the outside edges catch up with the inside's spin. It's the perfect balance of torque and friction launching the car to 200+ miles per hour in two seconds.

But bad things happen when either torque or friction are out of balance. If friction is too low, the tires spin, wasting precious rpms. If friction is too high, the outside edges stick as the insides continue twisting tight like a rubber band. Then, all at once, that energy is released, launching the tail end of the car into thin air. That split second of frictionless airtime is enough for the tires to overcompensate, causing yet another unbalanced interaction between rubber and track, sending the car up again and again.

Many times, a driver recovers by rocking the throttle, many times they don't. Either way, shakes are violent things, at best leaving drivers with bruised forearms from holding on so tight, at worst leaving them unconscious. One crew member's sole responsibility is to measure the track's temperature and adjust the tire pressure accordingly in a finely tuned effort to reduce the risk of shakes. Races are lost by some, and won by others, with the smallest of shakes.

Pride is the only thing at stake, and bragging rights the only prize, for a match race. Pride and bragging rights were all Robert needed to go searching for that line of chaos, and he found it more often than not. It could get downright frustrating with a blow up here, or a shake there. The damned Nitro dragons were so much different than the alcohol cars. alcohol cars are just a step up from souped-up street cars. Everything is defined, refined, documented, and predictable. When something goes wrong with an alcohol car, all you do is consult the manual.

There are no manuals for Nitro Funny Cars. When something goes wrong, well, you have to figure it out, and there is no room for error. Was it the tune? The clutch? Was a cylinder running too hot, too lean, or too rich? An adjustment here called for tweak there, and so on. It could be frustrating to say the least, but it was the only way to get experience, so he chalked it up to that.

Robert's ego was taking a beating on the track, but he was making valuable connections with quality drivers from across the west. He always won the silent competition of the crews. The car required a complete tear down and rebuild after each run. Back at the pit, the crew had sixty minutes to tear her down and build her back up into racing condition. Watching them in action was an exhibition of efficiency, a demonstration of precision, and a shining example of leadership and teamwork.

Together they'd swarm the car; off with the body, the ballistic shields, drip pans, super charger, headers, engine, clutch, and tires. Each crew member specialized in one or the other. They worked independently, yet together. They used no words, just looks, glances, grunts, and motions. Within minutes, all that remained was a bare chassis, a thousand parts and pieces systematically scattered about, and pure concentration. Every cylinder was examined, each piston was inspected, all cranks were verified and replaced. The clutch was dismantled, sized, and rebuilt, then gently heaved back into position. Not a bit, piece, or part was left uncleaned.

The quiet race was won by the team who broke the silence first, and the silence could only be broken by the car. There is no mistaking the iconic sound of a Nitro engine roaring to life. No crowds cheered, no lights flashed, and no purses were won. But crews celebrated with high fives as the distinct thunder rolled across the park, telling the competition "We win!" Pride and bragging rights were enough to inspire any crew.

Robert learned something with each exhibition and match race. He obsessed over every part, dialed the tune, tweaked the cam, and refined the clutch on his relentless quest to completely understand the fundamentals of the simple mechanical beasts. He knew if he understood the fundamentals, he'd make good decisions, and it showed. Soon he was blowing up, breaking, and replacing parts less and less.

Over those years, Robert became something of a celebrity. He loved the crowd. He loved putting on a show. He loved watching the shock wave travel through the hearts of everyone within earshot at the speed of sound. It was the same every time; the rev, the jump of fear, the stunned looks quickly melting into smiles, followed by cheers for more. Yes, the crowd knew him, and they cheered him.

Over those years, he'd come to know who he was. He was a working-class kid from Adelaide, blessed with a dream in his heart, a plan in his head, and an unshakeable will made of stone. He knew what he had and what he had to do, and he was always running full speed to do it. Some thought he was running from something, or some part of himself. He'd tried that once by turning left at Threeways, and he knew running away was no way to live life. He wasn't running from anything; he was running toward something. Toward his dream.

By some standards, he'd arrived. He had a Nitro Funny Car with a top-notch crew and a sponsor. He was racing exhibitions and had a following down at the local track. But that was never the plan. The plan called for a life on the NHRA Circuit and racing week-in and week-out at tracks across the country.

He was just a working-class kid from Adelaide, with no money or resources. He'd been blown up twice and burned up once. He was doing match races and knew the big leagues were still so far out of reach. Even with Wheeler's sponsorship and the arrangement with the track, he was digging into his own pockets to keep things going. But he was cursed with an unshakeable will made of stone that he could not stop.

That is why, at the beginning of the 2004 racing season, Robert stood on a chair in the shed and announced to the team, "IT'S TIME, boys. This is the year we make our national debut. We've been dialing in this combination and perfecting our rebuilds long enough. This year we're heading to Denver in July." The crew cheered.

"What's after Denver?" one called out.

"Well, we'll see. If things go well and we make it in the money? Well, we'll see."

OFF TO DENVER

It's an eight-hour drive from Salt Lake City to Denver. Nine if you're dragging a utility trailer, eleven if you're dragging a racing trailer loaded to the brim with a car, equipment, and crew behind a borrowed pickup. That's a long time to think; especially when you're used to doing. Robert spent the entire time inside his own head, questioning the integrity of their logistics, and worrying about a million other things. "Did we get everything? What did I forget?" he asked himself over and over. Every now and then he'd holler aloud, "Hey Brandon, did you get the fittings?"

"Yep!"

"What about the clutch plates?"

"Yep!"

He couldn't help but stress over logistics. They'd been in such a hurry with the match race Saturday night. The way the rebuild spilled into the wee hours of Sunday morning didn't help. He knew the generator was in. He spent Sunday afternoon loading it, and Sunday evening patching the hole it left when it dropped through the floor. The way that job spilled into the wee hours of Monday morning didn't help.

He wasn't alone. None of the crew got much sleep Saturday, Sunday, or Monday. They were focused on either tending to the final details in preparation for their first big league appearance, or worrying about it. The plan was to head out right after work Tuesday evening and take turns driving through the night. But things never work out as planned.

Robert was so nervous sleep never entered his mind. But the self-talk never left, and it was all over the place. Starting with the glaring fact that this was their first national event. Inside his head sounded something like, *It's a fine line, your first trip to a national event. One of those lines that get all blurry and there's no telling if you've crossed it or not. Things could go perfectly. You could impress them all. Or they could blow up in your face and you'll be the laughingstock. There's just no way of telling. I'll settle for anywhere in-between.*

Then there's the pressure of presence. This is the first time any of these teams will be seeing us. They say first impressions are everything. I can't help but wonder what their perception of me and the team will be. All the other teams have multi-million-dollar budgets with big name sponsors like Snap-On, Coors, Castrol, Budweiser, and Ford.

And here I am, working as a mechanic, skipping meals, and forfeiting root canals for car parts. Thank goodness we have Wheeler. We've given them the paint job on the car. Sure, we've taken a few liberties with the use of CAT yellow and logos and all. But it was meant to give them as much exposure as possible. So, we have that going for us. The car looks like a million dollars, and we are expecting to perform like it too. The only problem, we're not, really. But that's all right, what we're lacking in money, we make up for with quality maintenance, intelligent tuning, and endless effort.

And a new crankshaft. Yeah, I'm glad we got that new crankshaft in. It was worth the extra work. I've never actually owned a new crank shaft, though I always wanted one. I've always wanted a lot of things, like a new truck and trailer. Oh, I'm tired of borrowing trucks for every appearance. Man I'm blessed with people around me with trucks who like hauling race cars around the country.

This trailer is way too heavy for the pickup rating. The springs are straining, and I think I've bottomed out a couple of times. I should paint this trailer sometime. I wish I had a new engine; one that wasn't built of other's parts. But ya gotta be smart and get deals where you can find them.

I'm proud of buying used parts, but I'm not this time. This time we're going in hot with a brand-new crank. And why not? This is it. This is the big leagues. This is the national stage. No, this is the world stage. This'll be televised around the world. People in Adelaide, Alice Springs, and Winnemucca will be watching. At least they better; I told them to. I can't believe it's been fifteen years since Jill and I drove away from the Kimberly Hotel. Yeah, it's time.

Yes, his head was a mess, but he snapped back to the present as he neared the Mile-High Raceway. He turned to wake the crew, but no one needed waking. They were all as wired as he and emerging from the same self-inflicted self-talk trances. He knew the answer, but out of courtesy he asked just the same. "Did you guys get much sleep?"

"No, not a wink. Been too nervous," was the consensus.

"Yeah, tell me about it. This is it! This is our first big show," Robert exclaimed, pulling through the gates.

There seemed to be a bit of confusion at the check-in station. "Yeah, that's right, Schwab Racing. Robert Schwab is the driver. Yeah, that's me. No, Fuel, Nitro Funny. No, not stock, Nitro Funny Car," he kept repeating.

Finally, the kid behind the counter handed over some papers. "Here's your registration, credentials, and slot assignment."

"This NHRA stuff is a bit different than Rocky Mountain," Robert said, concealing the fact that he didn't have a clue about the formalities or informalities of the NHRA circuit. The only times he'd been was as a fan, either walking the pits, watching from the stands, or listening from the parking lot.

Jerry, one of the crew from Wheeler, quizzed as they entered pit lane. "So, they didn't know we were coming?"

"No, they knew we were coming. We're registered, see?" he said holding up the registration papers. "I just don't think they were expecting us to actually show up. Besides, I registered last week, the last possible day. It's part of my plan," Robert replied.

"You have a plan?" asked Jerry.

"Yes, of course! I always have a plan."

"What's that?"

"The plan is to catch 'em off guard."

"Catch who off guard?"

"Them."

"Who's them?"

"Them, they, everyone. The officials, the other drivers, the crews, everyone," Robert said, digging deep into his stash of BS.

"Why's that?" Jerry asked, to which Robert replied, "Because I didn't want them to see us coming. It's called flying under the radar. We are dialed in to high-altitude racing. We know what we're doing at this altitude, and most of them don't. And they don't know who we are, or that we were even gonna be here. So, we are on the sneak attack."

"This is the fuel car row," Lisa interrupted. Robert steered the old trailer wide to make the turn. The entire crew were star-struck and took turns blurting something like, "Look! This is it! Look! There's Force! There's Kalitta! Pedregon! All the big teams, right here." They knew them all and waved to each. But, like Robert said, no one knew who they were, and they only got half waves and questionable looks as they sputtered their way down the row.

"Look, there's Ray, Ray Porter!" Robert hollered to the crew. Rolling down the window, he repeated, "Look, there's Ray, Ray Porter!"

"Hey Robert Schwab! Is that you?" Ray yelled in reply.

"Sure enough is. Man, it's good to see a familiar face. I mean, they're all familiar. It's just none of them know me back."

"Yeah, I get that," said Ray.

"Hey, you're having a fantastic year! Aren't you currently sitting number two?" said Robert.

"Yeah, it's been a good one, that's for sure. It's great to see you. So, you finally decided to leave Salt Lake and come join us out on the road?" Ray said in a humble attempt to distract from the standings conversation.

"Sure thing, just looking for our slot now. Hey, you know how these national events work; maybe you can help. Do you know where our slot is? This says Row B, number 47?"

"Oh man. Yeah, this is B alright, but 47? It's gotta be straight on down this row somewhere. Like, a way down there, I guess. I'd just keep on keeping on."

"Yeah, thanks, we'll do that. And we'll see you around."

"It's great seeing you, Robert, and good luck this week," Ray hollered as Robert puttered on down the row.

"That was Ray, from the match races back at home," Robert announced to Lisa and the crew.

"Yeah, we know Ray," they said in unison.

Robert and his calico trailer continued past the big teams, past the alcohol cars, and past the stock cars. "Aren't we supposed to be with all the other Top Fuel teams?" came a voice from the back.

"Yeah, I was thinking the same thing," said Lisa.

"Yeah, I think that was part of the confusion at the gate," Jerry quipped.

They eventually found slot 47 at the very end of the row, the last slot on pavement. Brandon piped in with, "Good thing we didn't get here any later; they'd have put us out in the field."

All Robert could do was sigh, "It's all part of the plan."

Robert knew his chances were slim, but he also knew he had a chance. He was serious about his high-altitude plan. He had been dialing in his car at high altitudes for three years. Most of the others hadn't given the altitude a second thought. He knew he didn't have to be first. But he also knew he couldn't be last, or second to last, or third to last, or even fourth to last. Number sixteen was the magic number that would put him in the money.

Qualification rounds were Friday and Saturday, and there were twenty teams competing for sixteen slots in Sunday's elimination rounds. Nineteen of those twenty teams had multi-million-dollar budgets. They had fancy new trucks, shiny trailers full of engines, and crews of twelve or so well-paid professionals. They would be swapping engines after each run, not rebuilding them.

Robert knew he was out of his mind to even consider what he was attempting, but he didn't let on to the crew. His truck was borrowed, his trailer was old. The crew were volunteers and he had one engine that would be completely rebuilt after every run.

Yeah, Robert knew his chances were slim. He knew only sixteen teams would be broadcast around the world on prime-time television. "It would be nice to be one of them. But, then again, we gotta be back to work bright and early Monday morning," he consoled himself.

The excitement of being in the big show coursed through their veins like caffeine; it kept them going all day and late into the night. There was so much to do. Each crew member had a job, and each did it with precision. They cared for the car and set up the trailer, generator, shop, and canopy. Even after everything was in order, they scurried about looking for something to take the edge off.

Finally, about 11:00 p.m. Robert called the crew together. "Okay, boys, we have one hotel room between us. We all could use a shower and a bed, but a shower's all that's guaranteed. Let's head on over and we'll draw straws for who gets a bed. The rest will come back to the trailer for the night." And they did.

Friday started precisely at 5:30 a.m. when Robert announced to the fully assembled crew. "Well, boys. This is it. Our first qualifying runs on the circuit, let's make them count. We have two runs today at 10:10 and 3:30, and two more tomorrow. We've been training for this for years. Let's focus on the task at hand and go do what we do," and they did.

They prepped and staged by feel. Once they made it to the track, they relied on habit. They knew what to do; tracks are tracks, no matter where they lay. The start, the burnout, the launch, and the trip down the track went off without a glitch, twice. Friday ended at 11:30 p.m. with the rebuild, the cleaning of the trailer, showers, and the drawing for straws for beds.

Saturday started at 5:30 a.m. and went on to have the same look and feel as Friday. By the end of the day, Robert Schwab and his team had qualified at slot number sixteen. They'd made it! They'd earned their way into the money and prime-time television!

Smiles erupted, excitement raged, and high-fives reigned as the car rolled to a stop in front of the tattered trailer. The excitement continued for five minutes, until Robert interrupted, "Come on, guys! We've got work to do and races to race. We have a car to strip and rebuild. We'll celebrate when we've won the last race of the day." The excitement turned to focus, and the crew worked with precision. But not until after getting the message out to all their friends and families.

Robert was no exception. Quietly, he too snuck off to spread the word. There was Andy in Nevada; the boys at the track in Salt Lake; Mum, Dad, and Adrian in Australia. He gave them the good news and encouraged them to spread the word. It was the first time a Funny Car built and piloted by a South Australian had qualified at a national event.

Robert looked on in amazement at his crew. The team was going on day four, or five, or who knows, without a good night's rest. They were weary, but the adrenaline was running so high, they just kept going like Energizer bunnies. With only one engine, one clutch, and two sets of heads, it was critical that the car was perfectly maintained. With their solid maintenance procedures, the quality remained impeccable.

Within an hour, Steve, the resident monster truck driver and designated clutch guy, cornered Robert off to the side. "Hey, ah. We have a problem."

"Yeah, I know," Robert replied without delay.

"You know?"

"Yeah, I know."

"What do you mean you know?"

"I mean I know we have a problem."

"What do you know?"

"I know about the clutch plates."

"Really?"

"Yeah, really. I know what's up."

"So, you know we have to race tomorrow, and we don't have enough clutch plates to build a functioning clutch."

"Yeah, I know."

"Well, are you concerned?"

"No, not really."

"What do you mean not really," Steve exclaimed, trying to keep his composure.

"It's okay. No worries. I have a plan," Robert responded nonchalantly.

"Well, would you mind sharing that plan with me?" Steve begged.

"Sure. What are the other teams doing right now?"

"Well, the same things we are doing. Tearing down and rebuilding."

"Right. What are they doing with their spent clutch plates?"

"I don't know, cooling them down I guess? Calibrating and rebuilding?"

"Yes and no. Yes, they are tearing them down, all right. But they are not rebuilding them. They're throwing them under their trailers and letting them rot. I've seen it; they use them once and throw them away. Monday evening, all that'll remain in this lot is a smattering of garbage cans and clutch plates."

"Really?" replied Steve with a tinge of disbelief.

"Yep. So, here's the plan. Tonight, when everyone else has packed up and gone back to their nice fancy hotels, I need you to grab the calipers and go collect clutch plates. Anything over .260 will work. But you'll need to do it quietly as there's still a chance someone might be around." And that is how Steve, the monster truck driver and designated clutch guy, came to be crawling around under the race trailers in the middle of the night at the Mile-High Nationals in Denver, Colorado.

The next morning, as the big teams stirred to life, no one noticed, or cared, that a few used clutch plates were missing from under their trailers. But what it meant for Robert and crew was, they were going racing! Their work was cut out for them. Having the sixteenth spot meant they were going head-to-head with the number one qualifier, who also happened to be the top racer on the circuit that year. Ben Bozeman, the track record holder.

SUNDAY DRIVING

THE SHOWDOWN

Sunday began precisely at 5:30 a.m. As usual, Robert rallied the crew and laid out the day's plan, laced with an enthusiastic dose of inspiration. It all seemed so normal, except it wasn't. There was something extremely unusual about the whole thing. A strange feeling followed him from the moment he woke and stayed with him everywhere he went. He couldn't shake it.

It was a level of excitement he'd never experienced before, and it came in waves. Higher and higher they rose as the morning ticked away. His mind raced at 300 mph, thinking through every part of the car. He visualized every nut and bolt, he replayed every adjustment over and over. Nothing he'd ever done in his crazy life had come close to the pure intensity he was feeling.

The thing about waves is, they have troughs, low points between the excitement where every fear, question, and doubt settle in. He wondered what the hell he was doing. *Who do you think you are? You're out of your league! You're going to crash! Besides, you're just some kid from South Australia; you have no business being here.*

He wanted to yell and scream, hide and attack, all at the same time. He needed air, he needed space, and he found it on the hill overlooking the staging area. There he stood alone, reflecting. About the time he thought he'd burst, he drew in a deep breath and held it tight. With that breath came a moment of intense clarity, and he fell into a very low key, calm, yoga-like trance. He was one with who he was, what he was doing, what needed to get done, and those on whom he relied.

Slowly exhaling, he thought, *This is it! This feeling right here. This is what you've been chasing your entire life.* In with another deep, controlled breath, followed by a long exhale. *This is the moment you've been chasing your entire life. This is Sunday morning at an NHRA event.* In with another clarifying breath. *Not everyone gets to race on Sunday morning; this is a privilege and you've earned it.*

He felt at home standing on the hill overlooking the organized chaos. Another breath of clarity. *Yes, this is it! This is the dream! This is 'what' I'm supposed to do. This is 'where' I'm supposed to be.* Just then, Lisa walked up from behind, quietly took his hand, squeezed tight, and quickly fell into rhythm with his breath. *And this is 'who' I'm supposed to be with.*

An hour later, Robert and his team sat atop the same hill waiting their turn.

"It's almost time," Jerry said with excitement.

"Yeah, I'm so ready for this. Been waiting my entire life," Robert replied.

A moment later, Ray walked up with a well-dressed, older, and quite distinguished gentleman trailing close behind. "Hey Schwaby, how's it going?" he said with a smile.

"Oh, not bad. In fact, quite good, I reckon," Robert replied.

"Missed you at the drivers' meeting this morning," said Ray.

"There's a driver's meeting?" Robert questioned with surprise.

Ray continued, "Yeah, there's always a drivers' meeting. Anyway. Maybe it's a good thing you weren't there. Old Ben pitched quite a fit this morning. He doesn't want to race you, and he let everyone know. He was talking all sorts of trash, saying you're an unknown commodity, a nobody, and questioned your abilities."

"Well it's a good thing I didn't know about . . . I mean, wasn't at the meeting. I'd have probably lost it right there and kicked his skinny ass." Robert replied.

"And, well, that's not all. He went on to say you were dangerous and shouldn't be allowed to race here, or anywhere for that matter," Rayl continued.

"For sure I would have kicked his skinny ass!" said Robert.

"Yeah, maybe it's a good thing you didn't kno . . . weren't there," Ray responded.

"So, what's up? You come by to tell me all of this just to piss me off? Is there more? Am I racing?" Robert quizzed.

"Yeah, don't worry. I stood up for you. I told them I knew you and we'd been match racing for several years in Salt Lake. I told them how you and the crew knew your way around a track and were no danger to anyone," said Ray.

"Oh, well, that's mighty nice of you there. Thanks for that," Robert said.

"No, it was nothing, my pleasure really, and it's the truth. You know that Ben can be quite a prick at times, and he was definitely one this morning," Ray said.

Robert soaked it all in. All the while, the well-dressed gentleman hovered close behind. Finally, Ray turned to him and said, "Robert, I'd like you to meet Frank. Frank, Robert." They exchanged handshakes and "howdys" as Ray continued. "This is my team strategist."

"Strategist?" Robert questioned.

"Yeah, strategist. All the teams have them," said Ray.

"Yah, of course," Robert BSd, pointing over to Jeremy, "We have ours, too." When really, he didn't even know what they were, or that teams had them.

"Good, well, bring him on over. You all need to hear this," Ray insisted.

Robert hollered and motioned to Jeremy, "Hey Jeremy! Come on over here, would you? And bring Jerry, he should hear this too." They came. "Okay, so what's up?"

Frank leaned in and said low and slow, "I have watched these guys for years. I know how they are and how they play." He paused, glanced suspiciously over everyone's shoulders, including his own, and continued. "These guys, they will try to burn you down."

"Burn us down?" Robert, Jeremy, and Jerry repeated in unison with a questioning glance.

Frank continued with his suspicious narrative, "Well, I've seen 'em do it before. Especially to a new guy, like you. They're going to wait until you start your car, then they're gonna start fidgeting and having problems. They'll dink around like something's wrong, but it ain't. They're just faking it, with the sole intention of burning you down."

"That bloody bastard's gonna burn us down?" Robert stated with disgust.

Frank continued, "Yeah, so whatever you do, do not start your engine until after they've started theirs. If you do, you're screwed. They're gonna piss around and stall until you don't have enough fuel to complete your hit, and it will destroy your engine."

Robert's mind raced. He knew exactly how much fuel and time he had. These cars idled at 4.7 gallons a minute, and 80 gallons a minute at full throttle. That was 1.3 gallons a second when moving down the track. He had a seventeen-gallon tank. He needed 110 seconds for the burnout and back to stage. That was nine gallons. The four second trip down the track would take 6.5 of those gallons, leaving him with just under two minutes of idle time. Everyone else knew it, too. That's why you always coordinated your starts and worked together; it was like a gentleman's agreement. He'd heard of this type of thing, but had chalked it up to a thing of legend as he'd never witnessed it.

Ray commented, "This guy, he can be a prick. He's sitting number one right now and he's going to try to intimidate you into starting first. Whatever you do, do not start until he starts."

"What a prick. Yeah. Thanks for the info," Robert said graciously.

"Oh, there is one more thing. The kangaroo. Its gotta go. He was saying how it's a safety hazard, and the NHRA guys agreed. So. It's gotta go. Sorry," said Ray.

"Okay, yeah, sure. Hey Ray, why would you do this? Why would you tell me this?" Robert asked.

"You. You're solid. You don't see that every day. You and the volunteer crew, you're in it for the love of the sport and it shows. It's cool that there's someone out here still like that," Ray replied.

Robert nodded.

"Besides, I'm sitting at number two right now, and that prick, he's the only thing standing in my way at the moment," Ray said with a smile.

Twenty minutes later, Robert was strapped down tight in the left staging lane with the question echoing through the stands, "Drivers, are you ready?" Robert signaled the okay and Jerry relayed it to the official. Ben's team concurred and both teams froze in their starting positions, eyes fixed on the official. He paused, glanced from team to team, then yelled loud enough for everyone on the property to hear, "FIRE 'EM UP!"

What should have happened was, both teams hit their starter motors. The big engines would whine for a split second under the pressure of a cold start, then quickly roar to life they spit flames high into the thin mountain air.

But what happened was nothing. Both teams stood frozen in their starting positions. Robert calmly held his hand up to the crew, signaling them to wait, wwwaaaaiiiitttt . . . Instinctively, his entire crew turned to Ben and his team, as if waiting for a signal from them. Well, almost the entire crew. Jerry refused to look over. Instead, he focused on his driver, Robert.

Ben and his team were all looking down their noses at the Schwabies, like they were a bunch of leakers who had no right to be racing at their level. Things got awkward as both teams waited for the other to do something. Finally, Ben's chief hollered, "Start your car!"

Robert knew the plan and he wasn't about to let anybody burn him down, not even the reigning champion. He knew he had to be the calm one on the start line. Continuing the hold motion, Robert looked to Jerry for moral support. Jerry smiled and hollered back without looking up, "Start yours!"

Stunned and bewildered, and with a tone of "do you know who we are," the chief hollered back, "Start your damned engine!"

To which Jerry calmly responded, "No. Go ahead. You first."

The next thing the NHRA knew, they had an old-fashioned stand off on their hands. Thirty seconds rolled by, then a minute. Each team stood waiting on the other, but neither budged. Every now and then an expletive-loaded threat was launched across the lane, but it was quickly batted down with a polite, "Yeah, once you've started yours."

It was a very ballsy move for the Schwabies, and the only reason they did it was because they knew Ray had their backs. Right out of the gates, they were experiencing both the ruthless nature, and the true humanity, of life on the National Circuit.

The TV cameras focused on Robert with his hand frozen in the "Hold" position. The spectacle was broadcast live around the world, and on the track's big screen. Robert saw himself pausing the entire event with his hand and smiled at the control he held. Oh, he hoped Ben was looking up to see the power he held in that hand; he hoped it pissed him off something fierce.

Deep down inside there was a part of him that knew his car and team were just as good as anything in the next lane. He'd spent half his life fighting battle after battle to sit in that seat. He'd gone without all the nice things normal people take for granted, like root canals, hot meals, and pickup trucks. He'd come a long way from the pool at the Kimberly Hotel and he wasn't about to let some prima donna burn him down before he got a chance to prove who he was.

Finally, the Official NHRA Chief Starter got involved, "If you don't start your engines within the next thirty seconds, you'll both be disqualified." The countdown began. Without flinching, Robert sat calmly with his hand in the hold position. Ben and his team fidgeted.

Twenty seconds left; Robert stared motionless into Jerry's eyes, knowing Ben had much more to lose than he, giving him the edge. Ben's crew chief fiddled with the starter motor.

Ten seconds left; the Schwabies stood strong as Ben's boys threw questioning glances at the chief.

Five seconds left; Ben's car roared to life, followed two seconds later by Robert's. The Schwabies had just won their first challenge! And it felt great!

There was a moment of fine-tuning where Jerry adjusted the fuel flow, checked the oil pressure, and inspected the pipes. As a mechanic, Robert tuned right along with him. But as the body was lowered and locked into position, the time for tuning had passed and the time for driving had begun. Robert the mechanic left the vehicle, and Robert the driver remained.

He rolled through the wet and lit her up for a perfect burnout. "Oh, that felt good," he said as Lisa guided him back into position. Looking up at the big screen, he saw he was ahead of Ben, so no rush. Reveling in the fact that he'd just beaten the top-seated Funny Car driver in an old-fashioned pissing match, he threw air punches inside the car and yelled at the top of his lungs, "F All you mother F-ers! I am here to race!"

With that release, he took a deep breath and began his self-talk, "Okay, focus. Drain the mind. Be one with the car. Be one with the lights. Be one. Be present." In with the second breath, and everything went away. Every part of him, inside and out, was completely focused on the lights. No sounds, sights, or distractions penetrated his focus.

His forearms flexed as he wrung the steering wheel. The lights flashed, and he kicked the beast, launching his dreams forward and his body back tight against the seat. Pure energy coursed through his hands, connecting him directly to the heart of the beast. He felt every breath and every beat of its heart. He and the car were one.

Deep down inside, there was another part of him that never expected to qualify. He never expected to be in a pissing match with the top-ranked driver on the circuit, and he certainly didn't expect to be racing him. But he had hope, and grit, and there he was, flying down the track at 250 mph, chasing a dream. At that moment, he expected to see a flash of red, blue, and silver as Ben blew past him. But he'd also become acquainted with expecting the unexpected.

The crowd in the stands, the long list of friends, family, acquaintances, and strangers watching around the world, went absolutely crazy as Robert crossed the line first. Somewhere back on the track Ben had a case of the shakes. Barely maintaining control, he eventually crossed the line. Robert had just beaten the top-ranked racer in the country in both a pissing match and a Top Fuel drag race!

People love a David and Goliath story. Robert had just served one up, and they couldn't get enough. The crowds went crazy, and the media went into a frenzy! The questions piled up; Who is Robert Schwab and where did he come from? How could a little-known dragster from Salt Lake City take down the top-ranked driver on the circuit? The crowds wanted answers and flocked to the Nitro trailers to find them. But where were they?

"Ok guys, they don't think we can maintain this old girl in sixty minutes, but I know you can," Robert hollered as the high fives faded into focus. He'd trained his volunteer crew from scratch and knew the workmanship of the professional Wheeler technicians was a step above many of the national teams. He didn't have a care in the world. He just leaned back and watched as the crew scurried with precision in the unassuming trailer on the far edge of the track.

Within one minute of hitting the pits, the body was off and the car was sitting on jacks. The clock ticked. Nick and Kelly busted off the valve covers, Steve and Jerry had the clutch can loose. It was a beautiful sight, like a perfectly choreographed dance.

At seven minutes, Tim announced, "The crank is good!" then pushed out the last of the pistons.

The clock continued to tick. Jerry had a quick look at the sleeves and rack to make sure nothing was damaged, then barked the orders, "Put it all back together!" By then, Steve had the clutch back in and was making final adjustments.

At fourteen minutes, the supercharger was lifted back into place, oil was put in, and the head guys adjusted the valves. Everything moved according to schedule.

At twenty-one minutes, Kim inspected the tires and torqued the wheels. Mark looked over and cleaned the entire body. Lisa packed the chutes and topped off the fuel tank.

At thirty minutes, they fired her up. The four years of match races showed. The only problem was, they were pitted so far away from the other teams that their perfectly performed maintenance was only admired by them.

Ray was the first to show. "Hey Robert! Great job! You did perfect." Out of the corner of his eye, Robert saw Ray's guys unloading a pickup load of beer. "Here, this is a gift for you and the crew, from the new points leader on the circuit! Drink it up; you earned it! And if you need anything, anything at all, you just go into our trailer. Anything you need is yours!"

Robert's first two thoughts, he kept to himself: *Where was that offer yesterday when we needed clutch plates?* and *Is the beer for me winning, or for Ben losing?* Either way, he thanked Ray graciously.

Turning to the crew, he hollered, "We'll get to this after the next round, boys. Next up is a Force car driven by Russ Stauffer. He's a very good and solid driver, backed by one of the best teams in the business. We gotta remain focused on the task at hand, and on our game."

By the time the press located the tattered trailer on the far end of the lot, Robert and the team were heading out for round two. Following the NHRA escort pilot, they wove their way through the frenzied fans and mobbing media. Reporters and fans alike cheered and fired question after question to anyone wearing the Schwab colors. Who was this guy who'd just beaten the top-ranked driver? They'd have to wait another round to find out. The questions quickly went from, "Who is this guy?" to "Can he do it again?"

To everyone's amazement, he did! Again, crowds and fans around the world went crazy. Robert and the crew won round two, qualifying for the Semi-finals.

From that moment on, there was no hiding from the press or fans. They were the talk of the race. Something big was going down at the Mile-High Nationals in Denver, and for the time being it revolved around the unassuming trailer parked on the edge of the blacktop on the far end of the pits.

The TV crew interviewed Robert and he explained how this was not his first race. His first national race maybe, but not his first race. "Some of these guys come to Salt Lake for match races. I've been studying these guys and watching them for years. And you know, half of my crew have never been to a national event before," that's where his voice cracked with gratitude for being there.

The cameras turned to Lisa, "We just wanted to qualify, and now here we are." She smiled graciously. She couldn't thank the fans or crew enough.

"What's the plan?" Jerry urged as Robert entered the trailer. "The boys outside are breaking her down; they'll realize a few things here pretty quick, if they haven't already," Robert replied. "Honestly, I didn't plan on getting this far. Clearly, we don't have the parts to go round after round like we're doing. But, here we are, we're doing it. I thought maybe we would qualify and then perhaps we could pull some parts together for one round, maybe. I . . . I . . .,"

"So, we don't have a plan?" Jerry whispered cautiously, as if someone might hear.

Robert looked back at Jerry, paused for a moment, and said with confidence, "Oh, yeah. We have a plan. We always have a plan. From here on out, the plan is to make it up as we go. But we're going to look good doing it. Make it up quickly, do it with purpose, and nobody will know." And they did. Jerry joined the crew at the car for some creative mechanicing.

With the car up on jacks and the clock ticking, it didn't take long for Jerry to stick his head back in the trailer to ask, "What do we do about the heads? We only have two sets; both have gone several runs and neither have been maintained."

Robert replied quickly with the confidence of knowing his car, "Put the first set back on. They'll be fine."

Jerry thought for a second and agreed with the same confidence, "Yeah, no argument here."

Robert followed Jerry out to the car to find a couple of things. First, quite the crowd had formed, with fans a few layers deep wrapping around their trailer. They respected the racers' space by not stepping inside the canopy. Most were strangers, with smiling faces and encouraging words. Many were familiar faces of team members they'd met through the week. It was quite the sight.

The second thing he noticed were the cracks forming in his dedicated crew. They'd spent the last week working long hours under the hot summer sun, breathing the thin mountain air, all with little sleep, and it was wearing them down. Fatigue was setting in and it showed, both on their tired faces and in the way they moved. Their willing hearts were no match for their weary bodies.

Some folks may have been surprised by what happened next, but not Robert. For him, it was just a way of life dating back to his dad's old shed on Baker Street.

Big Jeff was the first to step under the canopy. Kelly, the left Head Man, was struggling to pull the torque wrench to 150 pounds. Jeff watched patiently for as long as he could. Finally he walked right up to Kelly, took the wrench from his hand, and finished the torque himself. This opened the gates and before long, the pit was full of helping hands packing chutes, torqueing wrenches, and fueling the car. Soon Ray showed up with a brand-new clutch pack and asked if they needed anything else. All of these people pitching in when they didn't have to. It recharged the crew and left them with a sense of community in their hearts and smiles on their faces. It was contagious. It felt like home to Robert, and he loved it.

"Where's the escort?" he questioned while pacing the pit. "Screw 'em! We're leaving without 'em!" he announced, hopping into the car. The pilot car arrived about the time he'd strapped in. The official hung his head out the window and hollered for all the Schwabies to hear, "The crowds are a bit thicker than usual and you're farther out than I expected. We'd better hurry if we're going to make it." He then turned to the gent next to him, "We'd better call for help if we're going to make it." They didn't stop, or wait, they just rolled on past, and the Schwabies fell into formation behind.

PK and Mark led the way in the golf cart, followed by Jerry with Robert in tow. It was a long way from the farthest reaches of the parking lot to the staging lanes. The driver of the pilot car honked and motioned for people to get out of the way as they continued their slow crawl. Mark joined in by honking the beepy little horn on the cart and waving his hand for folks to get out of the way. It didn't help.

Everyone knew the event was televised around the world, everyone knew the schedule was tight, and everyone knew they could be disqualified if they were late for their time slot. The pressure was on. They continued to move along at a steady crawl. A pair of police motorcycles arrived with sirens blazing, they took the lead in an effort to part the crowds. It didn't help.

The pressure was getting to old PK. In real life, he was a quiet, peaceful, God-fearing elderly man, whose faith was matched only by his kindness and self-control. But he was no longer in real life. He was a vital member of a Nitro Funny Car race team at an NHRA Nationals event. His car was late for the Semi-final race being broadcast around the world. He had to do something. So, he leaned out his side of the cart, raised his fist to the crowd, and hollered at the top of his voice, "Get outta the way, you sons a bitches! Get out of the way!" It helped.

The crowds thinned and they picked up speed, and they kept gaining speed as they neared the staging area. Which would have been good thing, but somehow Robert had disconnected at the top of the hill. With nothing holding him back, he rolled up next to the tow car. Jerry's eyes met Robert's as he passed. Jerry gestured "what the hell," as Robert shrugged a "what are you gonna do?" He had the same exchange rolling past Mark and PK in the golf buggy, again as he rolled past the NHRA official, and yet again as he sped past the two cops near the bottom of the hill.

With three minutes to spare, Robert rolled to a stop next to Cruz Pedregon, prepping in the water box. One of those minutes was spent waiting for the crew chasing him down the hill. Some ran while others hung off the golf buggy. Eventually they all arrived and immediately began prepping for the race.

With a mighty heave, Steve raised the car body up over his head, and realized he'd left the body pole back at the pit. Panic set in, knowing he was stuck in that position until the engine started. It's funny how life can be a series of hurry-up and waits, all strung along one after the other. After hurrying to reach the staging area, they waited for the commercial break before proceeding with the starting sequence.

Steve squirmed under the pressure of the heavily damaged and heavily repaired body, which weighed twice as much as a new one. Glancing back and forth for some type of support, his eyes locked on Robert's, but all he could give was an empathetic shrug of the shoulders and a half-baked thumbs up. Steve stood his ground with the body up over his head and sweat dripping from his nose. He was twitching and wavering quite a bit when the official finally announced, "Light 'em up!"

Robert rolled through the wet and lit it up for a perfect burnout.

He began his starting ritual as Lisa guided him back to the line. *Drain the mind. Focus on the lights. Be one with the lights.* And he did. But then he did a very bad thing. He had another thought. *Huh, I wonder if I opened up that second flow too much?*

The thought lasted a thousandth of a second, but that's as good as forever at a drag race start line. The lights flashed like lightning, Cruz's car roared like thunder, and Robert snapped back to the present. Kicking the beast, he launched himself down the track a thousandth of a second behind Cruz. A thousandth of a second is an eon in a 3.5 second race.

It would have been nice if he'd been focused on the lights rather than some arbitrary thing over which he had no control. But there are a million things to think about at the track, and one can easily get lost in their own head at the most inopportune times. It would have been nice if Robert continued the Cinderella story. But that's what happens if you think at the start line.

There was no celebration, hooting, or hollering when the crew returned to their trailer on the far end of the lot. There was no maintenance either. They simply left the car in the pit, found a suitable spot, and collapsed. No one acknowledged the magnificence of the past three hours, or the remarkable event that had just taken place. They simply collapsed from exhaustion.

Robert stirred first, driven by his desire to analyze the race data, to make things faster for next time, and to make it to work on time. "Come on, boys, let's go. We've got a lot to do. Leave the car as she is; we'll tear her down at home. We need to be packed and ready to head out by 5:30."

That time was no arbitrary number. Ray had told him, and the words echoed over and over in his head, "They cut the checks at five p.m. on Sunday. You have an hour to pick it up; otherwise, they'll mail it to you." Robert needed that check desperately. So, at precisely 4:50 p.m., he and Lisa left the boys to finish packing, walked to the start line, and took their place in line out front of the NHRA trailer.

The crowd at the start line was thick with drivers, TV crews, race teams, NHRA officials, and fans alike; all coming and going for one reason or another, and they all seemed to know who he was. The check line moved quickly and soon enough they greeted the nice lady behind the window in unison, "Hello. Robert Schwab."

"Congratulations on a great day today!" she replied with a wink and a smile, handing over a white envelope with a big NHRA insignia.

"Thank you," they replied. Turning back toward the trailer, their eyes were fixed on the envelope.

They hadn't taken more than fifteen steps when Lisa finally asked, "Well, are you going to look at it?"

"I'm not sure," he replied.

"What?" Lisa questioned.

"I mean, yeah. Sure," he said, slowly opening the envelope. Peeking inside, he stopped without warning when his eye caught the figure on the amount line. Shock and disbelief shrouded his face as he looked up at Lisa, who'd stopped a half step later. They paused, then together their eyes traced back to the half-open envelope. They stood speechless in the crowded raceway.

Finally, their eyes locked, and shock faded to excitement and laughter. The entire world and everything in it faded into the background, leaving them alone in the crowd in their own little world. They smiled, laughed, hugged, giggled, and yes, like a couple of kids, they even broke into a swing dance right there in the staging lanes of Bandimere Speedway in Denver, Colorado. Lisa stopped mid dance and asked with a smile, "Do you think we could go out for dinner now, just once?" Robert just smiled and continued the dance.

It was one of those fleeting moments in life where all good things come together in the same place and at the same time to create a perfect moment.

Nothing the crowd did or said could steal their moment. Well, almost nothing. Out of the corner of his eye, Robert saw a lone figure walking their way. There was something familiar about him, so he did a double take. It was Connie Kalitta, a legend he'd watched on TV and admired for years. Connie had watched their entire celebration from the start, and, in some way, it was as if he'd joined in as their eyes met. He wore a warm smile and pointed right at them as if to say, "Good job today." That was the moment Robert knew that Connie knew just how much that moment, and money, meant to them. With that, they did one last swing before heading back to the trailer.

It would have been nice if they could have stayed for the after party, but he and the crew had work at seven a.m. the next morning. It would have been nice if they could have made it home Sunday night, but they were dragging an old trailer behind a borrowed truck and moving slow. Too weary to drive, they pulled off the highway somewhere out on the high barren plains of Wyoming to catch up on a week's worth of sleep they'd left on the track.

Robert was jolted awake at 7:03 a.m. by the ringing of his phone. "Oh no! It's Wheeler!" he yelled, shaking the rest of the crew awake. "Hello, this is Robert. Yeah. Sorry, we're running late. It'll be a few hours, but we'll be there." He rambled urgently, leaving no time for the other end. Panic threatened as the crew realized how late they were. But they were brought down by the change of tone in Robert's voice.

"What? You're not? Really? Really? What? You're kidding. Well, okay then. Yeah, we'll see you tomorrow. Bye." Everyone in the cab was fully awake and looking warily at Robert. He just sat there quietly gazing out the windshield into the wide-open nothing.

Lisa finally broke the silence, "Well, who was that, and what's going on?"

"That was Big T at Wheeler," he replied, still looking off into nothing.

"Are we in trouble for being late?" came a voice from the back.

"No. Not even a little. Big T, he said he'd just gotten off the phone with CAT Headquarters in Peoria. The weekend advertising numbers from all of CAT sponsorships had just come in. They called him asking, 'What's "Wheeler Machinery" doing on a pro car at the national level?' And then they asked 'who the HELL is Robert Schwab? They have just blown away an entire year's worth of the NASCAR marketing numbers in one four-hour event.'"

An awkward hush full of questioning faces followed.

Again, Lisa finally broke the silence by asking the question on everyone's mind, "So, is that a good thing, or a bad thing?"

"Good. Yeah, a very good thing. Big T said we could take our time getting back. I guess we made quite a mark for ourselves with television ratings."

Everyone in the cab cheered as Robert continued gazing out the windshield into the future. He was taken by how much the high plains of Wyoming resembled the Tanami at dawn. He put the truck into gear with a determination to meet the future, wherever it led.

Glancing in the side mirror, he saw the past. It was a couple of kids in an old XW wagon with six spare tires strapped to the top and a pair of barrels stowed in back. In a cloud of dust, they turned off the blacktop onto a dirt sidetrack.

He smiled, took hold of Lisa's hand, and thought, *Well, I didn't win, but I did it! Well, we did it! With a volunteer crew, a homemade car, and on a mechanic's wages, we raced a Nitro Funny Car at an NHRA National event in America.*

And man, I hope like hell they had it on the television at the Kimberly Hotel.

THE END

www.ingramcontent.com/pod-product-compliance
Lightning Source LLC
Chambersburg PA
CBHW061139120626
46546CB00005B/1848